RUTH

The

WEIR

"That was the place that you were home-
sick for, even when you were there."

Originally Published Feb. 1943
By William Morrow & Co.
Reprinted July 1986 By Blackberry
ISBN 0-942396-48-0

Blackberry Books
Chimney Farm
Nobleboro, Maine 04555

Printed in the United States of America

Cover photo by Beth Leonard

To

My Mother and Father

THE BACKGROUND of this novel is authentic, but I have not described in it any living person, nor would I wish to do so. It would be difficult to write a story about a place so well-known and beloved as the Maine coast without apparent character resemblances; but if anyone feels he recognizes himself or his neighbor in this book, he is mistaken, and such description is only a coincidence.

The WEIR

HARDY TURNER slid out of bed quietly not to awaken his wife, but as he put the quilts back around her shoulders, Josie moved a little and said, "You goin, Hardy?"

"Guess I better."

"Well, light the lamp then. No use dressin in the dark. I'm wide awake."

She could hear him moving around and presently she leaned over, fumbled for a match on the stand by the bed and lit the small kerosene lamp.

Hardy was standing by the window peering out, his eyes close to the glass. The window faced west and the soft muslin curtains were bowed out against the screen as if glued there. As he turned away, a gust baffled around the corner of the house and sent them flapping wildly out into the room. The window shade bulged, cracked loudly against the woodwork. Then the wind sucked away, drawing the curtains straining against the screen again.

"My land!" Josie put her feet out of bed, reached for a housedress to put on over her nightgown. "Tis blowin, ain't it? What time is it, Hardy?"

"It's half-past one. Wind's been breezin on hard since twelve."

"Tch, you been awake all that time?"

[3]

"Off an on. No need for you to git up, Josie."

"I'll make you some coffee and fry some eggs. It'll be cold down hangin onto them spilin."

"I'll drink some milk."

Josie snorted. "You won't drink no milk!" She put on her shoes over her bare feet. "There'll be some coals left in the stove, that good fire we had last night. You go down and poke em over."

Hardy knew there would be no coals left in the stove, and he would have preferred to drink his milk and leave the house without disturbing anybody. He'd have to wait for breakfast now, he thought, poking the cold ashes down through the stove grate with the hooker, and with this wind breezing on and piling up the tide in front of it, he wouldn't have much time to spare. He poured kerosene lavishly on the kindling to hurry up the fire.

"There!" Josie hurried in, jerking her head in the direction of the comfortable roar going up the chimney. "Now it won't take me a minute to have coffee goin."

She knows damn well I've had to build a new fire, Hardy thought. But he said nothing. Josie was just waiting for an opening. She didn't think much of his dropping down his weir nets every time the wind hauled out southeast.

"I think you'd better call Leonard," Josie said, breaking an egg into the big coffeepot, to settle the grounds. "The way it's comin on to blow, you'll need him to help you hold the dory."

"Leonard?" said Hardy mildly. "He just got to bed."

"Well, I'll just call him then."

"Chrise, Josie, I can't wait for him to git squared round. You know he was to the movies."

"You wait, Hardy. If you're goin to be fool enough

[4]

to traipse down there in the middle of the night and drop them nets, you ain't goin alone." She stopped and waited, but as Hardy turned silently to his eggs, she went out and he heard her heavy steps going up the back stairs to Leonard's room.

Hardy scraped his chair back from the table and sat a moment, indecisively. Too bad to get the boy up. Maybe . . . He got up quickly and went to the outside door.

The weather looked bad. Inky clouds raced overhead, but in the west a single star showed for an instant before it was snuffed out. Maybe Josie was right. Maybe the wind was just breezing up with the flood tide and would go down again toward morning. On the other hand, it was the time of year, and it might mean a bad southeast storm. Hardy wasn't sure. If only a man had a way of knowing. . . .

He ought to be starting. The tide was coming and he could hear the rote on the back shore beginning to thunder against the ledges. The higher the tide got, the worse the job of getting the nets down. Still, if Leonard went to the trouble of getting up, he supposed he'd better wait for him. He went back to the table, began to eat his eggs hurriedly and drink his coffee in gulps.

Leonard had pulled the quilts over his head until only a wisp of curly brown hair showed on the pillow. Josie gave his shoulder a gentle push. "Leonard! Your father wants you."

Leonard flopped over. "Huh?"

"Wake up. Your father thinks it's goin to blow."

"Godsake, Marm, is he goin to drop them nets again? He had em down all last week."

"He thinks he ought to."

"How's he expect a herring weir to fish if he keeps

his nets flat all the time? What time is it, anyway?" said Leonard crossly.

"Goin on for two. It *is* breezin up kind a hard, Leonard."

Leonard sat up in bed and listened. "Does sound kind a windy, at that. All right. But, heck, Ma, I ain't had but a couple a hours sleep." He had been across the bay to the movies at the Harbor, and after the show had taken Alice Lacy home. "Ahow-oo," he yawned. "Feel's if somebody'd hit me on the head."

He put his feet grumpily out of bed and followed them with his big lean body, scantily clad in the pants of an old pair of pajamas. "Blast and damn that weir," he mumbled, reaching for his undershirt.

"I feel the same way sometimes," Josie said. "I guess Pa does, too."

"Well, he ought to, the work he makes of it."

Josie went back downstairs, feeling her feet clump tiredly on the treads. She had put in a good hard day's work yesterday, and she felt, herself, as if she hadn't been to bed at all. She set the coffeepot back on to heat and broke Leonard's eggs into the frying pan. By the time they had begun to set, Leonard came down, his eyes red with sleep, his hair tousled and on end. He shoved his long legs under the table and ate for a while in glum silence. "Pa gone down?" he asked finally.

"No. He's out lookin at the weather."

"How long's he had that weir?" Leonard said suddenly. "Seventeen years, ain't it? He ain't made enough out of it to keep him in oilpants. I wish the damn thing would blow so far up the bay the devil couldn't find it to roost on it."

Hardy came in, closing the door behind him. "It's jest about kept you in oilpants, and any other kind a pants you had a notion to buy. You comin with me, or are you goin to set there pickin your teeth the rest of the night?"

"I got a goddam good mind to go back to bed," said Leonard irritably.

"No you ain't, Leonard. You go with him," Josie said. "I ain't goin to have him down in that dory alone."

"I ain't askin nobody to go," said Hardy, his hand on the doorknob. "It's my weir, and if I want to drop the nets down in the middle of church on Sunday, or any other time, I damn well will!" He stopped suddenly, a little too late to hide the nervous tremor in his voice.

Leonard grinned at him suddenly. "Oh, hell, Pa, don't git all tore out about it. We'll drop em."

"Well, git a move on, then. Here it is breezin on every minute, and the tide comin—"

"Go along," said Leonard. "I'll catch up with you." He buttoned himself into his oilskins and followed his father out into the gusty darkness.

THE herring weir was built on pebbly bottom, protected by ledges from all but the worst storms, but in a bad southeasterly on a high tide, the sea broke over the ledges and poured down in full force on the structure of brush and tarred nets strung between piles driven into the sand. Twice in the years he had owned it Hardy had lost the weir. Once he had lost two thirds of his nets through not dropping them down in time.

The wind seemed to gather strength as Hardy and Leonard rowed out from the shelter of the shore. Hardy kept the dory close under the weir wing for lee, but the long whistling gusts sweeping in unchecked from the

[7]

open ocean to the east tore at the boat, cuffed off the top of the rising tide and sent it down on them in drenching sheets.

Leonard shivered and swore, but Hardy kept his hands steady on the oars and said nothing. Now that he was actually doing a job, not worrying about it, his mind worked keenly and swiftly with his able body.

The tide was already a little too high. He could feel the strong drag of it under the boat as the big swells rolled in, without breaking, to race across the sand bar behind the weir and into the open bay beyond. In another hour, unless the wind moderated, they would be breaking on the bar.

Waited a little long, Hardy thought. Goin to have to hustle.

The night was thick and black, and he had to row by the feel of the wind and the push of the tide against the dory. But he thought little of that. As long as he knew which way the wind blew and whether the tide was flooding or ebbing, he knew where he was. Tending weir after dark was second nature to him. Besides, he had seen much worse storms than this, and been out on darker nights. Tonight he could make out the vague tracery of flimsy-looking poles that showed him he was close under the weir wing.

Inside the weir the seine poles with nets strung between them offered a partial windbreak. The water was quieter, but Hardy knew it wouldn't be once the tide rose over the inner ledge.

He laid the dory against the brush wall of the pound and began untying the tarred gangion that held the nets to the seine poles. The nets were fastened bottom, middle, and top, and the idea was to untie all but the bottom ropes and let the nets fall forward into the shelter of the brush wall. That way a seine pole or two might carry away, but unless the wall itself went, the nets were safe.

Hardy's hands found the knots and untied them by instinct, but he could hear Leonard fumbling and swearing down in the stern of the dory. Hardy had a special hitch, one he had devised himself, for the net ropes. The sea could maul at it until kingdom come and still it would hold, but a man could find the right end in an instant, give it a twitch, and the whole knot would fall undone in his hand. Except Leonard. Leonard never could seem to make out which end to twitch. Or maybe he could if he wanted to take the trouble, Hardy thought.

He knew Leonard hated the weir. He knew he hated it himself. But it was either tend weir or go lobstering, and he'd be damned if he'd eat salt water summer, spring, and fall and not get his seed back. Tending weir was as near as he could come to a job on the land, and when he'd begun it he'd planned to keep it up only long enough to make some money and set up in business on the mainland . . . a little store, or maybe a small hotel, and somehow get away from this dead hole of an island. He'd had a good course of training as a bookkeeper, in a commercial school when he was young. And he'd had brains enough as a young fellow to get to be first mate of a crack freighter in the South American trade.

What he'd done, Hardy reflected, his hands moving with skill and precision on the tie-ropes, all his life was waste his education.

They were finishing the last of the nets on the inner pound when the first of the big combers reared up over the ledge and came pouring through the weir. Hardy sensed its coming and sat down on the dory thwart, but it took Leonard by surprise. He grabbed the top of the

[9]

seine pole on which he was working, and the dory lofted from under him and fell away into the trough, leaving him hanging and kicking. Hardy swung the boat back instantly, so that it rose under the next swell and scooped Leonard safely and neatly off the pole.

"Chrise sake, Leonard," he said mildly, "what you think you are . . . a gull?"

Leonard was too wet and too cold to get mad, and too sobered to regard his loss of dignity. He was glad it had been his father in the dory. He had seen Hardy before in some emergency on the water function with split-second precision, as if something outside his brain told him the right thing to do. He had admired his father all his life for that ability and tried to copy it.

"No use tryin to drop down any more," said Hardy. "She's gettin too tough for us."

"Take em down if you want to," Leonard answered gruffly. "I guess I could hold the dory."

"No," said Hardy, getting out the oars. "Them few left, it don't matter if they do carry away."

The slow daylight was beginning to creep into the sky as they rowed ashore, so that they could see three miles away to the north the darker line edged with white which was the mainland. Comey's Island shore, a hundred yards off, was plunged in foam. In the village itself the houses showed whiter, the black spruces blacker in the half light. Pallid, angry water sluiced through the weir and out across the sand bar into the bay.

" 'Tain't breakin on the bar, is it?" said Hardy meditatively. "You run along home, Len. Need your sleep, I guess. I got a few odds and ends to tend to over to the fishhouse."

"Oh, come on home," said Leonard impatiently. "You ain't had no more sleep'n I have."

"H'm, well," said Hardy. He dropped the dory anchor on the beach rocks, turned and went off along the path to the fishhouse.

Now what can you do? Leonard said exasperatedly to himself, watching Hardy go. I won't be any more'n out of sight before he'll be out on Crab Point watchin the weather.

The wind was beginning to slacken as Leonard went up the path to the house, and as he undressed in his room he saw that a clear amber streak was showing in the cloudy eastern sky. When he woke up at ten o'clock in the forenoon, the air was flat calm. The tide was low, and Hardy, he saw, was off in the weir, in the dory, tying up the nets again.

JOSIE could not find the set of box tops she had saved, with which she intended to send for six oatmeal dishes. She had her money order for fifty cents all made out, but when she went to get the box tops, they were gone.

"I could of swore I left them box tops on the mantelpiece in the green pitcher," she said, puzzled, going back to look again. "I *know* I left em there. Mother, have you seen my Blast Borax box tops?"

"What?" Grammy Turner, bent over her knitting in the rocking chair by the west window, shook her head irritably and very fast. "Sh! I'm countin."

"Well, I don't see . . ." Josie stood in the middle of the room glancing about for any place they might possibly be. She did not miss the sidelong look Grammy gave her, nor the gleam in Grammy's eye.

Grammy Turner and Josie had never got along. They

put up with each other, Grammy because she felt she was entitled to her place in the house as Hardy's mother, Josie because of her essential kindliness and her sense of duty. Sometimes she felt a little wronged because Grammy did not seem to fail any as old people should. For sixteen years of her married life with Hardy, Josie had had the old lady in her house, and at eighty-six Grammy was as hale in body and lively of mind as she had been at seventy. Each year the tough texture of her face seemed to add another network of wrinkles and her body seemed to shrink a little more on its bones. But her shrewd old mind went daily and in detail over the affairs of each member of the family.

And what she don't see, Josie told herself grimly, she guesses at.

"Nine . . . ten . . . 'leven . . . fifteen," Grammy murmured. She looked up, meeting Josie's steady regard. "What's the matter with you?"

"I've lost my tops I saved from the borax boxes. You seen em?"

"From what?"

"From the Blast Borax."

"What'n time's that?"

"You know what borax is as well as I do, Mother," said Josie patiently.

"Oh. That new stuff on the radio, ain't it? Tallicum powder in it."

"It ain't that old-fashioned kind that took the skin off your hands, no."

"S'posed to make your hands smell pretty while it takes the skin off, ain't it?"

"Now, look, Mother, we've had this all over about that borax. I know you don't like it, but I do, and I use it. It's advertised on the radio as the best washin borax there is."

"You'd use a cow-tird if the feller on the radio said to."

"Mother, you watch your tongue. Mildred hears enough of that talk down around the shore."

"Yeller soap was always good enough for me," said Grammy. She spread out her dry old claws and regarded them. "When you write the feller on the radio after one a them prizes you don't never git, you can tell him that Mrs. 'Lonzo Turner always used lye soap, and look at her be-yootiful hands today. As for Mid, I guess Mid wouldn't know what a nasty word meant, now would she?"

Josie felt her temper going. She was tired and nervous anyway, what with getting up so early with Hardy and Leonard, and she had promised herself the treat of sending for the new dishes. She liked to keep something nice in reserve against the time when she needed it. And this morning when the wind had gone down and she knew Hardy had dropped his nets uselessly again, she figured she needed it. Grammy knew where the box tops were, she was sure of it, and Grammy knew that she knew.

"You never heard any of the children talk nasty around the house," she snapped.

"Oh, ain't I? Hah! That Haral's foul-moutheder'n a Portygee, and you just ask Mid what she said when she slopped the pot over this mornin!"

"Mildred!" Josie called. "Come in here a minute."

"Wha-at?" Mildred appeared from the shed, dragging the word and her feet after her. She was a leggy girl of eleven, with a sharp impertinent little face and a cloud of curly yellow hair. Her incessant and violent activity kept her thin and stringy, and a likeness to her grandmother, not apparent in her babyhood, but inherent in the bone structure of the two faces, was beginning to show as they both approached vital turning points in their lives. She had on a pair of ragged overalls outgrown by her brother Haral, and her feet were bare. "What you want, Ma-a?"

"If the's anything I'd wallop the stern of, it's a whine-y youngone," Grammy observed with distaste.

"Mildred," said Josie calmly, not to be diverted. "You been talkin nasty where Grammy could hear you?"

"Why, I ain't! I never did!"

"Don't say 'ain't,'" said Grammy. "It don't sound good. For the lord's sake, Mid, why don't you go put on a dress like a lady? You look like a dose a salts."

Mildred eyed her grandmother with venom. "If you want to know where your box tops are, Ma, they're in Grammy's knit-bag."

"Why! The idea!" Grammy looked incredulous and amazed, but in spite of herself her hand stole down to the knitting bag in her lap.

"She took em off the mantulpiece and put em in there!" Mildred danced up and down between her grandmother and the door. "I see her do it, but she never see me."

"Tch!" Grammy shook her head sorrowfully. "I dunno what your kids'll grow up to be, Josie, the way they've took up swearin and lyin."

"All right, Mother," said Josie. "Just let me look in that bag, will you, please?"

"I got all my private business in this bag," said the old lady. "My will and my letters from 'Lonzo before he died. I'll look myself." She fumbled about, producing a suspicious tearing sound from the depths of the bag. "I declare, Josie. They *are* in here. Well, we know who done it. The one that knew where they was. And look at that! One of em's tore right in two! If that ain't the hatefullest youngone . . ."

"Fault's in the finder, stink lies behind her," chanted Mildred. She ducked for the door, but too late to escape Josie's firm hand on her arm.

"Tell your grandmother you're sorry for that sarse," said Josie.

Mildred's mouth set in a stubborn line. Then she muttered, " 'M sorry," under her breath, and slid out the door as Josie let go her hold.

"Praps you can glue that tore one together, but I dunno. It's tore quite bad, ain't it?" said Grammy brightly.

"What's the matter, Ma?" Leonard, in trousers and shirtsleeves, had come down the back stairs. "You and Gram havin another fight?"

"No. Just the same one," said Josie. "It's been goin on for sixteen years, and I guess it won't stop till one of us plays out." She went past him into the shed, her firm cheeks bright red with anger.

"Don't count on it's bein me!" Grammy shrilled after her. "Shut up, Leonard. I been tryin to turn a heel for three hours and can I git a chance to count? I can *not!*"

Leonard grinned at her. "Go on, Gram, you could keep count turnin a heel if your pants fell off. You been raisin the deuce again?"

"No," said Grammy. "All I ask is to spend my declinin days in peace and quiet. I'm an old woman and I don't amount to nothin . . ."

"Okay," said Leonard. "I'm cryin. What was the idea, you yellin down here and makin such a racket, when I was upstairs tryin to sleep?"

"What was the idea of spendin all your daylight hours

sleepin?" retorted Grammy. Her good nature had quite returned to her. Leonard was the apple of her eye. "The time to sleep is in the night, when the lord knows last night I tried to, but the' was so much noise I couldn't."

"That was me," said Leonard. "I fell upstairs."

"Rantin home from the movies at all hours," sniffed Grammy. "Prob'ly drunk."

"Mm-hm. Awful drunk. I nigh ended up into the bed with you."

Grammy cackled, delighted. "You'd a been welcome as the flowers in May." She looked speculative, following out the train of thought this provoked. "Where's your father?"

"Down tyin up his nets," said Leonard, rummaging in the cupboard. "Marm! What can I have to eat?"

"Your breakfast's in the warmin oven," said Josie from the other room. "That is, if you could call it breakfast."

Leonard wrinkled his nose at the platter of dried-up baked beans. "For gosh sakes!"

"No, I wouldn't call it breakfast, either," said Grammy, peering around his elbow. "Give it to the cat, Leonard. I'll fry you an egg."

"I had eggs. Look, Gram, I'll have some doughnuts and coffee. I ain't very hungry."

He ate in a hurry, knowing that he had already wasted what should have been a busy day. Morris and Joe Comey would have been working on the haddock drag since six o'clock, and he could imagine what Morris would have to say about his being so late.

"Where's Haral . . . you know?" he asked Gram, swallowing the last of his coffee and picking up his cap.

"Nobody knows," said Grammy. "And that's where he always is. If I was your mother I'd bat them two youngone's heads together, but, there, the youngest always gits ruint. Your Grampa 'Lonzo and I certainly did spoil an awful good man in your father."

"What you want Haral for?" Josie called from the shed.

"Well, I can't go out and give Pa a hand, and somebody ought to. I've got to help Joe and Morris mend net."

"If he comes home, I'll send him down," Josie said.

"She thinks them nets is too heavy for the poor weak little feller," said Grammy sarcastically in a stage whisper. "She's out there writin her billy ducks to the feller on the radio. Don't know what she wants oatmeal dishes for. Ain't none of us likes oatmeal."

"Take it easy, Gram," said Leonard, eyeing her. "Marm'll cut your guzzet out one of these days, and I don't know's I'd blame her."

He hastily closed the door behind him and went down the shore path in search of his younger brother.

✦

THE August morning after the gale had turned clear and cool, with a few shredded clouds drifting across a mildly blue sky. The light breeze barely wrinkled the surface of the broad bay that stretched out to the islands and the mainland, which, on the western side of Comey's, was fifteen miles away. Canvasback Island, Comey's nearest neighbor, a mile and a half to the southwest, so called because of a bare granite hill which reared up in the middle of it, showed a light dusting of spray at the foot of its beaches. But that was the only sign of what last night had looked to be the beginning of the early fall gales.

[17]

Be good weather for a while longer, Leonard thought. He went steadily down the path, his rubber boots clumping on the hard-packed dirt. He hoped Joe and Morris hadn't raised too much hell with the dragnet yesterday. It would be good if they could get the benefit of fine weather as long as it lasted.

The New York House, he figured, was the best place to look for Haral. That was where the Comey's Island males headed for when they were in from fishing, and the regular loafing place of any who felt they hadn't much to do.

The New York House was a kind of community fishhouse on the east beach of Comey's Island Pool, the almost landlocked little harbor, where they kept their fishing boats. It was owned by the men of six or eight different families, its gear-cluttered rooms passed along through the years from father to son. An out-of-state man named Gray had built it, long ago, for a summer camp. He had started with a single room, but each year, for a time, he had added on, doing the work himself and for some reason of his own—possibly because it was easier—setting his rooms end to end and making them all the same size, until he had a one-storied structure eight rooms long.

Old Man Comey, who had been alive then, had said that the place was a "New York" house and nothin but a damn frig, and that the first good gale would blow it down. Old Man Comey didn't think much of a summer cottage anyway unless it had laths and plaster and an upstairs and at least two gables, and was built by local labor at the going prices.

Gray, dead now, had been bankrupt for years and his property sold for taxes—to no one's surprise, it might be said—and only a few of the older people on Comey's remembered where the New York House had got its name. But it still stood, weathered silver, a little sagged into the beach rocks on the north, where Old Man Comey's grandsons had let the sill rot away under their end of it. The men built lobster traps there and painted buoys and baited trawl and stored bait and gear; but more than anything, they gathered there for talk.

Haral was loafing in the sun with his chum, young Saylor Comey, listening to Perley Higgins and one or two others egg on old Jarv Willow to talk about the government.

The gov'mint, Jarv said, didn't pay enough pensions and never would, Republican or Democrat. Besides, taxes were too high. The time was a-comin when every man, woman, and child would have a little meter right on his breastbone to measure the air he breathed, and by Jeezus, if you didn't put your quarter into it, you wouldn't git your breath. What the gov'mint used the money for, Jarv didn't know. He'd jest as soon live under one a them damn kings. Now a old king, when he frittled away the tax money, he done it accordin to law and order. He hat to, because it was the law for a king *to* spend money. But Hoover, he spent it all on doctor's bills, had diabetus the day he was 'lected, from all that sugar he et durin the war.

"Haral." Leonard gave his brother's shoulder a nudge in passing. "How about goin off and givin Pa a hand with them nets?"

Haral gave him the enigmatic, slightly inimical glance that Leonard had learned to expect from him, and edged away. "Sayl and I've got some trawls to bait. We git paid for that."

"Okay. Then you better make some plans for gettin across the bay to the movies Saturday night, because you ain't goin with me," said Leonard. "You'll find the rowin's fine." He said no more, knowing the futility of argument with Haral. He went on to the end of the fish-house, where Joe Comey and his brother Morris were mending the dragnet. Out of the corner of his eye he saw that Haral had pulled himself away from the fascinating pastime of waiting until Jarv got around to Roosevelt, and was deep in conversation with Sayl Comey.

Haral, he had guessed, had been going, as usual, to beg for transportation across the bay and back on Saturday night. Pay him enough and you'll get what you want, Leonard thought. That's the only language he speaks.

At fifteen, Haral Turner, christened Harold, seemed to his elders to live in an absorbed world from which he emerged briefly when spoken to loudly enough, and to which he returned without hearing what had been said. He was at home only at mealtimes, unless forcibly detained to do chores, which was not often, because he had an Indian's skill in vanishing silently and without trace.

When Hardy or Josie took him to task because the weeds were crowding out the vegetables in the garden, or because Hardy after a day's work had to split kindling and fill the woodbox, Haral would pull a few weeds or fill the woodbox for one day. Somehow he didn't seem to understand that the same work had to be done *every* day.

"But you didn't tell me to," he would say, gazing at his father reproachfully. "You didn't say you wanted it done."

Hardy felt he did not understand the bringing up of Haral and Mildred. He himself had had his own skiff for lobstering when he was thirteen, and had taken care of chores around the house as well. But he seldom mentioned that, because Grammy, who heard everything, was sure to remark that she couldn't see where *he* had amounted to much. Leonard was turning out all right, but he and Josie had both seen to it that Leonard learned how to work around a house and boat as soon as he had been old enough. And now Leonard was considered one of the smartest young men in the village. He was making money at fishing—had a hand for it, the oldtimers said.

Leonard, at twenty-two, had an eight-hundred-dollar fishing boat of his own, and he owned a third of Joe and Morris Comey's haddock drag. Hardy had wanted him to go to high school, and Leonard, under protest, had spent two winters over on the mainland, where he had done well enough and had been second or third in his class. But when the third fall rolled around, wild horses couldn't have dragged him back to school, and Hardy had finally given in, though sometimes he wondered if he would have if money hadn't been short that season.

Hardy didn't know why children growing up had changed, but it seemed to him they had. Haral and Mildred wanted more, and had more, than Leonard ever did. Hardy felt it in the increased pressure on him to make more money.

Haral didn't need a bicycle, for instance. It was kind of foolish to have a bicycle on Comey's Island, where there wasn't more than half a mile of road to ride a bicycle on. Of course, Haral was going to high school this fall, and he could use it over on the mainland. But it had seemed to Hardy that since money was so tight this year Haral might have been willing to put the price of the bicycle into his schooling. And then, after Haral got one, Mid had to have one, too.

Looking at his two youngest sometimes, seeing their blank withdrawn stares when he tried to direct them, Hardy felt a strange and, to him, disloyal sense of disaster. What would there be anyway in the world for two youngsters who didn't know how to work and couldn't be happy working?

Now he experienced a feeling of slight surprise as he saw Haral and young Sayl Comey come rowing into the weir in Leonard's skiff. The kids must either be just out rowing around or Haral wanted something.

"Goin fishin?" he asked, with mild sarcasm, as Haral laid the skiff alongside the weir dory.

"Sayl and I thought you might like some help, seein you been up all night." Haral turned a clear blue gaze of reproachful innocence on his father. "Where'll we start in?"

Hardy was touched. "I dunno's you and Sayl's hefty enough to handle them nets, are you?"

Haral looked regretful. "I dunno's we are," he said. "How's about it, Sayl?"

Sayl reared his near six feet of sixteen-year-old manhood off the stern seat of the skiff and peered doubtfully at the hanging nets, heavy with tar and sea water. "Try it, maybe. I could, all right, but my wrist's still kind a lame where I twisted it."

Hardy hid a wry grin. "Well, thanks for the offer." He turned back to his job, his hands moving smoothly along the stiff ropes. He blinked a little in the bright sun. Must be nigh dinnertime, and he was *darn* tired and hungry.

Haral let go the dory and the skiff drifted lazily off into the middle of the weir pound.

"Look!" said Sayl suddenly, his voice charged with excitement. "Ain't that a mackerel, Haral?"

Haral leaned over. "Where?"

"Right there by the edge of the pound. See? There he goes!"

"Yeah . . . there's another one!"

"Say, Hardy! The's some mackerel in here."

"Yes," said Hardy. "I seen em. Six of em. Big ones."

"Ain't you goin to git em?"

"Well, there ain't really enough worth runnin the seine for. I'm pretty tired."

"We'll git em," said Haral. "Look, Pa, if we git em, can we have em to sell?"

"Sure. How'll you git em?"

"Where's your big dipnet?"

"Ashore in the seine dory. You don't think you're goin to go along and dip out them mackerel without no seine, do you?"

He might have saved his breath, he thought. The boys tore out of the weir in a whirl of water as Haral bent to his oars, heading the skiff for the Pool and the seine dory.

They brought back the big unwieldy dipnet, with its ten-foot handle. Sayl held it, balancing in the stern of the skiff, calling out terse orders to Haral at the oars.

Hours later, when Hardy went ashore, they were still belaboring the skiff around and around the weir pound, sweating profusely, after two remaining fish that seemed always to dodge away from the dipnet.

LEONARD saw, sitting down on an inverted bait tub alongside Joe and Morris, that they had had really hard luck with the dragnet. Down one side of the big hundred-foot tapered cylinder of twine, a gaping irregular slit fifteen feet long had been torn and shredded. They had been dragging for haddock on the Mary Shoal and had got the gear hung down on something—possibly a big rock or a submerged wreck. Leonard wondered, seeing the hole, how they had managed to clear the drag without losing it.

"You was lucky," he said. "Been me, I'd have sunk the works." He wanted Joe and Morris to know he wasn't blaming them for wrecking the net. While the three of them owned it on shares and usually went dragging together, this summer Leonard had a string of lobster traps as well, and every other trip he stayed to haul his traps while Joe and Morris went alone.

"Hell," said Joe glumly, "warn't no luck connected with it. Took us three hours to clear, and look at the damn thing. Opened up like a tin can."

"Lucky to have it at all," said Morris briefly. "If I'd took Joe's advice, we wouldn't have."

Joe flushed. "That's right," he admitted. "I wanted to start up the engine and rip her loose, guts, feathers, and all, but Morris, he kept friggin, and he finally got her clear."

Morris laughed. "What really happened," he said, in his light, dry voice, "was, Joe cussed her loose."

He was put out, Leonard guessed, hauling a section of torn net across his own knees. Morris could practically take a man's skin off without raising that voice of his, and something in the tone of it now made Joe ridiculous, as if all he had done in a taut situation was sit around and swear.

[24]

Joe straightened his big shoulders and let out his breath with a smothered *pouf* of impatience. "Anything under God's green sky I hate it's mendin net," he stated. "Just as soon do a woman's crochet work, by God!"

"Maybe you better borry some of Cack's and practice up," said Morris, glancing over at Joe's row of knots. His own small flexible fingers moved without ceasing, intricately weaving the new twine into the jagged hole. With the possible exception of Hardy Turner, there was not a better man for ropework along the coast than Morris. He could, when he wanted to show off a little, perform the exceedingly difficult trick of "keeping the needle in the air," that is, draw his knot in the twine tight with one hand, catch up the next loop and make a knot so fast that the flickering needle seemed to be always "in the air." Joe's hands were too big and clumsy. He made something less than ordinary speed.

"Wonder what you fellas could have got hung down on," Leonard said hastily. That last crack of Morris's had made Joe mad, he could see that. He wondered if Joe would ever take a poke at Morris. He supposed not. Anyone who bothered Morris, or even twitted him about his size, was shortly made to regret it extremely, in one way or another.

No one, looking at Morris, would ever guess he was a Comey. The other Comeys were big and dark and heavy-handed, all of them except Morris over six feet tall. Old Man Comey, their grandfather, had been typical, and so were Joe and Saylor, who looked like him. Joe, at twenty-three, stood six-feet-two and weighed close to two hundred pounds. He had black eyes, set deep under bushy black brows, a wild shock of black hair, afid an Indian-dark skin that stayed tanned black the year around. Saylor was a younger edition of him, and Homer, an older brother, drowned with their father three years ago, had looked like that, too.

But Morris was a small, graceful man, scarcely five feet tall, sandy-haired and blue-eyed. His bones were delicate, almost birdlike, and he might have weighed a hundred and twenty pounds. Beside either of his brothers he looked almost womanish. But there was nothing feminine in the proportions of his little body, nor in the wiry effortlessness with which he could use it.

Morris was thirty, seven years older than Joe. He had run away to sea at fifteen and had knocked about the world for twelve years in ships of one kind or another. His family seldom heard from him and never knew where he was; but when his father and Homer had drowned in a squall off Grindstone Ledge, Morris had somehow got word of it. From whatever strange port he had been in at the time, he had come home to stay.

The Comeys, easy-going and haphazard, had not known what to make of him. Jasper's boys, Eddy and Will, his cousins, remembered him from schooldays and let him strictly alone, but some of the younger men tried at first to make him one of themselves, with the good-natured kidding which was second nature to them. They found out at once that Morris wasn't one of them and didn't intend to be.

He took his place as the head of the family, and after a while the others uneasily acknowledged him as such. For whatever superiority of size and strength the big fellows had over Morris, they couldn't out-think him and he knew it. It was significant that not one of them had ever laid a hand on him.

For a while the three mended net in silence, broken only when Leonard swore at seeing Haral and Sayl row into the Pool to get Hardy's dipnet.

"Look at that damn kid!"

"What's the matter with him?" asked Morris, glancing up.

"I sent him off to help Pa. Might have known he'd get out of it somehow."

Morris grinned. "Guess you'll have to show him, eh?"

The slight accent on the word "you" made Leonard squirm a little, but he said nothing. He had been expecting a dig or so from Morris about his late arrival at the shore that morning.

Well, he thought, now he's got that off his chest.

Morris laid down his wooden needle carelessly and stood up, stretching his arms. "Kind of cramped," he said. "Been at this since daylight. Guess I'll take a rest and let you fellows catch up with me. Got to keep your hand in, you know." He moved off lazily down the beach, strutting a little, his chest out.

"What's the matter with him today, Joe?"

"God, I dunno. Can't be the hole in the net, because he was all right this mornin," said Joe. "Somethin's happened he don't approve of, I guess. You can't ever tell with him. What wouldn't bother a common man, Morris'll take as a mortal insult, and the other way round. Matter of fact, I *was* to blame for gittin the gear hung down."

"Well, that could happen to anyone."

"Not on the Mary Shoal. I was steerin the boat and I let her sag off to the south'ard. We was onto rough bottom before I realized."

"Uh-huh," nodded Leonard.

"Morris never turned a hair, except he ribbed hell out of me. If the's anything he loves, it's to see me get my tail in a crack."

"Aw, you let it bother you too much, Joe."

"Sure. But when he horns me, I git mad. I wish sometimes I hadn't ever give up my own boat to put in with him."

"Ayeh, but without the big boat we couldn't go draggin. The only thing to do was to throw in together."

"Just the same, I'd rather be my own boss again."

Morris came back as abruptly as he had left. "I thought them kids was comin ashore," he said casually. "Had somethin to say to em. I feel like a hot meal, Joe. I'm goin up to the house. I'll be back by the time you slowpokes catch up to me."

"Guess he figures he'll even it up with me for bein late this mornin," said Leonard, looking after him.

Morris, as a matter of fact, did not return until three o'clock, taking off exactly the amount of time that Leonard had missed in the morning. He returned and picked up his needle casually, as if he had been gone ten minutes.

"Guess them kids have got a project off in the weir," he commented, looking off to see if they were still there.

"Not workin, I bet," said Leonard.

"Why should they, if they can get out of it?"

"Somebody's got to learn them two somethin besides plannin deviltry."

"I'll learn Sayl a few things," said Morris, his eyes narrowing. "Gi'me time. And your old man will likely tend to Haral."

"Haral been up to somethin?" Hardy had come up the beach from where he had anchored his dory. He sat down, mopping his forehead, on a plank laid across two pickle kegs beside the fishhouse.

"I sent him off to help you, Pa," said Leonard. "Why didn't you make him?"

"Oh, I was about finished," Hardy answered. "He's a little light yet for handlin them wet nets."

Morris said without looking up: "My dinner bucket's right around the corner of the fishhouse door, Hardy. There's a thermos half full of hot coffee in it."

"Thanks, Morris," said Hardy gratefully. "I can use it. Sure you're all through with it?"

Morris glanced at him briefly, his eyes expressionless. "Help yourself."

Hardy unscrewed the thermos cap, poured it full of the steaming drink and took a hearty swallow. For a moment he sat as if paralyzed. Then his face convulsed. He turned sickly green around the mouth and retched violently.

"Chrise, Morris!" he gasped after a moment. "What was in it?"

"God, I dunno," said Morris, getting up concernedly. "It was okay this noon. Le's see it."

"You all right, Pa?" Leonard looked at his father in alarm.

"Yes, I'm all right, but I thought for a while there I was goin to die," said Hardy. "What you tryin to do, Morris? Poison somebody?"

"Smells like fish oil," said Morris. He turned a little of the coffee into the thermos cap and held it to the light. "*Is* fish oil, by God! Now, who in hell done that? I'm sorry as the devil, Hardy. I could shoot whoever tried that scrummy trick."

"So could I," said Hardy briefly. He sat quietly for a moment, obviously swallowing.

"Somebody don't like you, Morris," said Leonard, eyeing him. Something screwy about this, he thought. It wasn't like Morris to apologize all over the place.

"Could be." Morris returned his stare, his cold blue

[29]

eyes blank as a platter. He had finished his section of net mending and was winding up his twine. He stowed the twine away on his workbench and took down a ball of gangion and began to rig a cod line on a pound lead. "You fellas don't git your share done before dark," he offered, "I'll finish it for you tomorrow."

Somebody's goin to up and slat the daylights out of him one a these days, Leonard thought. Yet you never could quite put your finger on Morris. You were pretty sure you had him, and then you always discovered he had an out.

Haral and Sayl came up the beach to the fishhouse, their string of big mackerel flashing bright sides to the sun.

"We got all six of em," Haral said proudly. "You didn't think we could do it without the seine, did you, Pa?"

"Why, no, son," said Hardy, "I didn't. You and Sayl didn't put the fish oil in Morris's thermos, did you?"

In the split second of silence which followed, an electric unspoken communication flashed between Haral and Sayl, and then was gone, leaving both faces blank, incredulous, and brightly shocked.

"Gosh, Pa, no!"

"Gee, Hardy, Haral and me wouldn't play no such lousy trick!"

"I got a swig of it," said Hardy grimly. "I'd lick who done it if I found out who 't was."

"Well, it sure warn't us."

"We never done it."

Morris sat idly swinging the cod line with its lead weight between his thighs. "I don't believe they done it, Hardy," he observed disinterestedly. "That Burncoat boat was in here this mornin, I see them fellas had a can of oil. Must a been their idea of a joke. Leave one of them mackerel for me, Sayl. I want it for supper.''

Sayl hesitated, glancing at Haral. They had been going to peddle the mackerel through the village to get spending money for Saturday night's movies.

"You better ask Hardy what to do with the mackerel. They belong to him." Joe suddenly spoke from the other side of the dragnet. His voice was slightly hoarse and his face black with anger.

"Oh, Pa give em to us off in the weir," said Haral, waving his hand expansively. "We can have em, can't we, Pa?"

"Yes, you can have em."

"I said I wanted one," said Morris. His voice had a soft, almost purring tone. "But never mind."

Sayl, suddenly startled, glanced at him, then got the point. Morris, for some reason, was covering up for him and Haral, but he wanted his pay for it. "Okay, Morris. Here you are." He picked out the smallest of the mackerel and laid it on the bench. "Come on, Haral." He jerked his head urgently. "Come *on!*"

Morris glanced at the mackerel. He seemed not to be looking at Sayl, yet suddenly the weighted cod line seemed to slip from his idly swinging hand, lashed through the air and struck Sayl sharply on the cheekbone.

Sayl cried out and clapped his hand to his cheek. Blood began to run slowly down under his collar.

"Godsake, bub," said Morris, coming over to him. "That sure was careless of me. You hurt much?" He took hold of Sayl's wrist and tried to pull his hand away from the wound. "I sure didn't realize you was standin so near me when I swung that."

[31]

But Sayl held his hand tightly over his cheek and blubbered.

Joe's big fist closed around Morris's small one. "Le' go, Morris. Morris, if you don't le' go, I'll squat your damn hand off your arm. Sayl, come down to the salt water and have that cut washed."

Morris watched them go, the curious blank look back on his face again. "Well," he said to Hardy, "I hope it ain't cut bad. I guess it ain't. I warn't swingin that line very hard."

"Good thing you wasn't," said Hardy dryly.

"Warn't it? Quittin time, wouldn't you say? If you're goin up the road now, I'll walk along with you."

Leonard and Haral waited while Joe washed Sayl's cheek and tied up the cut with his handkerchief. They were gone for quite a while. Joe seemed to be having quite a lot to say to Sayl. Once Leonard glanced at Haral, but Haral was sitting on the bench staring at the ground between his shoes.

When they finally came up the beach, Sayl had stopped crying, but his cheek, where the handkerchief did not cover it, was swelling and turning blue, and blood was beginning to seep through the bandage.

"Cut bad?" asked Leonard of Joe. Since they had gone to grade school together, he thought, he hadn't seen Joe so mad.

"Laid his whole cheek open. Guess it'll be all right, but he's likely to have a bad scar." Joe paused, then turned to look at Haral, who was watching him, wide-eyed and scared. "Sayl says you two did do that job with the fish oil."

"Er . . . yes." Haral was too taken aback to lie.

"Caused a lot of trouble."

"Yeah," said Haral foolishly.

[32]

"Don't never play no tricks on Morris," said Joe, speaking carefully. "He takes any kind of a joke on him like a deadly insult, and he gits it back on you. He got it back on you through your old man. He knew that oil was in the coffee when he offered it to Hardy, because I see him startin to swig out of it after you went off to the weir. Your pa'd been up all night, too. Sayl, he's had what amounts to a good lickin, but it looks to me like you had yours comin."

"Don't you touch me, damn you!" said Haral.

"I ain't goin to. Come on, Sayl. Le's go git some salve on that cut."

"He won't have to," said Leonard grimly, taking off his belt.

THE drink of fish oil, on top of twenty-four hours of worry and exhaustion, upset Hardy completely. By the time he had got home, he was too sick to eat any supper. He made a half-hearted attempt to do the night chores, but gave up after the second armload of wood and went upstairs to bed.

Josie was sorry for him and sympathetic, because sickness of any kind went straight to her heart. But at the same time she was furious with him. Since he had not explained about the fish oil, she put his illness down to his wearing himself out needlessly. Two or three times during the day she had gone to the upstairs window, which overlooked the weir, to watch his progress. At half-past two, sputtering, she had put up a hot dinner for him in a dinner bucket, planning to send it down to him as soon as she could waylay either Mildred or Haral. But neither of the children had come home during the afternoon, and just as she was preparing to take it down to the shore herself, Cack Comey, her next-door neighbor, had come in to call.

Cack had dropped one or two remarks, in a joking way, about Hardy's caution, and had succeeded in convincing Josie that the entire village was making fun of him.

It was hard for Josie to take ridicule from Cack Comey. Josie had a deep sense of family pride. There was no doubt in her mind that she and Hardy were well-born and, being so, had definite standards to maintain. Every ounce of her magnificent energy Josie threw into maintaining those standards. She was not a snob in the sense that she felt superior to everybody, but certain of her neighbors kept houses that were not spotless, their dooryards were cluttered with trash, and, worst of all, their children were neither well-trained nor very clean. Josie had a succinct word which included all such people, and which she used stingingly upon occasion. The word was "culch."

"What can you expect from that culch?" Josie would say distastefully.

She never went to call on Cack Comey until she had to, to keep up the goodwill between neighbors, not very stable in the village, people being as touchy as they were. When she did, she would put on a crisp, neat housedress and go the few hundred steps down the hill to "put in an afternoon" in Cack's frowzy, unaired kitchen. Once she happened along just as Cack's large family were having one of their irregular meals at the long kitchen table, and she had seen Weeza, Cack's six-year-old daughter, instead of asking for the potatoes, climb up on the table and walk the whole length of it to bring the platter back to her place.

[34]

"Barefooted," Josie told Hardy afterwards. "An neither Jasper nor Cack said one word."

They had chuckled together over it, but Hardy could see that Josie didn't really think it was funny. She worked too hard keeping her own establishment in order to have much patience with things like that. For himself, Hardy wouldn't have thought of it much except to laugh a little. Jap Comey was shiftless and he had never particularly liked him, but he had known him all his life. They had gone to school on the island together. Jap, son of Old Man Comey's cousin, had never been away from the island for more than an occasional trip to one of the mainland towns. Cack, his wife, had been an island girl. But Josie had been brought up differently, and naturally such things would bother her, particularly since Mid and Haral played a lot with the Comey kids.

Josie had come from Bellport, fifty miles away on the mainland. Her father had been Captain Hosea Scott, famous from Nova Scotia to Boston as a skipper and owner of coast trading schooners, and her grandfathers on both sides had been captains of clipper ships. Hardy, when she had married him, was the most promising and the smartest beau of a number who had been courting her at the time. He had been to school and he had been in most of the big cities of the world.

When she had first seen him to notice him, he was coming off the wharf at Bellport with his suitcase on his shoulder, his pea jacket over his arm, and his officer's cap cocked over one ear. He was on his way home to Comey's Island from the port of Brooklyn, New York, where his ship had docked the week before. She was a fast freighter in the South American trade, and Hardy was first mate of her, with a year to go before he went up for his captain's papers.

[35]

Josie had been down to the harbormaster's office to see if any word was there of her father's four-sticker, due any day now from St. John's, and she had heard Hardy before she had seen him, swearing bitterly and brilliantly because he could not find anyone to carry his slops. She knew who he was, because before he had gone away to sea she had seen him once or twice at Bellport dances.

"My goodness, Hardy Turner," Josie said, "is that all they learn you to the west'ard?"

Hardy hadn't batted an eye. He had set the suitcase down, touched his cap jauntily, and asked if she weren't Cap'n Scott's girl and where he was likely to find her father.

Since there was no word of Cap'n Scott, and since Hardy wanted very much to ask his advice about a new scheme he had for coast freighting, the best thing to do seemed to be to find a room in Bellport and settle down to wait for him.

By the time the captain arrived, which was in five days, Josie and Hardy had their courting done, and the question that Hardy asked him first was not anything about coast freighting but if he could marry his daughter.

The captain was outraged. His wife had been dead for three years, and he had counted on keeping Josie as his housekeeper for some years to come. She was only nineteen, but even then a magnificent worker, her house shining spotless, her cooking already famous in the town. Besides, she was the prettiest girl in Bellport, and he had other plans for her. He put up every logical argument he could think of, and some arguments which weren't.

Josie was too young for him—Hardy was twenty-six—

and she'd be better off with a boy her own age. Hardy hadn't a cent—as a matter of fact, he had five hundred dollars. Cap'n Hosea had gone shipmates once with 'Lonzo Turner, and 'Lonzo had had a terrible temper which he couldn't control and which had lost him a good vessel once. Hardy had to agree about his father's temper, but as to the vessel, she had gone adrift one night in a southeaster, when a careless deck hand had failed to make her moorings shipshape.

Finally Cap'n Hosea put his foot down with a flat "No, by God, you ain't goin to marry any damn Comey's Islander."

But Josie and Hardy were married by a justice of the peace, and the captain had turned up in the middle of the ceremony in his best blue uniform, standing in the corner by the door, glaring and muttering into his beard. When the muttering had become too loud and disturbed the marriage service, Hardy had stopped the justice in the middle of a sentence. He stepped down and confronted his father-in-law-to-be with a level eye.

"If you don't like my weddin, Cap'n Scott, I'd advise you to go som'ers else. I'm glad to have you here, but there's times in a man's life when he won't take meddlin, and this is one in mine."

All through the years of her married life that was a moment which Josie had remembered with swelling pride in her husband—Hardy in his new dark suit and white collar, standing up to hard-bitten, brawny old Captain Hosea. He had stared him down, too, eye to eye, until the old man looked away.

After that Hardy had had to change his plans. Obviously he couldn't ask old Scott to go in with him on his freighting venture now. He had planned, with considerable brashness, to suggest combining his idea with

Cap'n Hosea's vessels. There was no one else to ask, because Cap'n Hosea had the Bellport trade sewed up in his pocket.

Hardy was sick of going to sea. He had never liked the water, and he was convinced that his bent was toward a business on shore. But his five hundred dollars wasn't enough to buy out anything worth while. He thought at first of going back to the ship, getting his captain's papers, and saving money for a few more years. But Josie wanted him to stay with her, and he didn't feel like leaving her alone, either.

Finally he had suggested to her going back to Comey's Island. "I could get a lobster boat and a string of traps with this five hundred," he told her. "And we wouldn't have to live with Ma and Pa. I know a house over there I can get for little or nothin."

To his surprise Josie had burst into tears. "It seems like an awful come-down," she sobbed. "I don't want to go over there with them people, Hardy."

He was hurt and not a little shocked. "Judas, Josie, Comey's Island is all right. They're nice people. What'd you think it is—a Shantytown?"

"Well, no, but—"

"It's just like Bellport, honey, only it's an island and the town ain't but a little one. The's twenty families lives over there. It's only three miles off the coast, and they all send their kids over here to school."

In the end they had gone, and Hardy, after lobstering for three years, made enough to buy out the herring-weir privileges from Charley Warren.

At the time, the weir looked like a good investment. There were only a few herring weirs in those days, and with half luck a man could make a good season's work selling herring to the sardine factories and bait to the fishermen. Sometimes, if the fish were scarce, the buyers would bid a catch up to a dollar and a half a bushel. Charley Warren had had more than half luck. In his last season, due to a set of advantageous circumstances, he had made three thousand dollars.

"Enough to quit on," he told Hardy, the day he turned the weir privileges over to him.

The first years Hardy's luck went up and down. Five hundred dollars clear the first summer, a thousand the next. The third, he went in the hole. The year his father died, Hardy borrowed money, built on an addition to 'Lonzo Turner's old house, and opened a small general store. With Josie's help he farmed part of his land and raised enough potatoes and other vegetables for his family through the summer and to fill the cellar through the winter. He kept a cow and chickens and two pigs. At first, in addition to tending weir, he ran a string of lobster traps.

With all the irons he had in the fire, it meant hard work from before dawn until dark. But Hardy liked work. Josie did, too, and understood it. She put in as long a day as he did, helping in the garden as well as running the house, and in summers, when she could get summer people to come, cooking for sometimes as many as twelve besides her own family.

Just when the change had begun to come, neither Josie nor Hardy could say. It might have been the year when Leonard refused to finish high school, a bitter disappointment to them both. Josie couldn't see why he preferred to be a fisherman rather than to "make something of himself." She had hopes for Haral, but they would have to wait.

The store barely broke even, as the years went by. The population of Comey's was slowly dwindling. Each year somebody moved away, until there were only eight families left. Each year it took five hundred dollars of savings to rebuild the weir, for labor and replacement of nets. Josie and Hardy mortgaged the house once, one summer when the weir failed to fish at all, and they were three years paying the mortgage off. They never could seem to lay anything by, and Josie couldn't for the life of her see how, when money would be needed, for Haral's schooling, and something for Mid to start out with, they ever would be able to find it . . . unless some lucky summer the weir took the notion to fish the way it had for Charley Warren.

Josie went briskly up the stairs with a bottle of castor oil in one hand and a cup of hot water in the other in which a teaspoon of wintergreen extract had been diluted—her remedies for an upset stomach.

Hardy swallowed the wintergreen obediently, but at the mention of the oil he muttered incoherently and buried his head in the pillow.

"Well, I don't see how you'll get your stomach to rights if you won't take dosin," said Josie, mildly surprised at his display of temper. "Where *do* you feel bad, Hardy?"

"I'll be all right. Just need sleep."

"I should think so!" She said no more for a moment, but stood regarding him. He did look bad, and her heart smote her. But to save her life she couldn't keep quiet, after the day she had had. "Cack Comev was in here this afternoon."

"Was she?" Hardy's voice, muffled by the pillow, registered a deep indifference.

"Yes, she was. And I wish she'd keep to home with her slurs."

"Who she slur?"

"Us."

Josie went to the bureau, took out her sidecombs and began to comb her hair with short, raking strokes. She was usually careful with her hair. It was light and fine and graying, and little tendrils of it curled softly about her face and in the back of her neck, in "scolding locks." But now the comb squeaked as she pulled out a snarl here and there without stopping to untangle it.

Hardy rolled over on the mattress and pulled the bedclothes away from his chest. He certainly did feel rocky and he wished Josie'd go downstairs and let him sleep. "What we been doin that Cack don't approve of?"

"She just said that there was them around the island had quit takin a long breath for fear the wind would make you go and drop your nets down." Josie waited, putting her sidecombs in with little stabs. She turned, but Hardy was lying with his eyes closed, his breathing deep and regular. "H'm! I know you ain't to sleep!"

As he did not reply, she pulled the bedclothes over his chest, her hands gentle, out of habit, and went downstairs to get the boys' supper on the table.

It did not ease her annoyance any that Leonard and Haral were late. When at six-thirty they had not come, she left Mildred to superintend the supper in the warming-oven and went out to do the night chores herself. She milked the cow, and carried in wood, and split kindling with a kind of outraged righteousness. The hens were only languidly interested in the corn she threw out, and she discovered from the empty nests that Gram must have already fed them and gathered the eggs.

"I wish you'd let me know when you feed up," she fumed, coming into the kitchen with her pail of milk. "I've gone and wasted a whole feedin of corn on them hens."

[41]

"Eat it for breakfast, won't they?" said Grammy. "How come them smart, lovely boys of yourn is lettin their mother do the barn work?"

"You have to remember that them smart, lovely boys of mine is part Turner," said Josie icily. "I don't recall doin any of the heavy luggin when the Scott menfolks was around."

"H'm, I never knowed there was any Scott menfolks," said Grammy. "Well, here's Leonard now."

Leonard came in, looking harassed and a little shamefaced. He had waited, wanting Haral to get home first. He thought it likely that Haral would keep his licking to himself, considering the scrape he had got everyone into, but with Haral you never knew. In case he did tell, Leonard was counting on his father. His mother, he knew, would be upset. She had never allowed him to punish either of the children.

"Where's Pa?" Leonard asked, hanging his hat behind the door and taking the tin dipper out of the water pail to get himself some washing water from the reservoir on the stove.

"Your pa's to bed sick. He's wore out. Did you see Haral anywhere?"

"He's down to the New York House." Leonard buried his face in a basin of soapy water.

"Well, for the land's sakes, Leonard, why didn't you make him come home?" said Josie irritably.

"Ain't he got sense enough to come home to his meals?" put in Grammy.

"He'll be along," mumbled Leonard. "You have to milk, Marm?"

"Who do you think milked? 'T warn't you, was it?"

Josie put the supper on the table, setting each dish down with a distinct little thump. "Haral can just eat a cold supper, for I ain't goin to wait a minute longer."

They ate in silence, Josie growing more and more ashamed of herself, as she always did when she felt she had been unreasonably irritable with any of her children. Grammy occasionally cast a knowing glance at Leonard, trying to catch his eye.

Leonard avoided looking at her. Trust *her*, he thought, to dope out I got something on my mind.

They were finishing their meal when someone came up on the front porch.

"There's Haral now," Josie said relievedly. "Hand me the biscuits, Leonard. I'll just shove em into the oven while he washes. Where on earth you been, Haral?" she called at the opening door.

"It ain't Haral, I guess." Cack Comey put her head and her fat shoulders inside the door. "Oh, you still eatin, Josie? I thought you'd be up from the table by now. We was through two hours ago. Now, don't git up. I'll jest set till you're through."

"We're most done," said Josie.

"Well, if it ain't just like me, but I was over here all the afternoon and went home and clean forgot what I come for. I got to have a package of saleratus, but the' ain't no hurry."

"Mid, can't you go out in the store and get Cack a package of soda?" said Josie.

"You'll have to write it down on the book, Mid," said Cack. "Jap didn't have a cent a change, nor the boys, neither."

I'll bet they didn't, Josie thought. They better have pretty soon, the store bill you've got.

Cack sat down with a sigh. She was a short woman of much flesh, inclined to be uncertain when she walked because of the great weight put on her tiny feet. Cack was proud of her feet and of her small hands, on which her cheap wedding and engagement rings sank into the soft fat. Her little inquisitive eyes seemed sunk far back into her head because of the expanse of her round rosy cheek beneath them. Everything about her was fleshy— her nose, her chins, even her soft underlip. She was forty-two but she looked ten years younger because of her clear skin, creamy and without wrinkles.

"Eddy was wonderin if you knew where Haral was," Cack said, spreading herself firmly into the rocking chair.

"Why, where is he? Leonard, didn't you say he was down to the New York House?"

"Uh-huh." Leonard finished his tea and scraped his chair back from the table, lighting a cigarette.

"Eddy says he's hid away down in the loft cryin his eyes out, the poor little duffer," said Cack mournfully. "Eddy says he tried to git out of him what was the matter. Said somethin about somebody lickin him."

"Well, for the land's sake!" Josie got up instantly from the table, two red spots on her cheeks. "Who done it? People better lick their own youngones once in a while, from all the actions I hear about goin on. Leonard, you know anything about anyone lickin Haral?"

Leonard shoved his hands in his pockets and looked balefully at Cack through his cigarette smoke. "You couldn't wait to run over here and tell it, could you?" he said bitterly. "I wish you'd stay to home and mind your own business for once."

"Well!" Cack got up, trembling like a jelly with rage. "I never was talked to so in my life, outside my own home. I've always said you was a bad boy, Leonard Turner, ever since you busted Jap's fishhouse door hinges, and I guess I warn't no poor prophet. You ought a been in the reform school years ago!"

"All right, Cack," said Josie. "That's enough. We don't want to hear any more of it. People that live in glass houses had better not go throwin the reform school around. You better go home."

"Well, I certainly will! And it'll be the long day before I darken this door again!"

"And you can look right in your own pullet's nest," Grammy sputtered after her, "if you want to find somebody fit for the reform school!"

With this stab at the younger Comeys, Grammy banged the door behind Cack and, as an afterthought, bolted it.

"Gosh!" said Leonard, blinking, "I never meant to stir up no rat's nest."

"What's this about?" Josie confronted him. "I'm Haral's mother, and if he needs a lickin I'm the one to give it to him, not the neighbors!"

"I take notice you never do," said Grammy.

"All right, Ma," Leonard said. "I'm the one that licked Haral. He had it comin."

"Good!" said Grammy. "You use a club, Leonard?"

"Cut it out, Gram. I used my belt, and I didn't hurt him much. Now, wait, Ma." He held up his hand as Josie started to speak. "Wait till you hear what happened." He told the story faithfully, omitting nothing. "And that's why Pa's sick, too," he finished. "I didn't plan to tell on Haral unless you found out and was sore at me for lickin him. Maybe I hadn't ought to a done it, but I was mad. And he had it comin."

"H'm, he certainly did. And he'd have had it from me. But Haral ain't responsible for Morris Comey's bein

[45]

the next thing to a murderer. 'T warn't nothin but a boy's prank."

"That ain't the point, Marm. It's what come of it."

"All right. But you ever lay another hand on Haral, Leonard Turner, and I'll skin you. You hist yourself down to the New York House and bring him home, you hear?"

"Okay," said Leonard. "I'll git him." He took his cap and slammed wrathfully out of the house.

Halfway to the shore he met Haral, walking along sullenly, his hands driven deep into his trousers pockets.

"About time you got around to come home to supper, ain't it?" asked Leonard.

Haral did not look at him or speak.

"Don't worry," said Leonard bitterly. "It don't matter that Pa's laid up sick, or that Sayl's scarred for life, or that Joe's about ready to commit a murder. All you think about is poor little Haral, he's got his tail warmed."

Haral's shoulders shook, and sobs of rage choked in his throat.

Leonard looked at him disgustedly. "Hell, it's all over. I never hit you hard. You never got half what Sayl did, at that."

He went on down the shore path toward the fish-house. No use to go home and have it all hashed through again. Might as well light the lantern and paint buoys awhile.

He had gone only a few steps when he heard a swishing sound, and a rock the size of a teacup whizzed past a few inches from his head.

"Good God!" said Leonard, aghast. For a moment he was too shocked to be angry, and when he did move, Haral was out of reach, scudding for home like a shadow. Why, that could easy have killed me, thought Leonard. Sobered, he went in to the fishhouse and lit the lantern on the workbench.

HE didn't feel much like painting buoys, or anything else, Leonard reflected, puddling the paint around the inside of the can. If there were only some place where a fellow could go to spend his evenings it would help some. What he usually did was stay home and go to bed early—generally he wanted to, because he had to get up so early in the morning. Either lobstering or dragging, he had to be up long before daylight. Sometimes he and Joe and Morris started out as early as two o'clock. But every so often a fellow felt the need of a place to go where there was something to take his mind up—like someone to talk to, or the movies, or a girl to call on. What he'd like to do right now was get into his boat and go over to the Harbor and see Alice Lacy.

But like as not once he got over there he'd have his trouble for his pains. Alice was pretty popular and she probably wouldn't be home. She'd been going out with Orin Hammond a lot lately.

Darn livin to hell-an-gone away on this hole of an island, he said to himself. If he lived over at the Harbor, now, he could do a lot of things that he couldn't do here . . . drop in to Jake's when he felt like it, or go on a ride in somebody's car. Still, when you came right down to it, the island wasn't a bad place. He didn't know as he'd want to go so far as to move off of it.

Steps went past the front of the fishhouse and Joe

Comey stepped in over the plank doorstep, turning to shut the door behind him.

"Hi, Joe."

"Hi. I see a light down here. Thought it might be you." Joe went over and turned a bait tub upside down to sit on. He sat for a while, his elbows on his knees, not saying anything.

Leonard went on painting buoys. His lobster buoys were bright blue with white-striped tails, and he took pride in getting the paint on neatly. Joe would talk if he wanted to, and if he didn't, you might as well speak to a stone wall.

Leonard was getting worried about Joe. He supposed he knew Joe better than anyone else, and Joe knew him. Except for the two years Leonard had spent on the mainland at high school, he couldn't remember a time when he and Joe hadn't been together. Joe hadn't gone to high school. None of the Comeys thought schooling was very important. Well, Leonard didn't know as he would have bothered with it himself if his father and mother hadn't insisted on it.

"You seen Cack?" he said at last.

Joe grinned. "No, but I see Eddy. He said she come home from your house blowed up like a toad sculpin."

"I said more'n I meant to."

"Ayeh; anyone most always does."

"Don't know as I like the idea a havin Cack for an enemy."

Joe dug the big knuckle of his forefinger into his calloused palm thoughtfully. "Oh, Cack's everybody's enemy off and on. Leastways, I don't know nobody she thinks enough of so she don't go around stabbin em in the back to the neighbors."

"Ayeh. Guess so."

[48]

"Time she gits through tellin it, she'll have it over how you and your ma and gramma beat her up and put her out of the house. I dunno," said Joe slowly, "what gits into people."

"Neither do I, Joe. Seems like everybody on this island was gettin to hate everybody else."

"No worse'n it ever was, is it?"

"Well, yes. Seems to me it is. Oh, when I was a kid growin up they was fights around, like some kid would bust a window and their families would have a chew over it, but it would all blow over in a week or so. But you take now, it's different. Seems like you have to watch every minute or you'll make somebody mad. Even the kids is growin up poison."

"Them kids ain't bad, Len. An ordinary decent man wouldn't a took no notice a that fish oil more'n to cuff their ears a couple times, you know."

"That ain't what I'm talkin about. Haral just heaved a rock at me would a bust my head in, come an inch or so closer. I was back to him, too, Joe."

Joe unfolded his big frame from the keg and came over to the workbench for a paintbrush. "Might's well help you on them buoys, I guess, as set here and hate myself."

"Chrise, Joe, I did lick him, but a kid that'll do that will do anything."

"Oh, nuts, Len." Joe dipped his brush and picked up a buoy. "He was probably bloody-red mad at the time. Didn't stop to think. Kids don't."

"No, ti.. more to it 'n that." Leonard stopped, not knowing how to make clear to Joe just what he meant. Now that he was trying to put it into words, the uneasiness that he had felt growing up about him and in himself seemed foolish. It was as if he were trying to link up a

[49]

lot of unrelated incidents with a meaning that wasn't in them. "I guess I ain't talkin just about the kids. The kids is a part of it though, by God. Look, Joe. You take years ago, when Grampa 'Lonzo and your grandfather was livin."

"The good old days, eh?" said Joe.

"No, hold on. Le'me say what I mean. Suppose Grampa 'Lonzo had ten cords a wood or so to manufacture. What'd he do? He'd give a choppin match, and everybody'd get together and see who could saw and split the most wood, and the women would cook a bang-up meal, and they'd have square dances and play Tucker, and everybody'd have an oary-eyed good time. What'd you think would happen to a guy now, Joe, a guy with his dooryard full of cordwood, if he sent word around that he was goin to give a choppin match?"

Joe grinned. "He'd git the merry haw-haw from the whole island because he was tryin to git somethin done for nothin," he said.

"Well, that's what I mean."

"You mean that nowadays a man cuts up his own wood, and when he gits it cut, he likely as not has to go out and scooch down on top a the pile with a shotgun so it won't git stole. Well, what of it?"

"I'd just like to know why, that's all."

"I dunno why. People used to like other people and now they don't, so what the hell? You dope it out. You got a high-school education."

"Might be livin on this cooped-up island, but people has always done that."

"I wouldn't know. You git damn sick a seein the same faces."

"You sure do. You like it here on the island, Joe?"

[50]

"Like it? Well, I live here," said Joe. "Feller can make a good livin—if he don't want all git-out."

"Ayeh. But Grampa 'Lonzo had money laid by when he died."

Joe set down the buoy he had finished and reached for another. He drew his brush carefully around the blue edge, respecting Leonard's liking for a neat paint job, but the brush was awkward in his big hand and the blue slopped over on to the white stripe. "Chrise, look at that!" He tossed down his brush in disgust. "Can't even paint a buoy right."

"Don't matter, you slob." Leonard grinned at him. "Wipe it off and start over."

"The hell with it. I'm gettin so I can't do nothin. Len, le's you and me clear out a here for the west'ard and find us a job."

"Gee, I dunno." Leonard stirred the paint thoughtfully for a moment before answering. Joe felt lousy, he knew, and he didn't want him to feel worse. "Where to? I wouldn't know how to go about it. All I know how to do is go fishin."

"Ayeh; guess so. Same way with me," Joe said. He got up, hunching his shoulders. "Well, might's well be gettin along home."

"Oh, stick around. Marm's sore at me, and I don't want to go home till she's gone to bed."

Joe said nothing, and looking at the big unresponsive back, Leonard was suddenly furious. Most people would be okay, he thought, if other people would let them alone. Joe had been all right until Morris came home. He *was* clumsy, but he got things done somehow, and he was a hell of a good guy.

"Joe," he said, "take a poke at the little bastard. Turn him across your knee and wallop the pants off a him."

[51]

"No; can't do that. Morris don't fight with his hands." Joe did not turn around, and his voice came a little muffled. "Guess the only way you could fight Morris and beat him 'd be to kill him. That's why I'd kind a like to go off somewheres."

"Hadn't ought to have to do either, Joe."

"No. Don't know's I care about doin either. Jeezus, I wish the' was somethin to do tonight."

"Look, Joe. It's a nice night. Moon's comin up. What say we take the boat and strike out for the Mary Shoal?"

"Without Morris?"

"Yes, by God, without Morris!"

"What about grub? And gas?"

"It's early yet. Jake won't be closed till ten. We could stop in to the Harbor and buy gas and grub enough for two or three days. What say?"

"And not come back till we got a trip of fish? How much dough you got on you?" Joe hauled out his tattered billfold. "Le's see . . . I got two-eighty."

"Hell, I got some; but Jake'll trust us. Come on!"

Joe hesitated. "Hadn't we ought to let someone know?"

"Oh, they'll figure it out when they see the boat's gone. I'd be glad to see Morris's face, too."

They launched Leonard's skiff and loaded her with the mended dragnet. Then they rowed out across the Pool to the big dragger. The moon was just beginning to blacken the spruces on the east shore of Comey's and to whiten the rim of beach rocks around the Pool. The water was black and still, without a ripple. Joe got the engine started and went up on the bow to cast off the mooring. Leonard waited until the tide had dropped the boat back a few feet clear of the mooring buoy, then slipped in the gear and felt, with satisfaction, the big propeller begin to take hold, and the forward surge of stout timbers under him. She was a sweet job, this boat of Morris and Joe's.

You had to hand it to Morris for something, he had known how to design a boat for dragging. Harry Fenner, the boatbuilder at the Harbor boatyard, had built her to Morris's model and specifications. Forty-two feet long, powered with a big Packard engine, she was the next thing to a speedboat, and nothing except a few of the summer people's pleasure boats could touch her. Yet she was steady and light-footed in the water, and you could load her to the gunnels with fish and she'd take you home in any kind of weather.

That Packard engine Morris had shopped around for in half the automobile junk yards in the state. He'd bided his time until just the right kind of smashed-up car had been towed in—a big new one, driven less than a thousand miles, the car gone beyond repair but the engine not hurt much. He'd given the junk-yard dealer a hundred dollars for it, and it had cost a little better than a hundred to have it put into the boat. Leonard hated to think how much an engine like that would cost new. Oh, you had to hand it to Morris. He was smart and he had the luck of a fat priest.

Joe put his hand on the steering wheel and Leonard let him take it. Lord knows he never got a chance at it with Morris along. Leonard's teeth went on edge a little as Joe leaned on the throttle with a jerk that set the engine hard down against the timbers. Then he grinned to himself. Poor old Joe, he couldn't have opened her up slow and easy to save his life. Besides, he had a right

[53]

to run his boat and run her in his own way. He had twelve hundred dollars of savings in her.

The big boat flattened her tail down like a rabbit. On each side of her cutwater a gleaming fin of foam roared away into the still water, and moonlight crinkled after her along her wake.

Leonard could feel the big fellow alongside him beginning to let go, the tenseness going out of him, and he fetched Joe a clip between the shoulders. "Jeezus, Joe, she's a sweet thing! She's just sweet enough. She's been overboard just the right length of time."

"Ayeh, she is, ain't she? Handles good now."

They ate a hot meal at Jake's after they had gassed up the boat and stowed away the grub for the trip, and Leonard added to their list a half-dozen stubbies of beer. He'd make Joe have a few of them and then go below in the cabin and sleep on the run out to the Mary Shoal—be just what he needed.

Halfway out, along the twenty-mile run, Joe did begin to shake off his moroseness a little, but even four bottles of beer did not seem to free him from worry. He took the fifth bottle below and turned in on one of the lockers. In a few moments he came back on deck again, he said to have a look at the weather.

"There she is," said Leonard, indicating the bright still moonlight. "Look at her."

Joe leaned against a windscreen support, weaving a little. "You think we better drag the Mary Shoal?" he asked anxiously.

"Why not? Likely to be the best fishin there."

"Ayeh. But if we should get hung down again, I'd never hear the last of it. Morris's goin to be oary-eyed mad, anyhow, because I took the boat."

"Oh, forget about Morris! He don't own you. Don't own the boat, either, all of it." Leonard had had the remaining bottle of beer, and that together with the boat's swift passage through the water was making him feel just about right. "Sure, we'll fish the Mary Shoal. You don't get hung down there once in ten years. If we do, we'll fish up whatever we get hung on and take it home and hang it around Morris's neck." He sang at the top of his voice, to some unknown tune:

> *Instead of the cross, the Albatross*
> *About my neck was hung.*

"Huh?" croaked Joe, eyeing him dismally. "What in hell's that?"

"That? That's a poem. You was educated like me, Joe, you'd know it."

"What's it about?"

"Old feller went crazy. Went around tellin people his life history. They make you learn it in high school. Figure it'll make you ketch bigger fish."

"They do?" Joe looked at him seriously. "Does it?"

"Sure it does. Go on down and turn in. Go on, you dope."

"Okay." Joe went down the step into the cabin and Leonard heard him rustling around in the blankets on the locker. But in a moment he stuck his head out the companion door again. "You learn all of it?"

"What? The poem? No. Only a few verses. Forgot em long ago. No . . . wait. Le's see. Here's one:

> *The moon now rose upon the left,*
> *Out of the sea came he,*
> *And he shone bright and on the right*
> *Went down into the sea.*

"Chrise!" mumbled Joe, pulling his head in. "Why write it down? Any goddam fool'd know that."

MORRIS was sitting in the easy chair he had sent for from Boston, reading the paper by the light of the kitchen lamp, when he heard the engine start. The Pool was only a few hundred yards below the house. He did not stop reading or lower the paper, but Sarah, his mother, turned uneasily from the dishes she was washing at the sink and went to the kitchen door. She was just in time to see the boat slide out of the Pool in the moonlight.

"That was your boat, wasn't it, Morris?" she asked. "Where's Joe goin?"

"Yes," said Morris. "Couldn't say."

"Didn't you know he was goin anywheres?"

"No."

Sarah Comey went back to the sink, taking the dishes out of the hot rinsing water and turning their shining edges to the light. She was not, generally speaking, a very neat housekeeper, unless the boys made a fuss, and Morris would make one if the dishes weren't spotless. Even as a little runty kid, she remembered, Morris would get sick to his stomach and throw up if there was the least little bit of dirt got into his food. He wasn't any better now . . . worse, if anything. Sarah didn't believe in catering to Morris the way everybody else did, but she liked to be accommodating, and she hated a row. Peace—that was what she wanted above everything else in the world, and people liking each other.

The boys quarreling about the house she couldn't

abide, and they never did, except Sayl sometimes talked back to Joe when Joe tried to boss him too much. But a word from Sarah would silence them. They had felt the weight of her hand too often as children to think of disobeying her now. Morris might be the head of the family, but Sarah was the head of her household. Even now, at fifty-five, with three-quarters of a lifetime of killing hard work behind her, Sarah's big body was as tough as a string and as tireless as it had been at thirty. She was a tall woman, standing nearly six feet, with a voice as deep as a man's. From childhood the work of keeping house, cooking, dishwashing, and making beds had bored her. When Clyde, her husband, had been alive, she had liked nothing better than to go fishing with him, or into the woodlot for a long day cutting wood. Clyde had enjoyed having her along. She was good company, always amiable, always willing to do more than her share, and she could out-work most men.

But Sarah Comey came into her own when anyone in the village was sick. Over sick people her big calloused hands were skillful and compelling, and in her was a stout core of comfort which the frightened and helpless could hold to. Hadley, the doctor from the Harbor who was most often called to Comey's Island when someone was sick there, said he would rather work with Sarah Comey than with the best trained nurse that ever came out of a hospital.

It was strange, in a way, because with people in general Sarah was reserved, almost brusque. She never went calling on the neighbors the way the other island women did, and they seldom came calling on her. Sarah didn't care about talking—sustained conversation made her nervous—and she couldn't be counted on for a good sit-down gossip. Even Cack, her cousin by marriage, who could talk best when the other person just listened, petered out with Sarah. Because after a while it became quite plain that Sarah wasn't even listening. And, like as not, if you dropped in on Sarah in the afternoon you would find her doing outdoors work around the barn or fields, dressed in an old hat and overalls that had belonged to Clyde, and she wouldn't stop work to talk to you. She just stayed at home and minded her own business, and no one could remember a time when she had been off the island.

Sarah hung up the dish towels with a sigh of relief and went softly to the foot of the stairs to listen for any sound from Sayl. He must be sleeping, she thought. Ought to be, with that dose in him. When he had got home, his face was paining him badly, and she hadn't liked the look of that cut. She had undressed him as if he were a little boy, covering his big adolescent body with warm quilts and putting him to sleep with a dose of paregoric and aspirin. Probably he was good for all night, and she'd go to bed herself.

Sarah generally went to bed early. She didn't like to read or sew or do fancy work. She was happiest when she was using her hands and her body. She and Clyde had always gone to bed soon after supper, together in the big bed where she now slept alone, and they had got up together, early, before daylight, for the long hours of work that tired them out for another sleep.

But if Joe had been home tonight, she would have stayed in the kitchen until either he or Morris went to bed. No sense in leaving them alone together, with Joe in that black temper and Morris looking as if the last of the cat's cream had just gone in over his lip. Morris was the one who was mad now, she could tell by the way he held the paper. And with Morris mad, she told herself as she undressed, I'd just as soon set in the room with a snake.

Morris sat holding the paper in front of him, but since he had heard the boat go out of the Pool he had not read anything. He was indeed what his mother called "mad," but what went on inside his head was not anger. It was a systematic and cool evaluation of schemes whereby he might get back at Joe for taking the boat.

Morris considered that the boat was his. He had worked in spare time all one winter to perfect the drawings and model of her, a design carried in his head since he had been a boy. She was, in a way, the fulfillment of his life's ambition—something he owned and which obeyed him, something he had made, and made good enough so that the skill of his hands and eyes, patiently and painfully acquired, need not be wasted in the handling of her. But above all, she was the means by which Morris could make his living without having to work for someone.

Twelve years at sea, sometimes on passenger ships, more often on freighters, had taught him what it was like to be ordered around. Morris had never taken an order in his life without having to crush back hatred for its giver. He had run away from home in the first place because Clyde Comey made him toe the mark and would have no nonsense about it. Morris preferred not to remember his father. He had sworn he would not come home while Clyde was alive, and he had kept his word.

Because he had been a silent boy, uncommunicative and self-contained, he had been knocked around in most of the ports of the world, resenting the helplessness of his diminutive size, hating with a fierce pride anyone who joked him or laid a hand on him. He had too keen a brain not to develop in time the peculiar subtlety which must be a little man's protection among the rough and tough of his kind, and a grim and secret humor, come of having had to savor his personal revenges alone.

He had not wanted to leave Comey's Island. He had thought of it often—in the hot stench of a tropical port, or in his bunk aboard ship, his nerves prickling at the closeness of other bodies around him—not with sentiment but as a place that was clean and comfortable, where a man with a fishing boat was his own master. In those nights his own fishing boat had taken shape in his mind. When he had come back to Comey's Island he brought money enough to build her. To use Joe's money had not been a part of his plan. But as the boat on the ways in Harry Fenner's yard had taken shape, Morris saw how much better she could be if only a few dollars more could be put into her.

She had turned out even better than he had thought she might. The "few dollars," which in the end were all Joe's savings, had made the difference. Her sheer, for instance—Morris had taken infinite trouble in his design to get the curve just right, and at first Fenner hadn't built it to suit him. He had made Fenner tear the planks off and build it over. Her mahogany trim was all of hand-picked boards. She had electric lights, a built-in binnacle for the compass, and an automatic foghorn. And so on. Things like that had cost money.

Morris wasn't sorry he had called on Joe. He would have had to hire a man anyway to go dragging, and he could handle Joe. But the idea of not owning every stick and timber of the boat pricked at him, and Joe's awkwardness drove him to a nervous frenzy. Something in him curled up in cold disgust when Joe's big hands fumbled with the sensitively adjusted machinery. Things he had on board fixed just the way he wanted them, Joe was always knocking around.

So far Joe had been easy-going and had let Morris have the say. Taking the boat out alone was something new. Well, Morris thought, he could handle that all right. He folded the newspaper meticulously, laid it in a certain spot on the table, leaned over and blew out the light. Plenty of time. He'd sleep on it.

As he passed Sayl's bedroom door, the boy turned over and sighed in his sleep, and Morris hesitated a moment, then turned and went in. After all, Sayl was Joe's white-headed boy.

He kicked the leg of the bed sharply.

"What?" said Sayl thickly, sitting up.

"How you feel, bub?"

"Who is it? Morris?" Sayl's voice sharpened.

"Your puss ache?"

"No!"

"Want I should fix the bandage or anything?"

"Morris," said his mother from the darkness behind him, "you better go to bed, hadn't you?"

He turned and went quickly out of the room, meeting her in the doorway. "Yeah. I was just goin. Thought I heard the kid holler."

"Well," said Sarah, "I'm here now. Better go on, Morris." She put her hand on his arm, closing it experimentally, letting him feel the strength of her big fingers.

Morris pulled away with nervous distaste. "Don't, Ma!"

"Good night, Morris."

"Good night, Ma."

PART TWO

GRAMMY TURNER couldn't seem to help getting up early. As a young woman and through her middle age, when she had had a large family to tend and had to be up with the sun, she had hated it, for her wits came slowly back from sleep, and her body, however active after breakfast, in the early morning was heavy as a stone. She would stagger sleepily out of bed and into her clothes, moving more by instinct than anything else, so that sometimes she would not remember how she had built the fire and put the kettle on and got the things together for 'Lonzo's breakfast. For years one of 'Lonzo's best stories in company was a description of her getting breakfast asleep on her feet.

But now, in her old age, when she had no pressing reason to get up early and could have slept—with Josie's blessing—until past daylight if she liked, Grammy Turner waked up clear-headed and lively at the first feel of morning in the darkness. She herself was disgusted about it. It was only a further proof, to her mind, that in all important things the Lord was contrary.

She would get up and creep downstairs, light a lamp and build a fire in the chilly kitchen, get breakfast and have it by herself—or with Hardy, if it happened to be a morning when he had to get up early to tend weir. She always cleared away, too, and whoever got up first would find her sitting by the west window in the neat-ened kitchen, rocking and knitting, watching the morning come and the village stirring out of sleep.

This morning it was half-past three when Hardy got up to tend weir on the low tide. Grammy was already halfway through her breakfast. She was having ham and eggs, fried potatoes, and blueberry pie, and the kitchen was full of the smoke of frying. Hardy's stomach, still queasy from yesterday's upset, quivered within him, but he said nothing.

"You look like a skim-milk gull," Grammy observed through a full mouth. "You hadn't ought a got up. Why don't you let Leonard tend weir this mornin?" She knew quite well that Leonard hadn't come home last night, but she wanted to hear what Hardy thought about it.

Hardy, however, was not to be drawn into discussion. He didn't feel like listening to a string of comments and suppositions as to what Leonard was up to. "Oh, I'm all right. Nothin the matter with me." He was washing his face in the icy water from the pump and it was making him feel better.

"That's good," said Grammy meditatively. "Set right down here, then, and have your breakfast. The's plenty left." Her sharp little eyes twinkled maliciously as she noted his start of disgust. "Ain't hungry, hey?"

"Well," said Hardy from behind the towel, "guess I better go a little mite light on the eats this mornin. Coffee's all I want."

"There!" said Grammy in triumph. "If you can't eat, you ain't fit to be up. I'll call Leonard." She began to scramble herself together to get up from the table.

Hardy sighed. "Leonard ain't home."

"Ain't home? Ain't home? You mean to say that boy never come home at all last night? Well, where *is* he?"

"Fishin, I guess. I heard Morris's boat go out last night, so I guess they went a trip."

"They couldn't of. Leonard's dinner bucket's on the shelf and his oil jacket that he brought home for his mother to mend's still hangin behind the stove. He's gone off somewheres on a toot, that's where he's gone, and I don't know's I blame him, the goin-over your wife gave him last night. If I was Leonard, I'd never come home."

Hardy said nothing. He poured his coffee from the pot on the stove and drank it standing, without cream or sugar. The steaming hot stuff, strong as lye, felt good in his stomach. The stove gave off a deep, comfortable warmth, and he moved closer to it, feeling his sluggish blood begin to move through his chilled body. He had not slept well and had felt cold every time he had awakened.

He was deeply concerned over Cack Comey's being drawn into a row last night, part of which he had overheard, since his bedroom was directly over the kitchen, and the whole of which Josie had told him when she came up to bed. Josie was good and righteous mad with Cack for what she had said to Leonard; at the same time she was upset, for she knew what an island row meant. They started over trifles and snowballed on trifles until whole families took sides, down to the children, and for months, years sometimes, people didn't speak or have anything to do with each other.

Hardy didn't feel as Josie did about Haral's licking. He was grateful to Leonard. There had been other times when Leonard's loyalty to him had touched him deeply—times rare enough, for Leonard criticized him almost as much as the rest of his family did. But Hardy couldn't help feeling that there was something a little special between him and his eldest son; that there might even be a few things about him that Leonard still admired and looked up to. And Hardy had to admit to himself that if Leonard hadn't done the job, Haral would very likely have got off with a sound talking-to from Josie.

Don't know but it'd been better if he had, Hardy reflected, drinking his coffee by the stove and letting his mother's sharp nasal comments slide off the surface of his reflection. Better than having this kind of a mess stirred up.

Hardy hated to live in the kind of atmosphere where he had to watch his step or he'd be speaking to somebody he wasn't supposed to speak to. He had a temper himself that flew off the handle and was hot enough while it lasted, but he couldn't stay mad to save his life. The type of mind that holds a grudge and enjoys holding it for excitement's sake was incomprehensible to him. Had anyone tried to explain to him that Cack was bored to death and secretly looking forward to the row's development, he would not have understood. Hardy, as he left the house in the early morning stillness, was soberly searching his conscience. How much was his own family to blame, and how could he smooth things over with Cack?

The August morning was clear and cool, with a long bar of light whitening upward from the horizon. Against it the spruces behind the village were massed in solid black, broken here and there by the upthrust of a gabled roof. The houses at Comey's were not built along a street but dropped here and there on the west side of the island, wherever an owner of land thought might be his best building site. They were solid houses, built for the maximum of shelter, most of them with two or more gables faced to split the northeast wind.

Hardy's own house, receding behind him as he went down the sloping path to the Pool, looked neat and comfortable, the paint fresh on its white gables and dark green blinds. Years of snugging down on the sturdy stone foundations dug into the top of the low hill on which it was built, had blended it into the line of the hill, so that the eye followed the sweeping curve gently, with no sense of climax in the peaked gables of house and barn. From a distance it seemed almost as if the green turf, with a little extension of growing, could have closed over the roof, leaving no sign that a house had been there. Hardy's great-grandfather had built it, the same Andrew Turner whose date in the island cemetery was 1831.

The weir dory, anchored at the extreme lower end of the Pool so that it would not go aground at low tide, was rocking gently in the light bore, Hardy noted automatically as he drew in the painter and climbed aboard. In his younger days he would have given himself some slight credit at having judged the tide exactly right. A subconscious time-schedule in his mind paid attention to the working of the tides for him now. Yet if he had been asked at what given time the water would cover any one of the familiar ledges about the Pool, Hardy would have glanced at the tide marks and told instantly.

In his younger manhood, too, Hardy would have looked forward to rowing out in the early morning to see what the weir had caught during the night. A night like this one, clear and still, with low tide in the early morning, was when the big seagoing schools of herring fed into the coast bays and inlets with the flood and swam back on the ebb. And it was seldom enough that tide and weather served together. But Hardy, sitting on the high dory thwart and pushing the ungainly boat forward with his oars, would have been surprised to remember that he had once thought of the weir with pleasure.

He felt a certain disappointment in discovering no herring at all in the outer pound. A few silver hake flashed across the pebbly bottom. In the water directly below him a red lumpfish hung suspended, and a big skate rose inquisitively to investigate the dory bottom, then sank through the water, rippling its fins.

Hardy let the dory drift toward the gate of the inner pound, watching keenly through the clear water to see if there might be anything worth seining the weir for. He hoped there wasn't. He didn't feel much like breaking out the big seine and dipnet this morning. Still, Josie had asked him the night before to bring home some fish for dinner.

As the dory slid through the gate, something in the inner pound splashed sharply and shot across to the farther side before he could see what it was. A small school of terrified herring—perhaps ten bushels—dashed under the boat, streaking through the gate into the outer pound. Hardy sat perfectly still and waited while the troubled water subsided to a few ripples.

Across the pound, after a moment or so, a small darkness in the water which had seemed to be a part of the brush wall moved slightly, and an undersized brown seal poked his head out of water, looking cautiously about at first, then, as nothing stirred, relaxing and elevating his stubby mustaches with a kind of absurd dignity.

Hardy regarded the seal sourly. "Now ain't you raised hell," he commented. No knowing how big the school of herring might have been when it had entered the weir at high tide, but with a seal chasing them, the fish had probably circled the pound wildly a few times until they had found the gate they had come in by. It was a wonder there were any left at all.

At Hardy's voice, the seal stiffened, not knowing where the sound had come from, then for an instant its eyes met his with a look of almost comical despair and shock.

"Oh, you go to hell!" said Hardy. "Boo!"

There was a slight plop and a ripple, and nothing at all to see except the small dark shadow under the pound wall.

Grumbling, Hardy unfastened the lashings and closed the gate between the pounds, then swung back the one opposite that led to the open harbor.

"I ought to give you a good root in the tail with this," he muttered, picking up his flounder spear. "Prob'ly if any of us liked seal meat, I would." He lowered the blunt end of the spear silently through the water and gave the seal a slight prod under the hind flipper. The seal broke water with a rush, saw the open gate, and tore through it wildly.

"And don't come back," said Hardy. Methodically he closed the one gate and opened the other, then began to run the seine around the ten bushels of herring left in the weir.

He was dipping out the last of them when the lobster boats began to start up in the Pool. He was counting on their taking the herring off his hands for fresh bait. Ten bushels wasn't enough to run up the flag for. Hardy had a flagstaff on the end of the point toward the mainland. When he had a good catch he would hoist a flag on it and the sardine boats from the factory would call at his weir.

Jarvis Willow and Pogie Young, the first two boats out, bought three bushels apiece, paying Hardy fifty cents a bushel. Perley Higgins would have taken the rest but Hardy shook his head. "Sorry, Perley," he said, "I can't sell you but two."

"Goddam," said Perley, hanging his long jaw disconsolately. "Thought it was first-come-first-served with you, Hardy."

Hardy swallowed. This was something he had not thought of. The first-come-first-served rule when the supply of bait was limited *was* practically an unwritten law with the weir men, especially with Hardy. He had always been careful to preserve a scrupulous fairness. The practice of saving bait was bad custom and caused trouble all around. First thing a man knew, all the lobster fishermen were asking him to do it, and if there didn't happen to be enough herring for everybody on a night's catch, then the ones left out were mad. Hardy's idea had been to save two bushels for Jap Comey. He wanted, for one thing, to find out how Jap was feeling about the quarrel last night, and for another, to smooth him down if he could. Besides, he knew that if Jap really were sore, he'd figure that just for spite Hardy had sold out before he got there.

Well, Perley Higgins was a good friend. "I'll tell you, Perley," Hardy said, "I kind of wanted to do Jap a little favor this mornin."

"That don't help me none, does it?" The lines of Perley's face, assisted in their downward trend by a drooping handlebar mustache, took on a more somber melancholy. Perley was one whose only abiding faith was in his own bad luck. "You better sell me them fish anyway,

[69]

Hardy. Jap won't want em. Cack told May last night he was madder'n hell at your whole tribe."

"He is?" Hardy glanced toward the Pool where he heard Jap's kicker starting up. "Well . . ."

Perley sat down on the engine box in his boat. If this turned out to be as good as he thought it would, he wouldn't object to being a little late hauling his traps today. "I'll wait a few minutes. If he don't want them fish, Hardy, I'll take em. Funny you didn't get more last night, the tide right and all."

"Oh, there was a damn seal in here," said Hardy. "Prob'ly would have, hadn't been for that."

"Seal?" said Perley, interested. "You git him?"

"No. He got away."

"Goddam!" said Perley, astonished. "How'd he do that? Fly?"

Jasper Comey, with his son Eddy beside him in the boat, showed no signs of heading in to the weir as he came past. Hardy waved and hailed him.

"Hey, Jap! Got two bushels of herrin left."

Jap stopped his engine. "You stuck with em?" he inquired nastily.

Hardy flushed. There was a nice distinction between offering herring for sale and peddling them. "No, by God, I ain't," he said shortly. He picked up a bushel basket of herring and dumped it into Perley's tub. "Want the rest?" he asked.

Perley tried to conceal a smirk of satisfaction. "Sure do," he said.

Hardy emptied the rest of the fish, then turned to Jap and Eddy. "Go on and fish with whore's eggs for all I care," he said.

"Well, I would 'fore I'd use any bait a your ketch," answered Jap. "When you git any more, you know what you can do with em." He started up his engine and went chugging down the harbor.

Hardy did not glance after him. He started pulling the dory back into the weir to haul up his seine.

"Thought you was goin to kind a try and mog things over," Perley commented.

Hardy started a little. "By God, that's right. I was, wasn't I?"

⁂

AT the sound of his mother's voice, Haral rolled over in bed and answered sleepily, "Okay, Marm. Be down in a minute." He made no motion to get up, but lay regarding the ceiling with its brown blotch the shape of a cat's head over the bureau. The sunlight flooding through the window looked disagreeably bright. Probably it was as late as seven-thirty, and Josie would be calling him again in a minute. He figured it would be about the third call before Josie started upstairs.

He had had some kind of a dream that had been vaguely pleasant, something about dollar bills, but he couldn't remember it. He tried for a while, filling his imagination with a luxurious vision of new green dollar bills, a big basket overflowing with them. All he had to do was take what he wanted. He was riffling a handful nonchalantly and slipping them into a brand-new pigskin wallet when Josie called again.

"Haral! You get up!"

"Ayeh, I'm up." He slipped one foot out of bed and pounded it up and down twice, making a bumping which could be heard downstairs, then drew it back under the covers.

Huh, he said, aloud, bitterly. I guess that's all the

[71]

way I ever will have any dollar bills—make believe I found em.

Since school had closed in June he had had pretty slender pickings. While he was in school, his father had allowed him twenty-five cents a week, but now that Haral had time on his hands, Hardy figured that there were jobs around the shore a boy could pick up to earn his spending money. He could make fifty cents a tub any time he wanted to get trawls to bait, but a tub of trawl was pretty nearly half a mile long, with hooks every three or four feet. Haral and Sayl had figured out that it took too long and the pay wasn't worth a man's time.

Josie was generally good for a touch, but she always wanted the last detail on what he planned to do with the money. Twice lately he hadn't thought quite fast enough to get ahead of her when his stories hadn't matched up. Besides, this year, she had got it into her head that he was going to high school and that he ought to save up for it. He expected he'd better not ask Josie for dough again right away.

Last summer he had done a few jobs for the summer people, but, Haral thought scornfully, he sure was through doing that, ever since old Missus Whitewood had paid him a dime for working all the afternoon in her kitchen garden. The summer people who came to Comey's Island were a cheap crowd. They didn't have money enough to get into a rich place like Bellport, so they bought a little piece of land on the shore of one of the islands and made believe to the natives that they were rich.

Haral thought enviously of Sayl's second cousin, Bud Atwood, who lived at Bellport and made anywhere from a hundred to a hundred and fifty dollars a summer, caddying at the golf course. Got good tips, Bud did. Why, some of those big fat old red-faced fellers that Bud cad-died for didn't think any more of a five-dollar bill than Haral's folks did of a nickel.

Leonard, now . . . Leonard had plenty of money, but do you think he'd ever part with any of it, if you were choking to death and a drink of water cost a cent?

At the thought of Leonard, Haral suddenly remem-bered with a flash of humiliation the licking Leonard had given him last night. He felt cautiously down his back-side to see if there were any raised welts. There weren't, but he did feel lame. He stretched one leg down toward the foot of the bed as far as he could and was gratified to feel a definite twinge in the muscle of his left buttock. Well, there, he guessed he felt too mean to get up, and he'd tell his mother so when she came upstairs. By golly, he thought, it's somethin when a feller's only brother licks him so he has to stay in bed a whole day. His mother was sure going to be sore at Leonard when she found out how lame he was this morning.

Last night he could have killed Leonard, watched him die hard. This morning he didn't seem to feel so bad about it. His fury had gone out of him in terror when he had seen how close to Leonard's head the rock he had thrown had come. He was glad he hadn't hit him. But I guess he'll be pretty careful how he lays his big claws on *me* again, he thought. If he'd come home last night, I'd have been darn mean to him.

But Leonard hadn't come, and today was Friday. If he didn't get back before tomorrow night, there'd be no trip to the harbor and no movies. Ken Maynard was playing, too, in *Flaming Gulch*. And there'd be the tenth instalment of *The Green Archer*. Gosh, he couldn't miss that. Maybe Leonard would get back. Maybe some other boat from Comey's would be going over. Still, he knew

[73]

his mother wouldn't let him go unless he went with Leonard. As if I needed that big lug to look after me! If only we lived somewheres else besides this darn hole of an island.

Well, the fact remained that he hadn't a penny of money. If only he and Sayl—

Suddenly Haral remembered the mackerel. The last he'd known of them, they had been lying on the bench by the fishhouse door. Maybe they were still there, if the gulls hadn't found em. And if the sun shone on em they wouldn't be any good.

Haral tore out of bed and into his pants and shirt, hauled on his sneakers and hooked up one hook on each. He went downstairs three at a time, passing an irate Josie, who was halfway up, her mouth full of a good jawing because he hadn't minded when she called him. She spoke to him, but her words were lost in the slamming of the front door. By the time she got to the window, he was halfway to the shore, running at top speed.

"He's crazy," said Grammy. "It ain't on *my* side a the family."

The mackerel were not on the bench. Haral looked with a sinking heart, then got down on his hands and knees and peered under it. He sat despairingly down on the bench and leaned against the fishhouse. Sixty cents gone to hell.

Someone was moving around inside the building. Whoever it was might know where the mackerel were. But heck, someone, probably old Jarv Willow, had stolen them. Old Jarv wasn't a one to see a good string of fish go begging.

Haral got up and looked in the door, then recoiled and jumped away. Morris Comey was in there. He'd thought Morris and Joe and Leonard had gone dragging.

[74]

Morris came to the door. "What's the matter with you, bub? You act like you'd seen a ghost."

Haral drew back still farther, ready to run if Morris made a move.

"You ain't got no call to be scairt of me," said Morris. "I ain't mad."

"I ain't scared," said Haral. His voice went up into a falsetto squeak on the last word, and he stopped, furious at it. He'd thought last winter that he'd got all over that squeaking when he was excited.

"No, you don't look it," said Morris, grinning.

"I was just surprised," said Haral, in a deep bass. "I thought all you fellers had gone fishin."

"Nuh. I stayed in a trip. Had some things I wanted to do." Morris turned to go back into the fishhouse, then paused and looked at Haral speculatively. "You lookin for your mackerel? I hung em up in Leonard's fishhouse, back of the door. You must've forgot em last night."

As a matter of fact, it had been Leonard who had taken care of the mackerel the night before. Morris had seen them in the fishhouse when he had taken a look around there earlier in the morning. He rather liked to look around in the fishhouses when the owners weren't there. Sometimes it gave him advance information on things.

"You did!" said Haral, impressed. "Gee! Well, gee! Thanks, Morris."

"Oh, that's okay. I figgered one good turn deserves another."

Haral turned red. He poked a rusty tin can with his foot, then kicked it hard down the beach. "It didn't turn out as funny as Sayl and me thought it would."

"It don't, with me," said Morris briefly. "What you goin to do with them mackerel?"

[75]

"Peddle em," said Haral, delighted that the subject was changed.

"How much for?"

"Ten cents apiece, I guess. You think that's too much?"

"Hell's bells, them big mackerel? Use your brains. Clean and skyver em and you can get a quarter apiece this time of year. Anyway, ask a quarter and you'll get twenty."

"Gee!" Haral looked at the little man with something like awe. Everybody said Morris had brains and here was proof of it. Haral wouldn't have thought of asking more than a dime. His father, he knew, if he had seined the mackerel himself would have taken home a mess for Josie to cook and given away the rest.

He borrowed Leonard's sharp knife out of the rack over his workbench in the fishhouse and took the mackerel down to the water's edge to clean them. He had slit one open down the stomach and was laboriously washing the insides out of it, when Morris came down the beach.

"Godsake, bub, didn't your old man ever show you how to skyver a mackerel?" he asked scornfully.

"Well, yes," said Haral lamely, "but I ain't never done many to practice up on it."

"Gi'me the knife. Now, watch." Morris slapped the mackerel down and his wrist made two deft movements. It seemed to Haral that the knife blade flickered, it moved so fast.

"See?" said Morris. "Don't ever slit a mackerel down the belly. Cut from the back along the backbone, so's the fish'll lay flat in the spider. Then all you got to do is wash the guts out. You don't have to dig around for em and haggle your fish all up. Then if you want to

[76]

take the backbone out—" The knife said "Zsst!" and the bone fell away from the clean flesh. "Here," said Morris, "gi'me another one."

He finished up the fish and tossed the knife carelessly down on the beach at Haral's feet. "You seen somethin, bub. Ain't a man along the coast but I can bury him up in fillets, skyverin mackerel alongside of me."

He turned and went back up the beach into the fishhouse.

Haral gathered the dressed fish into a pile on the board. "Gee!" he said aloud. "Well, *gee!*"

He had seen his father dress mackerel many times with much the same economy of motion, only Hardy was always deliberate and casual, and it never seemed, with him, like much of anything to see. But Haral wished with all his heart that he could do the same kind of job with a fish that Morris had done.

By golly, he told himself, that guy's good! He's certainly good!

He went slowly up the beach, forgetting all about Leonard's knife, which shortly was buried in sand and beach rocks by the incoming tide.

Morris stuck his head out of the fishhouse as he went by. "Another thing, if you're goin to sell stuff, it don't cost nothin to dress it up a little and ask twice as much for it," he said.

"Ayeh," said Haral, nodding his head wisely. "Oh, ayeh; sure, Morris."

Morris looked after his important back, retreating up the path. After a moment the corner of his mouth drew downward. "Goddam soft little half-arsed fool! Don't amount to a sheep-tick. Just like the rest of em. Can't do a good job to save his life!"

[77]

Well, he'd sure made his eyes bug out. Besides, it wasn't a bad idea to have a friend here and there amongst the kids. You never knew.

～⊂∽⊃

HARAL sold his mackerel for a quarter apiece. He went Morris one better and asked thirty cents for them, which was really more than the market would bear, even for dressed mackerel. May Higgins, Perley's wife, lectured him roundly for overcharging, and Haral said innocently, after a little, "Well, golly, May, I guess that is high. How would a quarter do? That be too much?"

She was too pleased at having won her argument to make any more fuss, and Haral got the point. At each of the houses where he called, he came down to a quarter, either after the lady of the house had looked shocked or mentioned that the price was high. Sarah Comey raised one eyebrow at him when he said he'd had awful good luck peddling Sayl's mackerel for him, all but two, and he'd thought he'd stop by, and how was Sayl?

"Oh, he's all right this mornin," Sarah said. "Ain't up yet, but he et breakfast. How much you been gittin for the mackerel?"

"Well . . . thirty cents," Haral said, reluctantly. "But I'd make it twenty-five to you, Sarah."

Sarah grinned and paid him without comment, out of her battered old leather pocketbook.

One mackerel remained, and there wasn't any place left to sell it unless he tried Cack Comey. But golly, he didn't know whether he dared to go in there or not. Still, he didn't need to let on he knew anything about the row. He hadn't been around when it happened. She couldn't any more than throw him out, anyway.

He marched boldly up the steps and came face to face with Cack in the kitchen door.

"What you doin in here?" she demanded. "You git for home."

Haral permitted his jaw to drop and his face to assume a look of hurt astonishment. "Why, Cack! I ain't done nothin! I was just comin around with some mackerel—"

"Well, I don't want none of your works nor none of your ways. Your whole tribe makes me want to puke."

Haral turned slowly away. "Well, gee, Cack, I guess I done somethin I don't know about. But Sayl and I got these mackerel, and I know how well you like mackerel, and the' ain't been many around yet this year, so I saved this big one for you. But, gee, if you're sore at me—"

"I ain't sore at you! I'm sore at your damn tribe, if that's what you want to know."

"You had trouble up home?" asked Haral, unbelievingly.

"Don't you know about it?" asked Cack suspiciously.

"Why, no. I sure don't. Well, gee, Cack, I'm sorry. I'll git out of here."

He backed out the door, holding the mackerel in front of him. "Gee," he said, "I wouldn't a gone to the trouble to clean and skyver this fish if I'd known."

Cack loved mackerel. And as Haral had said, there hadn't been very many around this early in the season. "How much you want for it?" she asked sourly. After all, if he hadn't known . . .

"Well, thirty cents. No . . . a quarter to you."

"All right. I'll take it. But you tell your ma that if any of you comes in here again, I'll break their neck!"

She threw a quarter at him, intending it to fall on the

ground in front of him, but Haral scooped it expertly out of the air. He ducked out of the door and yelled, from a safe distance, "Fell for it! Yee-ow!"

As a result of his morning's trading, Haral had a dollar and a half jingling in his pocket when he came back to the house for dinner.

"Where you been?" Josie greeted him at the door.

"Why, down around the shore," said Haral vaguely. He washed his hands, dabbed sketchily at the sides of his cheeks, and sat down at the table opposite Hardy.

"Tell your mother where you've been when she asks you," said Hardy.

"He went out of this house like a skyrocket without a bite of breakfast this mornin," said Josie. "Ain't you most starved, Haral?"

"Uh-huh." He began eating rapidly, stuffing mouthfuls of fish and potato into his mouth.

"Don't guzzle so," said Mildred daintily. "Marma, look at the big pig."

"You'll have a bellyache." Grammy, next to him, leaned to peer.

"Aw, le'me alone. Eat your own dinner," mumbled Haral, kicking out under the table in the general direction of Mildred.

"Don't you gi'me any of your sarse," said Grammy spiritedly. "I'll fetch you a clip."

"I never. I said it to Mildred. Look at her—pork scraps all down the front of her tyer. Talk about a pig!"

"That's enough, now," said Hardy.

"What was you in such a hurry for this mornin?" asked Josie, returning to the original point.

"Oh, nothin. I just thought of somethin I promised Sayl I'd do. It wasn't nothin."

"Yes, but what was it?" Mildred stared at him inquisitively, her mouth open.

"What you got for pie, Ma?" Haral turned to his mother. "You ain't made any more of that lemon pie, have you?"

"Why, yes, I have. Want some?"

"Well, no. I guess I don't want any of that kind today." Haral pushed back his chair and got up from the table.

"If you ain't the worst thing to cook for!" exclaimed Josie aggrievedly. "I thought you liked it. You stuffed on it last time I had it. You come right back here and set till the rest of us gets through. Haral!"

"Aw, Ma! I got a lot to do." With a snort he came back and banged down into his chair. It was a tactical error. A quarter fell out of his pocket to the floor.

"Ooh, look!" Mildred was after it like a terrier. They rolled on the floor together, Haral getting in a good slap that resounded on Mildred's buttock. She began to cry loudly.

Grammy, watching with beady eyes of interest, began to giggle. "Go it! Go it!"

"Haral! Mildred!" Josie separated them with a firm hand.

Mildred rendered up the quarter with screams of protest. "It ain't his! It's mine. I found it and it's mine!"

"It ain't so hers. I earnt it sellin mackerel."

"So that's where you been this mornin, Haral," said Josie. "I don't see no reason why you didn't want to tell. I hope you brought one home."

"Well, no, Ma. I had a chance to sell em all, so I did."

"You did! And we ain't had a taste of mackerel this year!"

[81]

"But, Ma, they sold for a quarter apiece, and I didn't want to charge you that," said Haral unhappily.

"Well, never mind," said Josie reasonably. "There'll be more mackerel in the weir."

"A quarter apiece!" boomed Hardy suddenly from the table. "You mean to say you charged a quarter for them fish, Haral?"

"It wasn't too much, Pa. Most folks wanted to give me thirty cents, but I wouldn't take it."

"A quarter apiece! After dinner, young man, you take fifteen cents of that money back to every person you got it from."

"Now, Pa," began Haral in anguish, "I earnt it fair. I cleaned and skyvered em, and they was worth more'n a dime, all that work."

"I can guess how much they was worth if *you* cleaned and skyvered em," said Hardy drily. "You mind me now, Haral. Ten cents is enough."

Haral began to cry.

"Well," said Hardy.

"Oh, let him keep it, Hardy," Josie interposed. "If he's got brains enough to get twenty-five cents for mackerel, he's earned it."

"I don't like to," said Hardy, troubled. "I've always made a practice of chargin a fair price for fish. It'll only come right back on me."

"Sure," said Haral eagerly. His tears had vanished like magic. "Herrin ain't worth a dollar'n a half a bushel, but if folks bid up the price, you take it, don't you?"

"It ain't the same thing," said Hardy decisively. "No, Haral, you take that money back."

Haral went slowly through the sitting-room door and upstairs.

"Now he'll be misable all the afternoon," said Josie. "Why don't you let him keep it?"

"No," said Hardy. "But I'll make it up to him if he'll promise not to do it again."

"Give him all that money to spend foolish?"

"I'll see he saves some of it. He knows he's got to go to high school this fall."

Haral, who had been listening down the hot-air register that heated his room, called down loudly, "Half of that money belongs to Sayl, Ma."

"There," said Josie, her face clearing. "It won't be so much after all, will it?"

⁂

EARLY Saturday morning Joe and Leonard got back from the Mary Shoal. They were in high feather. They had had an excellent trip of fish, which they had sold for nearly fifty-six dollars at the Harbor fish wharf on the way home. The weather had been perfect and they had had no accidents whatever with the gear.

Morris, bland and expressionless as ever, came down the beach dressed in his good clothes, just as they were rowing ashore from the boat.

Joe gulped a little, but Leonard said in a low voice, "Keep your shirt on. He can't do nothin to you." He had been shocked and impatient to see how deep Joe's worry and real fear of Morris went. Generally speaking, Joe wasn't a nervous guy.

But Morris apparently had no intention of doing anything. He merely said, "Glad you got in so early. I wanted to use the boat this mornin." He would have gone on down the beach to his own punt, but Joe said abruptly, "We had a damn good trip, Morris. Figure your share of it, less expenses, come to seventeen-fifty-two." He held out a small sheaf of bills wrapped around some change.

Morris took the money without comment and put it in his pocket. "You leave any gas in her?"

The implication was that Joe wouldn't have had the forethought to think of gassing up for the next trip.

Leonard said pleasantly, "We had the tank filled and there's three extra cans. Figured it would save us a trip to the Harbor Monday morning."

Since this was the usual procedure, Leonard knew Morris wouldn't relish having it explained to him as if the explanation were necessary.

He was right. Morris didn't like it. He turned his head and regarded Leonard levelly for a long moment. "That was white of you," he said, and went on down the beach.

"Hunh!" said Leonard, looking after him. "He earnt that dough easy. Damned if I'm not sorry we give it to him."

"Well," said Joe, "it was the right thing to do, seein we took his boat."

"*His* boat! Oh, Jeezus, Joe, get wise to yourself. You own as much of that boat as he does."

Joe glanced after Morris with troubled eyes. "Now, where's he goin, all dressed up like that? He's up to somethin."

"Who to hell cares what he does? Go on home and get cleaned up and get a good meal into you. I'm slim-ier'n a jellyfish, myself."

"He wouldn't a took it as easy as that," Joe said,

[84]

knitting his brows confusedly. "Sure as hell, he's up to somethin. Well, maybe Marm'll know."

Leonard had expected things to be a little strained at home, but he found that everything had apparently blown over. Josie was unaffectedly glad to see him, and went to a good deal of trouble to have an early dinner so he wouldn't have to wait long for a hot meal after all those cold lunches on the boat. Grammy fussed over him as usual, and even Haral hung around the house after he had eaten, waiting expectantly for a chance to mention the trip to the movies.

Leonard felt warmed and comforted by his reception home. Whistling, he went up the stairs to his room, carrying a big pitcher of hot water and a clean towel. A bath was sure going to feel good.

Haral came pounding up behind him and bumped noisily into his own room across the hall.

"What you tryin to do—knock the house down?" Leonard inquired amiably.

Haral figured that now was as good a time as any. "What time you startin, Len?" he asked.

"Startin? Where to? I only just got home." Leonard went on undressing unconcernedly, pouring out the hot water into his washbowl.

"Why, to the Harbor. To the movies. You said you was goin." Haral appeared excitedly in the doorway.

"Gwan out a here. Can't you see I'm takin a bath?"

"Yeh, Len, but I want to know so I won't keep you waitin."

"Don't worry. You won't."

"Aw, Len! Can't I go? You said I could."

At the anguish in his brother's voice, Leonard looked up, startled. He had been in half a mind to bring up the matter of Haral's not helping Hardy tie the nets and also the matter of the rock. That rock-throwing incident puzzled Leonard and worried him. He wished there was some way of talking to Haral and finding out whether what Joe had suggested were really so—whether the kid had thrown the rock before he'd thought. But there wasn't anything in the world he could get across to Haral. He liked the little duffer a lot, too, he thought.

"Okay," he said gruffly, his mind shying away from even this much admitted emotion. "Gwan and get ready. Joe and I've got to load up some rope and stuff we ordered, so we're goin over early. You got any dough?"

Haral fairly teetered in the doorway. "Well, no, not to speak of. I sold them mackerel, but half the money was Sayl's." He thought it best not to mention the dollar and a half that he and Sayl had split between them. Hardy had not brought up again the matter of returning the money, and Haral figured he could say he had forgotten.

"Well, here's a buck. How's Sayl's face?"

"Oh, he's okay. Cut ain't so bad as it looked. Sarah, she put some stuff on it and hauled it together with adhesive. He wants to go too. Okay?"

"Okay."

Haral pocketed the dollar and plunged back into his own room.

Not even a thank you, thought Leonard. Oh, well.

Haral was thinking as he got into his best suit, Gee, I wish Ma would let me go to the movies in my old clothes, the way the Harbor kids do.

He almost forgot to change his money from his old pants into his good ones, and practically broke out into a cold sweat as he thought, Cripe, what if I had! He stood for a moment holding the money in his hand, feeling the round coolness of the quarters, the crispness of the dollar bill.

He was a tall boy, thin and angly, with long bones that now, in his adolescence, gave only slight promise of their future sturdiness. Some obscure defect in the cut of his ready-made dark blue suit, which only seemed to fit him, accentuated the lumpy boniness of his shoulders, the puppy bigness of his feet. His features, loosened from the compact beauty of childhood—as if everything had slipped slightly, the mouth a little wider, the nose a little thicker—had not yet tautened into the definite kind of lean face, like Leonard's which would be his in a few years' time. An untidy lock of chestnut hair fell over his tanned forehead as he bent lovingly over the money in his hand, his eyes dreamy and lost in some far-away project of his own.

❧

MORRIS'S boat was tied up to the town landing at the Harbor, but Morris was nowhere to be found. Joe went to all the places—Jake's, the pool hall, the loafing place on the fish wharf. Willard Hemple, who ran the general store, was the only one who could give Joe any clue.

"Morris?" he said, turning his faded blue eyes abstractedly on Joe. "Why, sure. Morris come in here about half-past nine this mornin an hired my car. I dunno where he went in it."

Joe, by this time in a definite state of jitters, went back to the wharf to find Leonard. Leonard wasn't there. He had loaded the rope and gear that he and Joe had bought and then had gone up the road to Lacy's, to ask Alice to go to the movies with him.

Joe sat down on a stringer and stared away over the blue harbor. He didn't know what was the matter with him, why he couldn't take Morris more for granted. After all, Morris had never done anything very awful to him. Yet, Joe added to himself, that was the trouble, Morris moved in the dark. Anything you did to him that he didn't like was paid right back, just about double. He admired Morris, couldn't help it, for the smooth way he did things. They might be able to get along swell if only Morris didn't ride him all the time. But three years of it, Joe had to admit, had sure got his goat.

I ought to go away somewheres, he thought. Get a job to the west'ard.

But the very thought of hunting work in a city like Boston or New York scared him stiff, and then there were his mother and Sayl. Sayl would sure go to hell without somebody to hold him down. He was a good kid, but he was a little hellion, and the Lord knew what would become of him if Morris had charge of his bringing up. Whenever Sayl got into deviltry, Morris would laugh at him and egg him on.

As for his mother, she would be too lonesome without him. He was the only one who understood the grief and the sense of loss which she carried around with her, even after three years.

She still misses Pa too much, he thought. No, I can't go. Well, he missed Clyde himself.

He got up and moved aimlessly up the wharf toward the village. With all there was mixed up in it, he guessed he could put up with things. He liked fishing and he liked the boat. That was a hell of a good boat. He grinned a little, remembering how he'd had the handling of her on the trip with Leonard.

Sayl, with the big white patch of sticking plaster on his cheek and the spectacular blue bruise running out from under it, was getting a lot of credit, Haral thought enviously. All the kids had asked him how he'd hurt himself, and Sayl was beginning to swell up every time he told the story.

Bud Atwood said, "Gee, I bet it will leave a dill of a scar, Sayl. You'll look like one of them German army officers that fights with sabers." Bud was seventeen and big for his age and he had been around a lot with the summer people, caddying and bell-hopping at the hotels.

"What d'ya mean—fights with sabers?" said Haral loudly. "They don't fight with sabers in a war no more."

Bud was silent a moment, then he spat boredly and professionally on the step in front of the pool hall. "The German army officers," he explained scornfully, "got secret societies. They meet in their clubhouses and have dools and cut each other scandalous across the face with big swords. The feller that gits the biggest cut is the best fighter."

"Sounds kind a foolish to me," said Haral. "What they want to do that for?"

Bud yawned and sat down on the step, leaning his loose-jointed frame against the sill under the plate-glass window. "You kids over on Comey's Island don't git around much, do you? It's well known what them fellers do. They git slashed and bleed till the' ain't no more blood in em than a turnup. And then the doctor, he sews em up without ether and they don't turn a hair."

Sayl flushed a little, remembering how he had bawled

over his cut. "Sounds screwy to me," he said. "How'd you know so much about it?"

"I seen one of the fellers," said Bud, looking Sayl up and down. "Caddied for him last summer. Von Hont, his name was."

"He have a scar?"

"Only from here—" Bud drew his finger from the top of his cheekbone to the point of his chin—"to here. Looked as if his whole cheek must've ben laid open and hangin down."

"Von Hont!" said Haral. "That's a hell of a name! Von hont, two hont, three hont—"

"The's a feller over on Gooseberry Island caught his hand in a winch last summer," said Sayl. "Took it right off at the wrist. Crushed." He made the word sound satisfyingly succulent, but Bud ignored him.

"This guy, this Von Hont, was high up in the German nobility. Y'oughta seen his car. Custom-built Lincoln Continental, seats all pearl-gray leather. And, boy! Would she travel! He give Trace Jones a ride in her, and Trace said that when they hit that stretch a straight concrete through Blair's Woods they was goin a hundred and two miles an hour."

"Must have dough," said Haral weakly.

"Dough! Jeezus, he could eat solid gold flapjacks seven times a week for breakfast and not notice it. He gimme five bucks once for findin a golf ball. Just for findin it." Bud got boredly to his feet. "You kids better git your tickets, if you're goin to waste your time seein Starkey's lousy movie-show."

Haral and Sayl looked at each other. Haral said, "Nothin else to do. Might as well see it."

"You'd think they'd have a decent show here once in a while," said Sayl.

[90]

"They do, when the summer people's here," said **Bud.** "Old Starkey knows damn well he couldn't git away with them lousy Westerns when the's anyone around that knows anything."

"What d'ya mean—knows anything?" said Haral, stung.

Bud turned a cold eye on him. "Them Westerns is the cheapest movies the' is. Starkey shows em all winter and the hick trade laps em up. Well, I ain't got no money to waste. So long."

"Where you goin, Bud?" said Sayl eagerly. "I thought you was comin with us."

"Nuh. Wouldn't be caught dead in there." He grinned knowingly. "I got a show of my own on."

"Any law against us comin with you?" asked Sayl.

"Ayeh, there is. Unless—" Bud appeared to consider, then shook his head. "Nuh. Trace'd be sore if I brought a couple of kids along."

"Unless what?" demanded Sayl.

"I was goin to say unless you had some dough to put out for treat. But I guess you ain't got any more'n the price of your tickets . . . have you?"

"Sure, we got dough," said Haral. "But I dunno's we want to put it out till we know what for."

"Okay," said Bud. He walked off down the street.

"Let him go," said Haral. "Who wants to go with the big blow? Him and Tracy Jones is prob'ly goin off with girls."

Bud turned around and came back. "What was that you said?" he demanded belligerently.

"I said you was goin off with girls," said Haral staunchly. He had had about enough of Bud's talk.

Bud thrust his hands into his pockets and teetered back and forth, heel and toe. "It'd prob'ly surprise you to know," he said scathingly, "that the's other projecks in the world besides wimmen and the movies." He came close to them and lowered his voice. "Trace has got his car," he said. "Him and me's goin to ride out to a chicken farm back of Blair's Woods and lift some chickens and take em down on the shore with some beer and stuff and have a feed. I guess Trace wouldn't care if you kids come along if you was to pay for part of the stuff."

"You mean steal the chickens?" asked Sayl.

"Sure. Old guy owns the chicken farm won't never miss em. We done it before, two-three times. It's easy."

"Gee, le's go, Haral," said Sayl.

"Aw, I dunno."

"He'd ruther set in a lousy show and *watch* guys go into action," said Bud. Intuition, and the fact that Sayl was holding back for Haral, made Bud suspect that Haral had most of the money.

"Nuh, that ain't it. I come with Leonard, and he'll wonder why I ain't to the show," said Haral.

"Leonard? He's out of this world," said Bud, jerking his head in the general direction of Lacy's. "He's gone up to see Alice. Besides, Trace'll bring you back by the time the second show lets out. You can mix with the crowd and Len'll never know you been gone."

The ride in Trace's car—and it would be an exciting one, for Trace was known as a fast driver—and the general glamorousness of the scheme began to make an appeal to Haral. The movies suddenly lost out. "Okay. I'll go."

Bud held out his hand, palm up. "Shell," he invited.

Haral contributed three quarters and Sayl fifty cents. Bud screwed up his mouth. "Jeezus!" he said.

"Thought you said you had dough!" He did not close his hand over the money until he was sure he had every cent the boys possessed.

Joe was in the poolroom, finishing a half-hearted game with Orin Hammond before starting for the movies, when Morris drove up in Hemple's car and stopped outside. He got out and came in, his eyes searching the crowd of eight or ten men who were sitting around the room waiting for the show to open.

"Thought you might be here, Joe," he said. He grinned knowingly at the men, as if to say that any loafing place, like a poolroom, was where Joe was most likely to be.

Joe laid down his cue. He had wandered around in a state of nerves all the afternoon, and now that Morris was back, he didn't know whether he felt worse or better. "You want to see me?" he asked.

"I'll say I do." Morris was jaunty, in high feather. "Lots of witnesses around, too, so's everything'll be aboveboard." He pulled a paper out of the pocket of his blue serge coat and tossed it across the pool table to Joe. "Like you to read that through and sign it. Here's my fountain pen."

Morris picked up Joe's cue and chalked it. "Anyone play a game?" he asked, sighting along the cue. "Prob'ly be some time before lame-brain gets the details through his head."

Nobody moved. Morris's brand of pool was too well known. Then Orin Hammond said, "I'll knock the balls around with ya, Morris, but I won't play for dough. You're out a my class."

"Okay. You first?"

Orin made four or five creditable shots. Then Morris took his turn and rapidly cleared the table of balls.

"Told ya you was out a my class," said Orin. He laughed good-naturedly, but the expression on his easy-going face was ironic. He was no bad shakes of a pool shooter himself.

Morris had been right. It did take Joe some time to get the details of the paper. He stood under an electric light bulb hanging from the ceiling, his hat pushed to the back of his head, his lips moving earnestly as he whispered each word he read.

Morris jerked a thumb at him. "Kid in grade school," he said to Orin.

Orin did not smile. He appeared to be studying his shot.

Morris was shooting when Joe finally finished the paper. He moved up to Morris's elbow with it clutched in his hand. "Come down aboard the boat and talk this over," he said.

"Nothin to talk over," said Morris, not looking up. He nudged the end of his cue into Joe's stomach. "Move, you lunk. Look, Orin, if you'd played your last shot like that, you wouldn't a missed it."

"Thanks," said Orin. "You got to gi'me time to learn, you know."

"This is private business, between you and me," Joe remonstrated. "No call to handle it before everybody, is they?"

"Nothin very private about it." Morris sprawled negligently and aimed for the six-ball nestled under the far edge of the table. His cue seemed scarcely to move, yet the cue-ball traveled straight as a ruler, nicked the six-ball and dropped it lazily into the pocket. "Ever play billiards, Orin?" he wanted to know.

Orin shook his head. He darted a glance at Joe and dropped his eyes, studying the game, his lips tight.

"I played billiards in Singapore once," said Morris. "There was a—"

"I say it *is* private," Joe said stubbornly. "I won't sign no paper, grade school kid or not, till I've had a chance to talk it over."

Morris, moving around the table to his cue-ball, stopped and felt in his breast pocket. "You ought a thought about that before," he said. "You lent me twelve hundred dollars to finish my boat, and you've yawped about it all over town for upwards of a year. Well, I figure I'd rather owe the bank, that's all. I'm payin you back your money before witnesses, and all you got to do is sign that quit-claim to all rights in the boat." He sent a flat package of new bills spinning across the table, where it lay on the green baize cover under Joe's fingers. "There's your dough. Sign the release and clear out, while I finish my game. Or get someone to write your name for you and you put a cross after it."

"I ain't never mentioned that money to a soul!" Joe stated, looking from the bills to Morris. "You ought a know I ain't."

"Pick up them bills, will you?" said Morris softly. "They're in the way of my shot. By the way, the twelve hundred's all there except sixteen dollars I took out for repairs on the engine, after you had the boat out for the last two days."

Joe's face turned slowly dark red. He picked up the bills mechanically and put them in his pocket, uncapped the fountain pen in his hand and wrote his name, "Joel C. Comey," in his painful round scrawl at the bottom of the paper. Then he turned and walked heavily out of the poolroom.

"Don't you ever get behind the eight-ball, Morris?" asked Orin suddenly, his eyes on the pool table.

Morris laughed. "Why, no, Orin," he said. "I don't."

It was dark when Tracy Jones's Chevrolet pulled up at the side road leading down to the chicken farm in Blair's Woods. The moon had not yet come up, but the starlight was clear and the night air was chilly and sweet. On either side of the concrete highway the tall spruce and birch growth banked in a black shadowy mass.

Tracy backed the car a couple of hundred feet down the side road, showing perfect familiarity with its hollows and curves. It was evident he had been here before. Then he throttled down the engine to an almost inaudible idle, and spoke over his shoulder to Sayl and Haral, who were in the back seat. "You kids know enough about a car not to let the engine die on ya?"

"Sure," Sayl assured him.

"Well, look, if she starts to miss, pull out on the throttle. Not much though. You pull it out too far and she'll roar like hell."

"Okay," said Sayl in a hoarse whisper. "Want me to get in the front seat?"

"Nuh, you can stretch over from there. When Bud and me comes back, we're comin a-runnin."

"Ain't it kind a early yet?" asked Haral nervously. "What I mean, hadn't you ought to wait till that old farmer goes to bed?"

"Nuts," said Bud. "He goes to bed before it gets dark under the table. Besides, if he bothers us, Trace, here, will wring him into a corkscrew, won't you, Trace?"

"Put him to bed with his own hens," said Trace. "Ph-tt!—like that!" He twisted his forefinger with his other hand and made a throwing-away motion, to show what he would do with the chicken farmer.

He and Bud climbed noiselessly out of the car, leaving their doors open. For an instant Haral caught the silhouette of his foxlike profile against the starlight. Then they were gone, stealing quietly down the dark road.

Haral shivered a little in the cold wind that came through the open car doors. The wind smelt good—like pitch and pine needles—but it sure was chilly.

That Tracy Jones certainly was something. He wasn't from around here anywhere—his home was in some town up near Salem or Lynn, but he bragged that he hadn't been there for five years. He was a waiter at one of the summer hotels—worked in Bellport from June to September, and then drove south to Florida to a winter hotel there. He had a year-round job. According to his tell, he had been around a lot of places—had even been in the navy and sailed all over the world.

Haral wondered a little if he had really done all the things and been all the places he said he had. Trace didn't look to be much older than Bud—a year or two, maybe, but he couldn't be more than twenty. Haral had never known him well, only through Bud and hearing Bud brag about him. Bud was always glorying in the scrapes he and Trace got into. Trace had been in jail for drunken driving—"And right now," Bud had boasted on the way up to Blair's Woods, "Trace is drivin without a license. He's just lost his driver's license for two years."

"Chrise," Trace said, "I would a got off easier if I hadn't taken a poke at the motorcycle cop."

"You didn't hit a cop, did you, Trace?" exclaimed Sayl delightedly.

[97]

"Hit him?" said Trace. "I'll say I did. That bastard's been after me all summer. He hauled me over to the curb and come pouterin up and started to shoot off his mouth. I had just enough of a load aboard so I let him have a honey right out through the car window. Gawd, mashed his nose flatter'n a fritter." Remembering, he burst into a loud guffaw.

Trace's Boston accent fascinated Haral. Usually he and Sayl made fun of the way the summer people talked . . . old Missus Whitewood, for instance, who came from Wilmington, Delaware, and said "neow" for "now" and "keow" for "cow," and one or two people from New Jersey who always called it "Nuh Jeisey." But Trace's slurred nasal syllables Haral thought, privately, sounded hard-boiled and sophisticated, and some of Trace's phrases he filed away in his mind for use later. Trace called the water-closet the "crappy," for instance. Haral intended to remember that.

It didn't seem to him that Trace drove a car with as much skill as Bud bragged he did. He had had one narrow squeak with a truck on the way up, and Haral caught himself watching the road a little apprehensively after that. He wasn't scared, exactly, though—the faster the better, so far as he was concerned, when it came to cars. But maybe if you were a pretty swell driver you *did* have narrow squeaks.

What pleased Haral, though, was that Trace seemed to like him. He had asked his opinion twice, so far, and once had told him that he wasn't so slow. What with the praise and the excitement, Haral had glowed. But now, sitting alone in the dark with Sayl, he shivered, and he couldn't help it but his stomach did feel a little funny.

"I bet that was cheap beer, Sayl," he whispered at last.

Sayl let out his breath relievedly. "I was just thinkin that myself. You feel funny, Haral?"

Haral bit down on his teeth to keep them from chattering. "Kind of," he admitted.

"Feel like pukin?"

"N-no. Not yet."

They waited awhile. Nothing happened. The wind moved rustling among the leaves and pine needles, and once in the woods off to the right, a stick cracked. Both boys sat up with a jump, the hair stirring on the back of their necks, but there was no further noise.

"Guess it must a been a deer," said Haral, relaxing.

"Ayeh. Or a cow."

"Where d'you suppose Bud and Trace is?"

"I dunno. Wish they'd come, don't you?"

Sayl gulped, his Adam's apple jerking up and down with a slight click. "Maybe if the's any beer left up front, we better drink it. They say some more'll keep a feller from bein sick."

Haral fumbled around in the front seat, but the cans were empty. "Trace said we'd have to get some more, remember?" he said. He was just settling back beside Sayl when the engine missed.

"What'd he say to do?"

Both boys leaned feverishly over the front seat.

"Pull out on that little gadget," said Haral confidently.

"This one?"

That was not the gadget. The lights came on.

"*Jee*-zus!" Sayl snapped them off hurriedly.

The next one was the throttle, and the engine resumed its even idling.

"Wow, that made me sweat," said Sayl.

"Me, too. I wish— Listen!"

Down the road behind them came a shout, then thumping sounds.

"They've caught em!" gasped Sayl. "What'll we do?"

"I—dunno. Can you drive?"

"Chrise, no!"

They sat paralyzed, listening to the commotion, which grew as they sat. Suddenly footsteps thumped on the road behind them—people running.

As one, Haral and Sayl opened the doors each on his side of the car and ducked into the bushes by the side of the road. The feet tore down the road—whoever was coming was running fast. Haral, peering agonizedly out of a bush, saw Bud's cap silhouetted against the patch of sky. It was Bud, and Trace was close behind him. They leaped into the front seat of the car, each tossing a brace of flapping chickens into the back. Trace threw off the brake, jammed the gearshift into low, and stepped on the accelerator.

"Trace, wait!"

The yell startled Trace so that he stalled the engine.

"What in hell! Quick, for godsakes get in the car!"

The boys plunged out of the bushes and into the back seat. A moment later Trace had the engine going again and they swerved wildly on to the main highway. He sent the car over the road unsteadily at sixty miles an hour.

"Bud," he drawled, "shut up. You'll die."

Bud was gasping with laughter and saying over and over, "Oh, sweet Jeezus! Oh, sweet Jeezus Chrise!"

"We thought we better duck," Haral offered a little tentatively. He felt pretty foolish. "We heard that yellin and we didn't know but you'd got caught."

"Not us," said Trace. "You done just right, though.

Gave ya a chance to get away if they had caught us and come huntin the car."

Bud half turned in his seat. "God, it was nip and tuck there for a minute. The old bastard was layin for us with a club." He pointed a hysterical finger at Trace and choked again. "He . . . he . . . he grabbed Trace and hit him . . . and Trace hit him back . . . right in the puss . . . with a live hen!"

"Stopped him cold," said Trace out of the corner of his mouth.

They were still weak from laughing a half hour later when Trace pulled up at a small sheltered moonlit beach a few miles from the Harbor. "Hand me out them pullets," he commanded. "I'll skin em, and then while you kids rustle some wood and start a fire, I'll take the car and go down to Jake's for some more beer."

LEONARD hadn't gone to the movies either. Alice Lacy, it turned out, didn't care for Western pictures.

"There's a swell show over to Bellport, though." She looked at him expectantly. "We could make the second show."

"I heard," said Leonard, "Charley Hemple's goin, but he may have a carful. You want to go?"

"Well, I'm not sure I do—with him. His crowd's kind of rough and he's an awful careless driver."

"Know of anyone else might be goin?"

"Well . . . let's see. Orin might, if we talked it up to him."

Leonard wasn't particular about going in Orin Hammond's car. He knew Alice had been going out some with Orin, and so far she hadn't made it plain just where she stood. But Leonard said amiably, "Let's go ask him."

They walked down the road together toward Orin's house, Alice stepping daintily along the tarred surface in her new patent leather shoes. She was a tall, sturdy girl, and the shoes were just a trifle small for her feet. They should have been sent back to Sears, she was thinking, but her other ones looked so awful, and she always liked to be dressed up when she went out with Leonard. He was always so dressed up himself. With Orin, now, you just didn't care. Orin always looked kind of slapdash, but he always told you you were pretty whether you had on good clothes or not.

Alice had been in Leonard's class in high school. She was one of a number of Harbor boys and girls who went up to Boston for winter jobs in the packing factories and came home from June to November. Some of them, Leonard thought, had seemed changed after a few seasons in the city—a little loud and tough, maybe —but Alice always acted quiet and nice. He liked to go out with her because she was happy-go-lucky and never had a tale of woe. He felt good when he was around where she was. Beyond that, he had never analyzed his feelings about her, except he damn well knew he didn't like Orin Hammond nosing around.

Orin was not at his house, and his mother said she didn't know where he was. "Gone down street somewheres," she said. "You might try the poolroom."

As they walked back through the town, Alice said, "I should think you'd want a car of your own, Len."

Leonard laughed. "Look kind of foolish, wouldn't it?"

"I don't see why. Most of the boys round here do have them."

"Ayeh, I know they do. But I live over on Comey's Island. What'd I do—drive across the bay?"

Alice lifted her shoulders impatiently. "You could keep it here in a garage, and have it to use when you came over."

"Nuh," said Leonard. "Matter of fact, Alice, I like cars all right, but I like boats better. Know what I'd do if I had money enough saved up to buy a car? I'd have me a boat built that would bug your eyes out."

"You would? You aren't goin to be a fisherman all your life, are you?"

Leonard looked uncomfortable, then annoyed. "I dunno. Why?"

"And live over on Comey's Island?"

"Why, I guess so."

"My goodness! I don't see how you could!"

Leonard turned his head and looked at her curiously. "What's the matter with the island?"

"Well, it's kind of a down-to-the-heel place, I've heard. Most of the people—oh, not your family, of course—but a lot of the people over there seem kind of . . . well . . ."

"You wouldn't want to live over there, I guess."

"Lord, no! That lonesome hole? I couldn't stand it." She realized from his face that she had touched him on a tender spot, and she laughed lightly. "But I'd be the last one to advise a man to change his life if he's satisfied with it."

"Satisfied? I don't know's I'd call it that."

"You just said you didn't want anything changed."

"Why, no, I don't believe I did, did I?" His voice held a kind of polite remoteness which would have warned her if she had known him better.

"I guess I don't get you," said Alice. She was a little

at sea. She had thought that the subject of cars was something that anyone would talk about endlessly. At least, any other young man of her acquaintance would. And going away from where you lived now, that was another thing. Everybody, that is, everybody who wasn't tied down with a family, or wasn't old, talked about going away somewhere.

When she was up in Boston, slopping around in the dirty winter streets, she longed to come home, was homesick for snow-filled woods and clean smells. But when she did come home in the spring, she was restless after about two weeks of it. There wasn't enough to do, and the people seemed dull and set in their ways.

This summer had promised better than most, now that Leonard and Orin were both coming to see her regularly. Orin had a car, and she had always had a secret admiration for Leonard, he was so kind of independent and self-contained. Leonard was good-looking, too. She did hope she could keep him interested—at least, until she went back to Boston in the fall.

"I guess I don't get you," she repeated. "But, then, people can't always understand each other, no matter how hard they try, can they?"

Leonard was flattered. If she was really trying to understand him, perhaps he'd better explain what he meant. "Well, look," he began, and stopped. It was going to be hard to put into words just what he did mean about living on the island. "It's a good place to live."

"A good place to die, you mean," said Alice.

"No, I mean most everybody over there has got enough so they ought to be—ought to be—"

"Contented?"

"Ayeh. Oh, not much cash, but they own their own

houses and most of em's got land to farm, and they've all got their boats. The's plenty to eat—fish and milk and eggs, and you kill a pig in the fall, and—gee, Alice, you ought to see Marm's cellar around the first of November. Shelves of preserves and ten-twelve barrels of potatoes lined up and apples and carrots—"

Alice put her hand on his arm. "Shut up, you're makin me hungrier'n a fool. Sure, I know what you mean. But I've sweat over jelly, and I ain't interested. I guess I don't agree with you."

"Don't sound like you do," said Leonard.

"Don't matter, does it?" She realized she had said too much, but she was honest about her feelings and she felt as strongly on this point as he did. "If a lot to eat and a house and land was all people needed to live, I'd say you was right. But, my Lord, Len, you can't even have a decent radio over there—just a battery set!"

"Look," said Leonard, "ain't that Orin comin out of the poolroom?"

Orin said, sure, he'd like to go to Bellport. He'd have to go up to the house, though, and bring down the car. "Have to round me up a girl, too," he said. "Don't know who I'll get, though, seein Leonard's walkin out with the prettiest one in town."

Alice gave him a sideways look. She liked that. It was more what she was used to—not lectures on cellars full of preserves. She couldn't think what possessed Leonard to be so old-fashioned.

"You seen Joe Comey?" Leonard asked Orin. "We got the kids with us, and I ought to tell him to keep an eye on em till I get back."

"Ayeh. I seen him all right." Orin glanced over his shoulder through the window of the poolroom, where Morris was visible, still concentrated on his game. "The

[105]

midget wonder!" he said. "I hat to get out of there or I'd a squat him like a bedbug."

Leonard glanced at him. Orin probably could have, at that, he thought. Orin stood over six feet, built like a boxer, with broad shoulders and narrow hips. He would have been a difficult man in a fight if he had had any temper, but he was sunny-natured and mild, and no one had ever known him to get mad.

He grinned now, sheepishly, as he noticed Leonard's surprised look. "It ain't my mix," he said, "except I do draw the line at bein learnt how to play pool. But you ain't heard what he done to Joe, have you?"

Leonard stiffened. "No, I ain't. What was it?"

Orin jerked his head. "Walk along a ways. I don't aim to do any tanglin with that little thug."

Leonard heard the story through in silence. "You know where Joe went?" he asked.

"Why, no, I don't. He looked to me like he was goin to hunt cover somewhere when he slunk out a the pool-room."

"Well . . ." Leonard looked at Alice. "I'll have to hunt him up. I expect that'll make us late for the movies."

"I'll take Alice to Bellport, if that's what you want," said Orin promptly. "I wouldn't be surprised if Joe did need ya."

"Gee, I dunno."

"I'll be glad to go with Orin," said Alice stiffly.

"Ayeh, I guess so. You go with Orin. I'll see you to-morrow night," said Leonard unhappily.

"That's what you think," said Alice. "Come on, Orin."

Leonard stood for a moment looking after them.

[106]

Then he turned and started down the road, his face set and hard in the light of the infrequent street lamps.

Joe was nowhere to be found. Leonard hunted in all the places he could think of where Joe might be, and finally gave up in exasperation and went to the second show of the movies.

There was still no light and sound aboard the boat when Leonard shinnied down the slippery ladder to go aboard. His feet thumped on the dew-wet planking. "Joe?" he called.

"Ayeh?"

Leonard peered down the hatchway into the cabin. Joe was sitting on one of the lockers. Leonard could just make out the white glimmer of his face. "Where you been?" he asked.

"I take it you heard the big news," said Joe bitterly. "All over town by now, ain't it?"

"Orin told me." Leonard sat down on the opposite locker. "Come on out a here."

"Don't believe I want to."

"It makes it worse, you crawlin down here like a sick cat," said Leonard.

"Feel like one, kind a."

"You ain't got reason to. Everybody knows what Morris is. The' ain't a man in town wouldn't be tickled to death to sock his teeth out through the back a his neck."

"Ayeh. I know. I ought to. But I don't do it, do I?"

"No, and people respect you for it." Leonard remembered uncomfortably the words Orin had used about Joe—"when Joe *slunk* out of the poolroom." "He's a little guy and he's your brother."

Joe sat up with a jerk. "Don't hand me that brother

[107]

crap. I'd mash him quicker'n I could spit if I dast to. But I don't. I'm scairt of him. I've been scairt of him since I was born. It warn't so bad when I was a little kid, but now he's got me so's I stick my tail between my legs in front a people. A hound-dog with a boot in his arse wouldn't a crawled outa there tonight any lower'n I did."

Leonard realized with a wave of hot embarrassment that Joe was taking it lying down. Jeezus, he thought, he'll be howlin in a minute if he keeps on. "Nuts, Joe," he said. "You got your dough back, free and clear, and damn lucky to get it. You don't owe a soul, and Morris owes the bank twelve hundred dollars."

"And I never yawped around town about his owin me money, either. I ought a hit him when he said that. Morris's hound-dog, that's all I am."

Actually, Leonard thought with amazement, and he'd seen it proved many times, he didn't know anybody who had more guts than Joe had. Suddenly he couldn't stand it.

"Jeezus Chrise!" he yelled. "You big bawlin calf!" His open palm described an arc and landed with a resounding smack on the white gleam of Joe's face. "Come on out on the wharf and I'll show you whose hound-dog you are!"

Joe came off the locker with a roar. His big paw closed only an inch or so behind Leonard's heel as Leonard fled up the ladder to the wharf. Behind a bait shed in an open space they fought silently and furiously, the only sounds the smack of fists on flesh accompanied by grunts of pain and rage.

Leonard landed a haymaker on Joe's chin that numbed his own arm to the shoulder. It was as if he had punched the side of the bait shed. Joe, breathing fire and brimstone, was suddenly all over him. A shower of jagged sparks let go inside Leonard's head. He felt himself falling, and then, unaccountably, he was lying relaxed and comfortable on a pile of crocus sacks in the shadow of the bait shed. Joe's big arm was under his shoulders. Hazily he made out the outline of Joe's shaggy head against the starlight, and then he realized that Joe was crying.

"Jeezus, Len! I ain't hurt ya, have I? Jeezus, you been out ten minutes."

Leonard started to grin, then thought better of it. While he had been asleep, somebody had taken away his chin and had substituted a big blob of broken glass. "That reminds me, Joe," he said thickly, "I got a boat I can sell for eight hundred dollars, and with your twelve hundred, that makes two thousand. That's about what Morris's boat cost, leavin out the fancy trimmins."

Joe let Leonard's shoulders drop with a thump.

"Ow!" said Leonard, sitting up. "Take it easy."

"By God, we got the dough to build one of our own, by God!" Joe said.

"Ayeh," said Leonard, getting to his feet with caution. "I've took another man's lickin to get that through your head. Now help me easy down that ladder."

"Jeezus, yes; I'll help ya, kid." Joe, in his eagerness, trod heavily on Leonard's foot, but at last managed to grasp him firmly under the arm. "Come on over to Jake's and get fixed up. I dunno how bad I hurt ya, but we both need a drink."

"We sure as hell do," said Leonard.

Under the arc lamp at the end of the wharf, the extent of the damage was apparent. Leonard's left eye was closed, the skin was gone off the bridge of his nose, and he had a lump on his jaw the size of his fist. Joe's shirt was ripped off the shoulder, his chin was bloody, and his right eye was black and swollen.

As they turned to go up the walk toward Jake's, two wan figures appeared in the radius of the arc lamp's light and proceeded uncertainly in the general direction of the wharf. Haral and Sayl, coming home from their evening, stopped and stared glassily at their brothers.

"Been fightin," said Haral thickly.

"Tha's ri," said Sayl. "Tch."

"*Look* at them kids!" breathed Joe.

"Been drinkin beer," said Haral, with a foolish confidential smile. "Don't like it."

Joe drove his bruised knuckles deep into his trousers pockets and stared ominously at Sayl. "Now, ain't you a handsome sight!"

"Nothin on you," mumbled Sayl, shifting uneasily. "You been fightin. I'm sure I dunno what Ma'll say."

Leonard shot out a hand and collared Haral. "Get em down aboard the boat, Joe, quick, before anybody sees em. This'll be glabbed from here to Bellport if it gits around."

Aboard the boat, they stripped off the boys' store suits and applied icy sea-water, scooped up in buckets and dipped out with wads of clean engine waste. Something about his brother's knobbly undeveloped body, lolling and helpless on the locker, tightened Leonard's chest with an emotion which he put down as anger.

"Goddam little fools!" he burst out, straightening up. "Come on, Joe. Don't bother with em. I don't care if they do get found out."

"Aw, no. That'd be too bad," said Joe. In the limited space of the cuddy, his big stern bumped into Leonard's thigh as he leaned over and turned up the lantern. "This ain't doin no good," he went on. "You feel like goin up to Jake's and fetchin down some black coffee?"

"Yeah, I'll go," said Leonard disgustedly.

"Bring a couple containers for us, too," Joe called after him.

Inside Jake's bar and restaurant, Leonard's appearance created a mild riot.

"Godsake," Jake commented. "You git run over?"

Leonard managed a grin, although he was about ready, he had to admit to himself, to crack almost anybody in the eye. He'd better give them a story, too, he thought, or the whole crowd would be down aboard the boat to find out what had happened.

"Joe and I had a fight," he explained. "He was feelin sorer'n a peep and I stuck my neck out. And now we need about four quarts a coffee, Jake."

"Coffee?" Jake raised an eyebrow.

"Yup. Coffee. And if that fifth of rum over there ain't half molasses, I'll take that, too. We're feelin like mixin our own." Leonard stuck his hands in his pockets and tried to look unconcerned. But I bet I look like a fool, he thought. He was feeling better than he had, though the walls of the room and the knot of inquisitive faces weaved in and out when he moved his head quickly.

Jake slapped the square bottle down on the counter and stuck covers on the pasteboard containers of coffee. "Who won?"

"Well—" Leonard gathered up his purchases—"all I remember is, I hit Joe three times." He turned to go and held up a warning hand at one or two who were getting up to come with him. "No riders. Joe's fit to be tied. He'd likely kill ya."

They settled back understandingly, and Leonard fled down the wharf.

The boat was dark and silent except for a splashing sound and a tinkle of water running from the scuppers.

"Joe?"

"Ayeh."

"Reach this stuff, will ya?"

Joe took the containers and Leonard swung down the ladder.

"We can put for home," Joe said. "Things is better."

"That's so?" said Leonard bitterly. "They couldn't very well be worse." He kicked the starter and idled the engine in neutral while Joe cast off the bow and stern lines. Then he backed away from the wharf and headed the bow out across the bay toward Comey's Island.

"They're pretty sober now," Joe offered. "I used the old finger treatment. Them two hunters, well—God, Len, I dunno what they et, but they sure was on one hell of a toot. I'll see 'f they want some coffee."

He came up out of the cuddy presently, ranged himself alongside Leonard and pried the cover off one of the remaining containers. "You didn't get anything to put in it, I s'pose?"

"Coat pocket," said Leonard. He heard the rich gurgle as Joe poured from the bottle into the coffee.

"Here you are," said Joe. "I'll steer."

Leonard took the hot container and sat gratefully down on the nearest bait tub. His tail came into contact with a pile of wet clothes, wrung out of cold water and piled in clammy twists on top of the tub.

"Jeezus! What's on this tub?"

Joe took his nose out of the other container. "Them kids clothes stunk like a brewery, so I soused em out in the harbor. I figured we could say, well, maybe that Sayl fell overboard and Haral went in after him. I dipped their underclothes and shoes over the side, too. They got on your work clothes and your oilpants."

The hot drink, laced with rum, nestled inside Leonard's midriff like a benison. He looked affectionately at the dark bulky outline of Joe, steering with one hand and upending the coffee container to the stars. "That warn't so dumb, Joe. You cover everything?"

"Think so. You might have a look around when you get your breath back. The wimmen-folks," said Joe soberly, "is goin to overhaul them kids like a patrol boat."

IN spite of his bruises and exhaustion, and not getting to bed until late, Leonard woke early the next morning. The clock on his dresser pointed to a little after seven. He was not so lame and sore as he had thought he might be, but he couldn't see out of his eye, and the lump on his jaw hadn't gone down any.

I bet I look like hell, he thought. He got stiffly out of bed and padded across to the mirror over the bureau. For a moment he stood regarding the reflection of his face with awe. The swollen jaw was purplish, and his sturdy night's growth of whiskers stood out on the taut skin like individual black spines. His eye was puffed shut and smudged with blue shading down his cheek into a sickly green.

Wow! said Leonard aloud. He thought with dismay of his date with Alice for that night. She hadn't seemed very keen about it, and he didn't know that he blamed her much, though he didn't see how he could have handled things any different. Anyway, he'd be settled with her for good if he didn't at least show up tonight.

On Sunday morning at this hour he knew nobody would be up but Gram. He'd better get some hot water or something.

Grammy, her breakfast over hours ago, was sitting by the west window peacefully knitting. At the sight of Leonard, she did not stop her needles, but stared at him with a grin of pure delight.

"Well, 'Lonzo Turner the second!" she cackled. "If this ain't like old times!"

"Ssh, Gram. You'll raise the roost. I kind a want to get fixed up a little before anybody sees this." He grinned at her lopsidedly. "What'd I better do for it?"

"Don't know nothin you *kin* do, less'n you cut your head off." She stowed her knitting carefully in the battered bag. "Haul up a chair to the sink. Blood meat is what that eye needs, but I doubt if your ma's got any."

She poked around in the supply closet and on the medicine shelf over the sink, and set to work on Leonard's eye, her misshapen old hands moving with surprising swiftness and dexterity.

"Does me good," she commented, slapping on a compress and steadying his wincing head with her other hand. "I ain't seen a shiner like this since your grampa had the chew with the Burnt Island feller over a barrel a pogies."

"Mouse, they call em now," said Leonard, in a muffled voice.

"Mouse? Does kind a look like one."

"How'll it look by tonight, Gram?"

"Worse," said Gram promptly. "Swellin might go down a little, but that eye'll be toad-color for a week-ten days."

Leonard groaned, and she glanced at him shrewdly. "What's the matter? Some girl?"

"M'm-h'm."

"Heh! Don't worry. She'll like it."

"Not this girl," said Leonard morosely.

"Then you stay away from her, Leonard! What for God sakes is she? One a the summer people?" Then as he did not answer, she went on, "That jowl a yours looks like a wood-hog, but if you could shave it, we could put some stickin plaster on and cover up the worse of it."

"I guess maybe I could if I was careful." Leonard got up, looking rakish in the white bandage she had tied around his head. His eye was better. She had put on some kind of poultice that felt cold and stinging.

He got his shaving things from the cupboard and poured hot water into a basin. Grammy had gone back to her chair by the window. She took out her knitting and waited expectantly.

"Joe Comey gi'me this eye," said Leonard, rubbing shaving cream tenderly on his sore jaw. "I'll tell you about it, Gram, if the's time before anybody gets up. But first, the's somethin else. Some guy tolled Haral and Sayl off on a binge last night and filled em full a booze."

"They did!" Grammy was indignant. "Now, what devil done that?"

"I dunno. The kids won't tell."

Grammy snorted. "Never had to do much tollin, I bet!"

"Prob'ly not. You know how kids is. But look, Gram. They spoilt their clothes and Joe washed em out with salt water. We figured we could tell the folks they fell overboard." In a few words he outlined Joe's plan.

Grammy nodded in approval. "That's smart. If it had to happen, it had to happen, and no use raisin a stink now it's over."

"You think of anything we maybe overlooked?" asked Leonard anxiously.

"M'm. Le's see."

There was a silence in which Leonard finished shaving. Now that the whiskers were off, he couldn't see that his jaw looked much better, unless perhaps a little less obscene.

"You wet their hair?" Grammy asked.

"Yup. Joe did."

"Haral get rid of it last night?"

"Most of it, I think. Joe ran his finger down his throat."

"Tch! Them little kids!" said Grammy. "I'd like to tar 'n feather whoever done it. Haral'll likely have a head on him this mornin. You better take him up a dose. Le's see . . . castor oil?"

"Castor—oh, my God, Gram!" Leonard, recalling one or two mornings of his own in the past, felt his stomach contract.

"Why not? Better in the wide world than in a narrow gut," said Gram virtuously.

"No." Leonard was firm. "Lay off Haral, Gram."

"All right, then. Lemon juice and saleratus. I'll fix it. You prime him up to tell his mother that he fell overboard with his stomach full a trash, like sody pop and hot dogs, and that's what's made him sick."

Josie, to Leonard's relief, swallowed the rescue story hook, line, and sinker. She dosed Haral and kept him in bed all day and was openly proud of him for jumping off the wharf to save his friend. Haral took her praise glumly, and after a while turned his miserable face to the wall and pretended sleep.

But Sarah Comey was something else again, as Joe

[116]

and Sayl should have known from past experience. Morris and Sayl slept late, but Joe, as he usually did, got up to have Sunday morning breakfast with his mother. His wounds, nothing like so spectacular as Leonard's, were scarcely noticeable against his swarthy skin, and if they had been, Sarah would not have bothered about them unless they had needed doctoring. Fighting was abhorrent to her and she wanted none of the details of it. She listened without comment to the story of Haral's going off the wharf after Sayl, and at its conclusion gave Joe a speculative look.

"I don't see why you're makin such heavy weather of it tellin me, Joe," she said. "Sayl can swim like a fish."

"Sayl didn't come up for a minute, and I guess Haral figured he'd caught a cramp. Anyway, he went off half-cocked and jumped in. I dunno—" he protested uncomfortably—"I warn't there when it happened."

"Oh, never mind." Sarah pushed back her chair, her eyes twinkling a little. "Long's everything's all right, I don't need to know everything. I don't s'pose you thought to change Sayl's dressin last night, did you? Standin watersoaked so long ain't goin to do that cut any good."

Joe's jaw dropped a little and he sat still, feeling the sweat start on the back of his neck. He'd forgotten about the dressing. He knew it hadn't got wet, because when he'd soused water over Sayl's head, he'd remembered to shield the dressing with his hand. "Why, no, Ma," he said, starting up. "But salt water's cleansin, ain't it? I'll go do it now."

"I'll do it." Sarah gave him an amused look. She took her box of dressings and salves and started for the stairway. "Too bad to wake him up, but I guess the sooner that wet gauze is off of there, the better."

Joe stared after her helplessly. He sure did hate to have her catch him lying like that. Not that she'd be mean about it. She wouldn't. She'd probably understand that he'd been trying to protect her as well as Sayl, on account of the way she felt about Homer's drinking so much the year before he died. And that, in a way, would be worse. Oh, well, maybe she'd think the damn gauze had dried overnight. He drank the rest of his coffee, listening nervously.

The murmur of voices drifted down from Sayl's room, his mother's deep tones, and Sayl's, sleepy at first, then raised in expostulation. Joe was not surprised when the sounds began, upstairs, of a violent chastisement.

Sarah came downstairs and advanced on him, and for a moment Joe thought she was going to light into him too, her cheeks were so red and her eyes so alight with anger.

"What was you and Leonard thinkin of, Joe, lettin them two kids traipse off that way and get drunk?"

"Well, Leonard was seein a girl. And I was so busy wonderin what Morris was up to, I clean forgot about the kids. Never entered my head but they was to the movies, like they always are. I'm sorry, Marm."

"Well, I'll put up with most things but not with booze, as you boys very well know."

"You . . . have any trouble lickin him? He's kind of big for you to lick, Marm."

"You well know I didn't. I could give you one like it if I took a mind to."

"Guess you could at that."

Something in his face, a kind of misery that in the last three years Sarah had come to watch for, warned her that there was no need further to punish anyone. "What's Morris done, Joe?" She moved to his side and

[118]

put her hand on his hair, smoothing the wiry mass backwards and forwards. Of all the rackety, violent-tempered brood she had raised, Joe was nearest her heart, though she would have died rather than admit it to herself or to anyone else.

"He borrowed twelve hundred dollars from the bank to buy me out of the boat," Joe said. "He— Oh, never mind what he done, Marm. He give it to me in the poolroom."

Sarah's lips tightened. "And shot off his mouth about it, I've no doubt."

"Well, sort of. But I don't care, Marm. Leonard's goin to sell his boat and put what he gets for her with my twelve hundred, and we're goin to have a new one built."

"That's the spirit." Morris strolled leisurely through the stairway door, his hands in the pockets of his neat gray Sunday trousers. "I was hopin you'd do somethin like that. No need to travel under my wing all your life." He glanced down at the used breakfast table with a little start of distaste. "Clear off the table and make me some fresh coffee, will ya, Marm?"

He sat down on the couch under the kitchen window, opening up the newspaper which he had brought from the Harbor the night before, to read while Sarah cleared the table. "I hope you thought to put your dough in a safe place last night before you went traipsin all over town," he said from behind the paper to Joe.

Joe's jaw dropped. "Gosh, I ain't thought of it since I put it into my pocket last night."

Morris lowered the paper. "You ain't? Hope to God you ain't lost it, then."

Joe went up the stairs two at a time, almost knocking

over a wan-looking Sayl who was creeping down to breakfast.

"Be just like the big lunk," Morris remarked. "I was goin to tell him last night to be sure to put it away safe, but he went out of there so kind a fast I didn't have time."

"Funny place to handle your business, Morris—in a poolroom," said Sarah. "Your father'd have the hide off a you for that if he was here."

Morris flushed darkly. "He ain't here," he said. He looked at her with an ugly little smile. "Is he?"

"No," said Sarah steadily. "I wish he was. But I am, Morris. You don't want to forget it."

Joe came back through the stairway door. His face, in the warm sunlight which streamed through the kitchen window, was greenish tan. "It ain't there, in my pants," he said hoarsely. "It's gone."

"It is?" Sarah went swiftly to him. "You sure you looked good, Joe?"

"I looked everywhere. Floor and . . . everywhere. Maybe it's down aboard the boat. I'll go see." He banged the kitchen door behind him and tore down the path to the Pool.

"More like it's gone overboard," said Morris.

Sarah glanced at him sharply. She had known that smooth, ready-to-pounce look of his ever since he was a little boy, and there was no mistaking it now.

"I better go look in his room," she said, putting down her cooking fork. "He's excited, he prob'ly ain't half looked. Sayl, you tend these eggs for me, and don't let em burn."

Sayl gave a howl. "Oh, my gosh, Ma! Let Morris tend his own eggs. The sight of em makes me sick."

[120]

"Set em back," said Morris, without moving.

Sarah went upstairs, but not to Joe's room. She went along the hall to the big sunny bedroom which had been Homer's, and where Morris now slept. The room was as neat and impersonal as if nobody had used it. Morris always took care of his own things, and he kept most of them locked away in the bureau drawers.

Sarah opened his clothes closet door. The suit he had worn yesterday was hanging smoothly, the pants in a press. She felt in the pockets and found them empty.

"You lookin for somethin, Ma?" Morris stood in the door regarding her. "Ask me, will ya, when you want anything out a my room?"

"Yes, I want Joe's money, Morris."

"Hell, I ain't got it."

Sarah stepped closer to him. "I know you too well, Morris. I seen you look like a cat suckin up cream too many times. Hand it over now. A joke's a joke, and this has gone far enough."

Morris looked at her. The eyes that looked at him out of Sarah's face were his own eyes, cold blue, steely. Once or twice in his life Morris had seen that expression on Sarah's face. He moved a little away from her and laughed uneasily.

"Okay. As you say, a joke's a joke. I was just tryin to learn the big muttonhead a lesson." He took the packet of bills from his hip pocket and laid them in her hand. "You'd a had a sweet time findin em in the room, wouldn't you?"

Sarah said nothing, and after a moment Morris turned and went silently down the stairs.

Then she stirred, sighed deeply, and moved to a chair and leaned against it.

The time's comin, she thought, when I ain't goin to be able to handle him.

After a little she went to the front window and called out to Joe, waving the bills. He was rowing dejectediy ashore from Leonard's boat when he looked up and saw she had them.

PART THREE

HARDY'S idea in going down to Jap Comey's house on Sunday morning was to make peace in a situation which seemed to him foolish and unnecessary. He figured he knew Jap pretty well. Cack had worked on him in the matter of the row, and Jap's dignity was injured.

I can talk him out of it, like as not, Hardy thought.

He stepped up on the rickety porch and went in at the back door without knocking. Knocking wasn't a custom of the country, and if he had thus announced himself, the Comeys would have thought him crazy.

Jasper was lying on the couch in his shirtsleeves and stocking feet, smoking his pipe. He did not get up, but regarded Hardy coldly and without change of expression. The kitchen was blue with pipe smoke and frying smoke.

Weeza, Cack's youngest, scrambled up off the floor where she was playing with a dirty kitten, and pattered into the pantry, where Hardy heard her whispering loudly.

Cack came to the pantry door, filling it with her bulk. She had on an old bungalow apron, white down the front with flour, and she had left off her corsets for Sunday morning relaxation.

"What you want?" she demanded of Hardy.

"Kind of wanted to talk things over with you and Jap," said Hardy, forcing heartiness into his voice. "Seems too bad for old friends to be at swords' points."

"Well, you might's well go home," said Cack. "I've done all the talkin with your crowd I'm goin to."

"Now, don't feel that way, Cack."

"I'll feel any way I damn please. You go home and lick some manners into them sarsy youngones a yours and maybe I'll feel diff'rent. That Leonard's always been a tartar. If you'd tended to him when he warn't too big to lick, he might a turned out partway decent."

"If he was my kid, I'd thrash the devil out a him now," said Jap, taking his pipe out of his mouth. "And your ma said things to Cack we ain't goin to forget in a hurry."

"Yes," said Cack, "if she hadn't been a old woman, I'd a slapped her right in the face. I'll know enough to stay away from there after this, and any store tradin we got to do we can do off to the Harbor. And you can tell Josie that if her hens git into my garden again, the way they been doin I'm goin to shoot every last one of em with Eddy's shotgun. I can't keep one thing around here that them damn hens don't scratch up. That's a warnin, Hardy. Either you and Josie shut them hens up, or I'll shoot em. Every last one of em. I don't plant dahlias and nasturtians for Josie's hens to dig up."

"I didn't know the hens been botherin you," said Hardy.

"Well, they have. Your folks been decent to me, I'd a kept my trap shut about it, but I'm all through. The's a good many things I've kept my trap shut about, too. The first time I ketch that little slut of a Mildred eggin Weeza on to dirt up my woodshed chamber again, she'll hear ducks quack. I'd lick her just as quick's I would my own. Up there, rummagin round in my things! I'll learn her! If I hadn't been too much of a lady the other night to speak my mind, I'd a give Josie an earful that would make em burn. She thinks she's so nicey nicey. You ask any of the school kids what Mildred was doin down on the Southern Neck beach the other day. I guess I know, for Weeza told me."

"I will," said Hardy. "But I warn't exactly interested in kids' doins when I come in here, Cack. What I did want was—"

"Maybe if you was a little more interested in kids' doins, your girl would get a good slapped arse."

"All right. Will you let me say what I come in here to say, or won't you?"

"The' ain't nothin *to* say. Jap and I don't want no more truck with you and Josie, and the first time I catch up with that Haral, he's goin to give me back my quarter or I'll take it outa *him*. The idea, comin in here and lyin to me about—"

"Oh, shut up!" Hardy's patience snapped. "If you was as long on brains as you are on gab, Cack, you'd be God's wife."

"Oh, is that so! You git outa here!"

"Yes, by God!" said Jap, getting up from the couch and putting down his pipe. "Maybe I ain't God, but I can put you outa here, like Cack says."

"Oh . . . blast!" said Hardy explosively. "If you ain't unreasonable, I never saw two people more so. I come in peaceable to patch things up, and you act like a couple of kids. All right, stay mad if you want to." He turned and went, shutting the door firmly behind him.

Jap followed him into the shed. "And what's more, you needn't cart no more freight acrost my place,

[125]

neither. You can haul it around. I got a right to say who's goin acrost my land."

"That cart road across your place has been a right a way for years," snapped Hardy.

"Well, it's goin to be shut off," said Jap threateningly.

"That so?"

"Yes, that's so. I'm going to build a fence between your place and mine. Cack 'n I've stood your kids and your hens runnin over our garden long enough."

"Build a fence for all I care," said Hardy. "You're a damn fool, Jap, and always were. A right a way's a right a way, no matter whose land it goes over. You better save yourself trouble and expense and find that out before you go crossin up the law."

He went down the path toward the Pool, walking rapidly until his anger lessened a little, slackening his stride as the rage went out of him. The way he felt about fights, he thought, he ought to be feeling pretty bad. He supposed he was. But down deep he had a sense of excitement. Things would tear wide open now, he knew that. Cack was probably already getting on her things to go visiting. What story she would tell he shuddered to think.

Actually, when he thought of it, nothing had happened. Little quarrel like that, why, it ought to blow over the next day and be forgotten. But it wouldn't. Well, it wasn't his fault. He'd done what he could to stop it.

He might as well go off and take a look around the weir, seeing it would be an hour or so until dinner. He'd noticed yesterday that a couple of tie-ropes looked frayed. He could fix them up before it was time to go home, and then he wouldn't have it to do tomorrow.

Hardy got a ball of tarred gangion from the fishhouse,

launched his dory, and rowed methodically out of the Pool and along the brush wing into the weir. Inside, he let the boat drift a little while he looked around for the ropes he wanted to replace. But when he had spotted them, he made no move to fix them.

The early September forenoon was clear and the light breeze smelled of salt from blowing so many miles over salt water. The bay sparkled and the wooded islands stood out in crisp light and shadow. The houses on the island looked clean and peaceful, standing white against the bright green of the second-crop grass in the neat hayfields.

A feeling of disgust so strong that it was almost a sickness swept over Hardy, disgust for his life and the way he was living it, for his work done day in and day out without much return, disgust for the island with its smallness and its hemmed-in-ness and its everlasting monotony.

I'm fifty years old, he thought, but if someone was to come along and say to me, Will you go to sea again? by God, I'd go, bad's I hate goin on the water.

The idea called to his mind a picture of himself as he had been as a young man, in his pea jacket and officer's cap, and he remembered suddenly how eagerly he had quit the sea to come back to Comey's Island.

But there wasn't nothin in it, he said to himself. There won't ever be nothin in it. If I was ever goin to do anything else, I'd have to start pretty soon.

ALICE was sitting in the hammock on the screen-porch when Leonard drove up in the car he had hired from

Hemple. She had the porch light on and was reading. When she looked at him, intending to be cool and remote, his bruised, rueful face was too much for her and she burst out laughing.

Relieved, Leonard sat down on the doorstep. "You must like the way my puss looks," he said, with his crooked grin.

"Well," she said, giggling, "it is kind of a relief after so many just plain faces."

"Want to go somewhere?" He hoped she would realize that the hired car was a peace offering. He had an idea that she was figuring him all wrong, and it rankled. A car was all right, and someday he meant to own one, but not if it meant mortgaging everything else he had. He wanted to get that across to her somehow.

"Why, I don't know," said Alice, riffling the pages of her book. "I was all over Robin Hood's barn last night with Orin."

"Be a moon later on. I'd come if I was you."

"We-ll. But not far, Len. Somewhere and watch it rise, maybe."

Leonard drove out along the state highway toward Bellport. He was a good driver, Alice had to admit, watching his smooth handling of the car—better than Orin was by a long shot. She wondered where he had learned, and asked him.

Leonard looked at her in the dim light and she saw the dark arc of one of his eyebrows shoot upward into his tanned forehead. "Engines come kind of natural to me," he said. "I drove a delivery truck one fall when I was over here to school."

Suddenly he swung the car sharp left off the highway and down a rough dirt road. The heavy branches of spruce trees interlaced above it, and the car lights bored into a dark, woods-enclosed tunnel.

"Where on earth you going?" asked Alice.

"Down to the Smelt Brook. You've been here, haven't you?"

"Oh, my goodness, yes. But not for a long time."

"Go somewhere else if you want to. But you said you'd like to see the moon come up."

Alice said nothing, and they bumped along in silence for a few minutes over the uneven grass-grown ruts. Then the road ended abruptly in a small field. As Leonard let the car roll to a stop and cut the lights, the field took shape out of the darkness, its grass close-clipped even of the second crop, and beyond it the dark smooth expanse of the ocean. Almost at their feet the brook was a gash of blackness between shallow banks. Its water tinkled lightly down the rocks, for now, at the first of September, the brook was low. The air smelled damply of moss and ferns and salt.

"No fish this time a year," said Leonard. "But, boy, do the smelts make this a busy place in May! I've seen em piled up in the mouth a this brook so thick you could dip em out by the bucketful."

"Mm," said Alice softly. The smell of the wet sweet air made her think of the times she had come down here in the spring, when the smelt were struggling up the brook to spawn. "We used to wade along where it was shallow," she said, "with a bucket and a flashlight and pick em out of the water with our hands. I got a bullfrog by the leg once," she added, chuckling. "Like to scared me to death."

Leonard laughed. "I'll bet. You like things like that, Alice?"

"I used to. Now I'm always up to Boston in May."

"You like it up there better?"

"I guess it depends on the time of year."

"What's the time of year got to do with it?"

"Boston's nice when I get back in the fall. But along toward April I get homesick." She laughed again, as if making a little fun of herself. "Then I spend the summer down here and I'm crazy to get away again. I guess I just don't make sense."

"Yes, you do. It's natural," Leonard said. "But it's a funny kind a life for a girl. What does it get you?"

She looked at him a little impatiently. "I can't sit at home all winter, doing nothing. I'd go crazy, and besides, Pa would have a catfit. He thinks a 'woman's place is in the home'—but not when she's 'an extry mouth to feed.' "

Her mimicry of old Brad Lacy's nasal pronouncements was accurate and without malice, and Leonard laughed appreciatively.

"I can see how you feel," he said.

"I don't think you see anything, Len," she said. "Your idea of what a girl ought to do is to live on her folks, I guess, till some man comes along and marries her."

"Why, for gosh sakes, it isn't!"

"Well, that's what it sounds like to me. I could have stayed here and married some . . . some . . ."

"Fisherman?" supplied Leonard in a quiet voice.

"Yes."

"Nothin wrong with that, is there?"

"Of course there isn't. I didn't mean there was. My own folks is fishermen. But I had to fight my own father every step of the way through high school, and most of the men around here think the way he does. Boy!" she added with feeling, "the royal old battles we used to have!"

"I'll bet you did," said Leonard, grinning. Brad Lacy

was a die-hard in all his notions, and when it came to women, he figured they had one use in the world and that was that.

"He used to take out after me with a lath," said Alice, chuckling again, "until one time I hauled it out of his hand and busted it over my knee. I told him he was lucky it wasn't his head I'd busted it over. After that he gave in, but he never misses a chance to twit me about being educated. He says now I'm a damn freak—I know too much for any man to want to marry me."

"He's mistaken there," said Leonard warmly. In the white reflection which was begining to grow in the sky before moonrise, he could see the blur of her face and the luminous texture of her hair. "I didn't know you had such a time with Brad."

"Oh, I had a time. I fought for everything I got," she said.

He liked the way she talked about herself—as if she were amused at her troubles, not bragging.

"Oh, I won't say that going to Boston every fall and packing canned stuff is the happiest thing I could do," she went on honestly, "but it's the best I can do, Len. I started out to do better, but I don't know enough to teach and my spelling's awful, so I can't get a stenog's job. I'm not very bright, you know. About a C-plus average."

"You don't have to be," said Leonard.

"There you go. Just like Pa. 'All a woman needs to know is how to wash dishes an cook.' Well, I can wash a mean dish if I have to. But if you want to know why I go to Boston, you take a look around the Harbor at some of the girls who were in school with us. It would curdle your blood. I want some say about my own life and to have it kind of decent, that's all."

[131]

"Well, darn it," said Leonard, "that's the way I feel, too. I dunno why you jump on me and tell me I think like the old shellbacks."

"Well, you sound as if you did. That line about jars of preserves that you gave me last night, for instance. I've heard about that from Pa. Gosh, I put up three hundred jars the fall I was fourteen."

"Oh, hell!" said Leonard disgustedly. "Skip it, will you? I was only tryin to tell you about somethin I thought looked kind a good. Smoke?"

"Thanks. I will."

"You smoke kind a nice. Most girls act like a fool with a cigarette."

"That's because their menfolks tell them they do, if you ask me."

"You just won't let me get straightened out with you, will you?"

"Why should I?"

Leonard laid his cigarette down carefully in the dashboard ashtray. He slipped an arm around her and his mouth was over her startled one before she realized what he intended doing. For a moment her lips lay warm and relaxed under his, then she pushed him firmly away.

"Okay," said Leonard. He did not attempt to hold her. "But that was the reason I figured I wanted to get straightened out with you."

"I don't see but it's a good one," said Alice. "If I was most girls, I'd cut up and cry and make you take me home. Being me, I tell you I liked it."

"Doggone!" said Leonard, his jaw dropping. "Good for you!" He put out his hand tentatively again, but Alice said, "You know you smell like a drug store?"

Leonard was horrified. "It's all that stuff Gram put on

my eye. I'm sorry, Alice. I guess I must look like Joe Palooka."

Alice laughed. "I don't think you can help the eye," she said. She figured it might be a good idea to get the subject changed. "Joe Comey was kind of ungrateful, wasn't he?"

"He was just tore out. I happened to be the first one to come along, that's all."

"Morris ought to have that eye, not you. What's Joe going to do for a boat now?"

"I was goin to tell you," said Leonard. "He and I's throwin in together—his twelve hundred and the eight hundred I can get for my boat."

"Oh," said Alice, in a small voice.

He went on, not noticing her withdrawal, eagerly telling her all the details of their scheme. "Chuck Hamblie down on Burncoat will gi'me eight hundred any time for the boat I got now. And Joe and I together've got enough saved to buy a slick marine engine—maybe a Gray. We're going to build a dragger on Morris's molds and model, and you put a big Gray into a model like that and—"

"You meant it when you said you'd build a boat if you got some money."

"Sure I did. Ain't that a good idea, to your way a thinkin?"

"None of my business, is it?"

"Why not? What *would* I do? I s'pose you'd buy a car. Well, a car's nice, but a boat's my livin."

The tip of the moon sparked at the edge of the horizon, sending an uncertain squiggle of quicksilver into the black water just beyond the hood of the car. Alice watched it for a moment in silence. Then she said,

"Well, the moon's up. We've seen it, and now let's go home."

Leonard's arms went around her again. "Don't talk, Alice. We're all right if we don't talk."

For a little she seemed about to push him away, then she put her head down on his shoulder. "I know it," she said. "Seems kind of foolish, doesn't it? You want one thing and I seem to want another. What'll we do?"

"Figger out a way not to fight about it," he said promptly. "You've got a lot of sense—"

"So have you. But look around, Len, at the men who thought twenty years ago that a boat was a livin."

Leonard's jaw under the blue bruise went hard. "What are you tryin to say, Alice? I ain't got all the dough in the world; most people ain't. But Joe and I and Morris cleared twenty-five hundred last season. With only two of us to share, and a new boat, I can do better."

Alice took her head away from his shoulder. "Boys up in the city with brains like yours make twenty-five hundred all by themselves in a year, and they work under cover and in comfort."

"My God!" said Leonard, staring at her. "Under cover? I'd go nuts! I've always been my own boss, too, and I always mean to be. Stop talkin like a fool, Alice."

"You just aren't used to it. It's not so bad."

"I wouldn't live in Boston if you gi'me the place."

"All right, nobody asked you to."

"I know what I want," he snapped.

"You can't know when you've only tried one thing."

"Who for God sakes would know if I don't? You're a good one to talk. You went up there and got movie crazy—"

"I'm not! If that's what I seem like to you—"

"Why else would you harp so on goin to a city?"

"You take me home!"

"Okay, I will. Glad to!" Leonard started up the engine and jerked the car around in the narrow field.

Neither of them spoke on the way home, and Alice left him with an icy "Good night."

Leonard was half-way home, chugging in his boat across the moonlit bay, before he began to wonder why on earth he had got so mad. He didn't see much reason for it. Still, what right had Alice to belittle the way he lived his life and what he wanted to make of it?

He couldn't see much wrong with it himself, except he didn't make a lot of money. He knew perfectly well that he was a good deal like the rest of the men who fished out of Comey's and the Harbor—he'd gripe and growl and say that it was a lousy way to live and the pay was stinking. But when it came to quitting dragging or lobstering or trawling, he'd think a long time before he would. The people who lived over on Comey's spent a lot of time telling about how they hated the island and going on the water; but if they had the best chance in the world to leave—a well-paid job on the mainland—he doubted very much if they'd actually go.

Women always seemed to feel a man could do better than he was doing if he wanted to take the trouble. Well, he figured he was doing about the best he could, right now. Certainly he couldn't work much harder, and fishing was something that took brains and skill if it was done properly. He'd like to see some of Alice's city friends who made twenty-five hundred a year all by themselves try to get a dragnet inboard with the wind northwest and a flood tide making.

She could plain go and climb a tree. He was through. But even as he made the decision not to see her again, he realized with amazement that he couldn't solve the problem that way. They'd been going around all summer together, off and on, when he could spare the time. Not that he was in love with her. It was just that this wasn't any row with any girl. He really respected Alice's brains, and he cared what she thought about him. This misunderstanding was something he'd like to straighten out between them, and straighten out quickly.

Alice went to bed in the grim ell room where she slept when she was in her father's house. She sat for a while with her knees snugged under her chin, watching without seeing it the patch of moonlight moving across the shabby wall.

That kiss tonight had been special, and it had meant something to her, too. She hadn't really thought what it would mean if Leonard fell in love with her. With Orin, it was different. Orin *was* in love with her, or he thought he was. She supposed she could marry Orin tomorrow—he certainly talked enough about it. But she wasn't going to. Orin was easy-going. When she went back to Boston the first of November, as she surely was going to do, Orin might feel glum for a few days and then he'd forget all about it.

She sighed, hugging her knees, hating to put her feet down into the damp sheets. Even in summer the bedding in this ell room always felt clammy. In winter it was like going to bed in a tomb. The hall bedrooms up in Boston weren't much either, but at least they weren't horrible, and she was her own boss up there.

She knew well enough what it would mean if she got married and stayed here at the Harbor. The tired, discouraged women and girls whom she saw every day were evidence enough. They kept house for their menfolk and children at night and worked in the sardine factory in the daytime. The day's work most of them put in was too much for any woman to stand, and they showed it in the way they looked and the way they dragged around.

Not that she minded hard work—she'd certainly done enough of it; but to struggle along like that, to know your menfolks expected it of you, would take the heart out of a woman.

Her own mother had died years before her time—tired out, and glad she didn't have to live any longer. Time after time, when Alice was little, she had seen her mother start off for the factory, when Brad Lacy would be sitting with his stocking-feet up on the stove tank.

All the men weren't like that—it would be unjust to say so. Some of them worked like dogs from morning to night. Most of the ones who did admitted that there wasn't enough in fishing to support their families, though, and their womenfolks *had* to help out by working in the factory. Some were stubborn and wouldn't admit it, but their wives worked just the same.

Leonard was one of those. Leonard was a worker. He'd be nice to his wife, too. But would he make a companion out of her, let her have a part in the important things of his life? From the way he talked, she didn't think he would. He'd look on her as something he possessed, to make love to, to keep his house and make him comfortable, something less than a person who had the same kind of brains and feelings he did. The men around here all felt that way about women.

Well, she'd go back to Boston. She didn't feel at home there any more than she felt at home in this house or in this town. To look ahead and see that kind of life stretching out for years wasn't pleasant. As Leonard said, it was a funny life for a girl. This place here, this countryside, was what she loved and wanted fiercely to be a part of, yet the way she was now, divided, it hadn't anything to offer her.

I guess I'd like to belong somewhere, she told herself forlornly. But I'd have to guess again to know for sure where.

HARAL wasn't particular about going to high school, but the idea of spending the winter off the island had interested him tremendously. The Harbor wasn't much of a town, as towns went, but compared to Comey's Island in the wintertime it was a lighted metropolis. And so in all the discussion about whether or not he was to go, and how the money was to be found for his expenses, Haral had taken an interested and enthusiastic part.

His mother was on his side. Practically, Josie didn't see how it could be managed, unless Haral got a job and worked his way through. But she was determined that he was to go. He was her one hope, now that Leonard had decided to keep on fishing. She had schemes for Haral's future that would have surprised him.

To Haral, the "future" was a state of being in which he would have plenty of money and be his own boss, like Leonard. How this was to be achieved he had no idea, unless you waited and the "future" happened to you. If going to high school would help him to make something of himself more quickly, Haral was willing.

Josie hated to say anything to Hardy about it when he looked so kind of glum, but after all, school opened the Monday after Labor Day, and that didn't leave much time. So Sunday night, when Hardy went out to milk the cow, Josie followed him, to be out of earshot of Grammy.

"I just don't see how we can manage it," Hardy said, the downward lines of his face setting in more deeply. "The best we can board him for is five dollars a week, and he'll have to have some new clothes."

"We *got* to manage it," Josie said grimly. "I won't have any more of my youngones growin up happity-hazard."

"I don't see's any of them have," Hardy said, glancing up at her curiously from his seat on the milking stool. "Leonard's doin all right, ain't he? What'n time you want your youngones to be—the President?"

"I want em to be somethin," Josie said. "Leonard could be somethin besides a fisherman if he was a mind to. *You* always wanted to be somethin else, Hardy."

Hardy winced. "Did me a lot of good," he mumbled.

"I never meant that against you, Hardy," said Josie gruffly.

"I don't object to Haral's goin," Hardy said slowly. "Only thing is, we ain't got the money."

"Your mother has."

"Ma?" He grinned suddenly. "Would you like to ask her for it?"

"You well know what she'd say to me. She might listen to Leonard, though," said Josie speculatively.

"Hell, Josie, she ain't got much. She's savin a few dollars for her funeral."

"She's got enough to start Haral in with. By that time maybe you'd be doin better with the weir, or Leonard would have his new boat paid for."

"I'm willin to ask her," said Hardy, "but we'll never hear the last of it. We could mortgage the house again, Josie."

Josie looked sober. "I'd be willin to do that if there ain't no other way."

"H'm," said Hardy, getting up with his full pail of milk. "You stay out a the kitchen, Josie. I'll see what Ma says."

Josie listened shamelessly just outside the shed door.

"You gone out a your mind, Hardy Turner?" she heard Gram say in a shrill, shocked voice. "Here we are, livin on the skin of our teeth, and you think a borrowin money to send that boy to school? If I didn't know you was such a fool, I'd think you was a bigger one than I thought you was. Josie's behind this."

"I want it as much as she does," said Hardy staunchly.

"When you went to school, you worked your way through. What's the matter with that lazy shitass? Let him git a job." Grammy retired into her knitting and refused to discuss the matter.

Haral had talked the whole thing over with Sayl, lying sprawled in front of the brush camp they had started to build on the shore for a duck blind. Somehow the project had palled, and they never had got the roof on. Now that this high school business had come up, it didn't seem worth while finishing the blind, since they might not be on the island this winter.

"Joe says I gotta go," Sayl said glumly. "He's goin to pay my way. Wish he'd just gi' me the dough and le' me take it and go find a job."

"You're lucky he's got the dough at all," said Haral. "My folks is dead broke . . . as usual."

"Wish Joe was." Sayl hurled the rock he held in his hand at a tin can lying on the beach. "Hunh, he never went. How's he think he's goin to make me study in school if I don't want to? Hell, I never even got through eighth grade till I was sixteen."

[140]

"Well, look, Sayl, if we don't go, we got to stay here this winter. At least the's a movie off to the Harbor."

"Ayeh. It ain't like this dead hole. But to hell with school!"

"If we're there, and a job turned up, we could take it."

"Le's run off and enlist in the navy."

"No money in it."

"Ayeh, but you git to go somewheres."

"That's right. Trace Jones was in the navy once. He said in all the best places, like Brazil, they never let you go ashore."

"Oh, crap!" said Sayl. "Of course they do."

"Now, look, Sayl. You quit bein stubborn. You want to stay here all winter doin nothin?"

"I ain't goin to stay here all winter. I'm goin to school, ain't I? Joe says he'll kill me if I don't."

"Well, all right then," said Haral, relieved. "Maybe it won't be as bad as it sounds."

JOSIE was really good and mad on Monday morning when Hardy told her about Cack's threat to the hens and Jap's threat to cut off the right of way across his land.

"Why," she said, "they know I keep my hens shut up in a yard. They did get out the other day when Mid forgot to close the gate, but they didn't do any harm. I put em right in again as soon's I found it out."

"Well," said Hardy, "the way Cack feels right now, they practically went to roost on the rim a her flour barrel."

The cart road, as Hardy had said, had been used for years. It did go across Jap's land, as it must, since Jap's acre lay between Hardy's house and the shore. Hardy's family not only had to use it to get to the Pool, but every month when he brought over from the mainland his supply of goods to stock the store, he hauled them by team up this same cart road. To go around Jap's land was possible, but it made for a longer haul and considerable trouble, as the road was bad.

"You goin to stand for it, Hardy?" Josie asked. She had got up earlier this morning, since it was washday, and was eating breakfast with Hardy.

"Why, no," said Hardy, not looking up from his breakfast. "I ain't. You want wash-water lugged, Josie? It don't look to me like it was goin to be a chance to wash."

"It ain't," said Grammy. "It'll rain in an hour's time."

Josie got up and peered anxiously out the west window. "It does look kind a frowy," she said. "Well, no, I s'pose not, Hardy; not if it's goin to storm. Which way's the wind?"

"It's out," said Grammy. "Hauled out in the night. I heard it. Southeast."

Hardy bestirred himself nervously from the table and went to the door to look at the sky.

Josie, worried, glanced after him as he closed the door and went to stand at the end of the porch, studying the big bulging clouds that hung low in the west. "Oh, dear," she said, "I s'pose it's only a matter of minutes before he starts out to drop them nets down."

"Humph!" Grammy stowed away her knitting and came over to help pick up the dishes. "He better keep em up and earn some money so he won't have to go round beggin."

She cocked her head for Josie's reply, but Josie said nothing. She didn't feel like a row with Grammy this morning and she knew that Grammy was all agog for one. Josie was beginning to regret that she had let Hardy say anything to Grammy about money. As he had said, they'd probably never hear the last of it.

"Girl and woman," stated Grammy, stacking plates and cups and saucers with deft skill. "I never missed once washin on Monday. If it rained, I dried em in the suller."

"Well, never mind," said Josie tolerantly. "I don't like clothes dried in the house. They never smell good."

"Mine always smelt clean as snow. But then, I always took pains to air mine."

"If you don't mind doin the dishes, Grammy," Josie said abruptly, "I've got some outdoors work this mornin." It seemed to her that if she had to go on talking with one single person she would jump out of her skin. She wanted to keep quiet and to think. So many things, all coming at once, always did make her feel that way. If she had time, she could deal with her problems one by one and do a good job on all of them.

"I do mind," said Grammy, "but I s'pose that's all the good it'll do me. If you're goin out to think out some way a weaselin me, you needn't bother, Miss Josie. You ain't goin to git my money!"

Josie went out the back door and stood for a moment by the big pile of stacked cordwood in the yard. The wood smelt faintly resinous, and she put out her hand to touch the rough bark of a stick of it, feeling it tough and sandpapery under her fingers.

The weather did look bad. The sky in the east still glowed a faint pink where the sunrise had been red, and in the west the low clouds had begun to disperse in a

gray, ugly-looking mist. She didn't know as she'd blame
Hardy if he did drop his nets down on a day that
looked as bad as this one did. Well, he probably would.
She didn't need to worry about that. He was still stand-
ing on the porch, looking troubledly at the sky.

Josie walked slowly on through the yard and out into
the back field where the vegetable garden was. The land
was neat, everything in its place, but there certainly was
plenty to do in the garden. The weeds had got a head
start. Too bad the boys weren't more interested, but
then, they had their own things to do. She did think,
though, that the way both of them liked green vege-
tables they might buckle down and do a little of the
work it took to raise them.

She settled her ample body down at the end of a row
of carrots and began pulling the weeds out from among
the plants. Josie liked the vegetable garden. Secretly she
was glad that the boys hated it, because it gave her an
excuse to take care of the plants and to be alone while
she did it. If she could do something useful with her
hands, something that they did well by themselves, then
her mind was free and she could think things out.

Something would have to be done, quickly, about
Haral's school money. Of course they'd mortgaged the
house before and got the debt paid off finally. It would
help some if Cack Comey was to pay her store bill.

She had always had her private opinion of Cack, and
if the time had come now to state it outright, Josie didn't
think she'd hold it back.

I ain't lived alongside of her for twenty-three years
for nothin, Josie told herself. She's made more trouble
than any other three women on this island, and she'll go
on makin it until the day she dies. I've put up with her,

but if she thinks she's goin to lay a fight on my doorstep and have me knuckle under, she's mistaken.

She stirred the newly weeded soil around the carrot plants, and sniffed appreciatively as the smell of the richly manured earth rose under her grimy fingers.

I don't know's I care if we do have a good rain. Things is gittin kind of dry. This gardin's been an awful good one this year.

Hardy probably wouldn't do anything very much if Jap did cut off the right of way, she reflected. Hardy's too easygoin when he ain't mad. If the time ever come when Hardy's actions and his gettin mad should come at the same time, he'd get somethin done. But his trouble was that he couldn't stay mad.

Thin rain, more like mist than rain, began to filter down from the increasingly overcast sky. It made the spruce woods on two sides of the long field she worked in look a darker green, and the birch trunks spotting them here and there a whiter white. Josie turned her back to the rain, feeling its coolness pleasant on the tight-drawn back of her housedress.

Jap could certainly build a fence, legal or not, between his line and Hardy's. If he did that, what would be the best thing for Hardy and her to do?

She weeded steadily along, changing her bent position only at the end of a row, pausing only long enough at intervals to wipe the moisture from her spectacles with the corner of her apron. Her cheeks grew pink with exercise and the soft hair around her face and in the back of her neck drew up into little tight ringlets misted with tiny drops of water. She left behind her the damp black soil clean of weeds and cultivated, punctuated by the clear green of the maturing plants. As she worked, she felt the turmoil within her die and move far off, like discordant and ugly sounds left behind as one walks away from them down a road. After a while she did not even think of it any more.

It was nearly noon when Josie stood up, straightening her kinked back with a groan. She had done the carrots, the turnips, and two rows of beets—eight long rows in all. Also she had thought out her problems, and her courses of action were clear in her mind.

Haral must go to school, and if Hardy was willing, they would mortgage the house again. It was, after all, a little mean to expect a woman as old as Grammy to part with what few savings she had. If I hadn't been upset and nervous, Josie said to herself, I'd never a thought of askin her. And if Jap Comey builds that fence across the cart road, we'll just take an ax and chop a gate through it.

Through the now heavily falling rain she walked on stiff and protesting legs back to the house.

Grammy eyed her with sour disapproval as she came squelching in soaked shoes through the woodshed door.

"Don't you come howlin round me with the rheumatiz," she stated. "I won't have one mite a sympathy for you. You gone crazy?"

Josie laughed richly. "I've come back from bein," she said. "What do you want for dinner, Mother?"

"H'm," said Grammy suspiciously. "Don't you 'Mother' me. You ain't goin to git my money by mealin me up."

"I been thinkin about that," Josie said. "I don't believe it'd be right for me and Hardy to take your money, Mother, even if you was willin to give it. So you better forget about it, and we'll think of somethin else. What *would* you like to have for dinner?"

The old lady's eyes shone with malice. "Flapjacks,"

she said promptly. Flapjacks would be hardest to cook.

"All right," said Josie, as promptly. "But don't come howlin to me with the bellyache. I won't have a mite a sympathy for you."

⟨ formula ⟩

FROM his usual point of observation on Crab Point, Hardy watched the ugliness of the gathering storm. The tide was on the ebb, about half out. At any time now he could begin to drop his weir nets. But he stood for a while watching for weather signs in the curdled clouds that came driving in over the islands from the open sea.

Suppose he took the nets down now and by sunset it cleared off? It often did, this time of year. He could imagine what people would say. He could imagine Jasper and Cack having it over and Cack telling it around the town. "Somebody broke wind and Hardy dropped his nets down."

The wind blowing in fitful gusts tugged at his sou'-wester and sent a slap of rain off its brim into his eyes. Hardy fished for his handkerchief and wiped them dry. The weather signs were all bad. Wind coming in gusts, sea making up fast on the ebb tide, clouds black and roily-looking over Canvasback Island. Well, they had been last time too. He'd wait a little while longer.

Maybe in an hour or so it would either begin to clear or get worse enough so he could tell. So many times he'd taken precautions for nothing. And so many times he'd taken precautions and something had happened. Twenty years ago he could have told in a minute just what he wanted to do and when he was going to do it. Twenty years ago he'd have dropped them or left them up and wouldn't have given a hang. Now the problem nagging at him left him feeling foggy, so that the sense of wind and weather he had always depended on didn't seem to tell him anything.

People had said that Hardy Turner could smell a storm three days away, and he'd always thought he could. Now, with the clouds rolling out over Canvasback and the combers beginning to put up their heads so you could see them over the outer ledges, the *feeling* of storm eluded him. He felt storm in the air these days whenever a cloud blew up on a bright day, or the wind in its ceaseless searching around the points of the compass blew for an hour or so from any of the danger spots between east and south.

He stood uncertainly, a little stooped and weary in the drooping lines of his loose wet oilskins, trying to convince himself of the signs which now bewildered him.

A scrambling on the rocks made him turn. Mildred, in raincoat and rubbers, was climbing up to him, agile as a monkey over the slippery boulders.

"Pa," she shrilled, "Ma wants to know shall she put away dinner or are you comin up to eat?"

Her bright little eyes slid past him to the gray-green water, spotted here and there now with white rags of foam, then returned to fasten on his face with enjoyment and a kind of inquisitive malice.

Hell, thought Hardy. Even the kids. Even my own kid. "I'm comin home to dinner," he said aloud, more loudly than he needed to. "How'd you and your mother happen to run of an idea I wasn't?" He began stalking down the rocks, slipping a little as he went.

"What's it goin to do, Pa?" Mildred came lightly down behind him, racing on ahead when he went too slowly. "Ain't it goin to be a bad storm?"

"Oh, I don't think so," said Hardy firmly. He thrust out his chest and looked grandly up at the sky. "It'll clear off before night. Don't look to me like no more'n a whisper."

AT three o'clock Leonard and Morris and Joe, in Morris's boat, came in from outside along the lee of the islands and shot up to the mooring in the Pool. It had been too nasty to drag fish, with promise of being a good deal nastier, and they had given up the trip.

Morris had made it clear on Sunday night that he expected Joe and Leonard to finish out the fishing season with him or at least to go dragging until their own boat was finished, and Joe had persuaded Leonard to do it.

"After all," he said, "we do own thirds on the drag, and we'd lose the rest of the season if we didn't."

"It's up to you, Joe," Leonard conceded. "As long as Morris acts human, I'll go."

Morris had acted very human—in fact, for him he had been almost pleasant. He had wanted to stay outside longer, even in the teeth of the rising weather, but he had given in with good grace when he saw that both Joe and Leonard thought it was best to come in. He hadn't, either by word or raised eyebrow, implied that they might be just a little white-livered for wanting to quit.

Ordinarily he would have suggested something of the sort, Leonard thought, although Morris knew as well as anybody that the thing to do was to quit and come inshore when the wind and sea started to kick up like this.

Now, as they rowed ashore from the mooring, bending their heads against the rain that slashed across the

Pool, Joe suddenly said, "Godsake, Len, what's the matter with your old man? He ain't got his nets down."

"He ain't!" Leonard half stood up to look out at the weir, rocking the punt precariously as he did so. A bucket or so of water splashed in over the side and Morris let out a yell.

"Hey! Maybe you know how to swim. I don't, and I don't care about the idea."

Leonard looked at him startled, and Morris glared back at him. "Rockin a boat like that!" he said. "Damn fool!"

"Ain't but five-six feet of water this far inshore," said Leonard. "What's the matter with you?"

"I said, I can't swim," said Morris, in his usual bland voice.

"Maybe Hardy's sick or somethin," interposed Joe. "He sure ought to have his nets down."

"He must be," said Leonard, with concern. "Look, Joe, if you don't mind, I'll let you do my share of the stowin away, while I hop up to the house and see where he is."

"Sure," said Joe. "Look, if ya need any help, let me know."

"Thanks," said Leonard.

At the house nothing seemed to be amiss. Grammy made a face at him through the window, and Josie was sitting at the sewing machine placidly stitching.

"Where'n hell's Pa?" said Leonard breathlessly.

"Out whitewashin the tie-up," said Josie. "Why, what's the matter, Leonard? Somethin wrong?"

Leonard dumped his dinner bucket in the sink and started for the woodshed door. "He ought to be down droppin his nets, that's all," he fired back over his shoulder. "It's hellish outside, and blowin on every minute."

Hardy was in the tie-up, methodically working white-wash on to a beam with an old broom. Leonard was taken aback by his unruffled calm.

"Hello!" Hardy said, glancing at him briefly. "Have engine trouble or somethin?"

Leonard sat down on a barrel, wiping the sweat off his forehead with his handkerchief. Seeing his father all right made him feel better. "Too rough outside to drag," he said. "Thought maybe I'd get in in time to help you drop the nets."

"Why," said Hardy, dipping his broom in the bucket, "I don't believe it's bad enough for that, is it?"

"My God, Pa," Leonard burst out, "the spray's comin in over Ram Island Head in sheets! It's flood tide now, and if we don't hurry we won't get em down. You crazy?"

"No, I ain't!" snapped Hardy. "I ain't goin to drop em, that's all!"

"You'll lose em," said Leonard desperately. "This looks to me like the worst summer storm in years."

"Well, it ain't. I guess I know weather signs. I watched off the Point awhile before dinner, and it didn't look so bad to me."

"Well . . ." said Leonard. "Well . . ." He didn't know what to say or what to make of his father not being worried, not even bothering to go and look at the weather for three hours. "You . . . you ain't sick, are you, Pa?"

Hardy whirled around so sharply that the whitewash from his broom spattered on Leonard's pants. "Sick? Sick, hell! Your ma and you 'rangue the daylights out a me when I do drop them nets and now you're startin

[151]

in on me cause I don't. Get to hell on out a here and let me alone!"

Leonard stared at him open-mouthed. "Look, I'll go drop em for you—"

"You touch them nets and I'll wam the hide off you. I can do it, too. I've had the hell'n enough of people tellin me what to do."

Leonard backed out of the tie-up and stamped into the house. All right, by God, he muttered to himself, if that's the way he feels.

He had not noticed in the dim light of the barn that his father's hands on the broom were shaking, and his face was set and strained and white as a sheet.

THE weir must have started to go sometime in the early part of the night, probably around high tide, at nine o'clock. As darkness came on, the storm grew worse instead of showing any signs of the clearing that Hardy had promised himself. He ate his supper without saying much to anyone, and when he had finished, he left the others eating, put on his hat, and went out of the house.

"Maybe I ought to go with him," Leonard said morosely, as soon as the door had shut behind Hardy. "But I don't feel much like it, the goin-over he gi' me this afternoon."

"I don't know what's got into him," said Josie. "I never knew him to act this way before. Most always he wants people to give him advice and tell him what to do, but all day he ain't listened to one word I've said." She got up and went to the window, peering after

Hardy's retreating figure as it dimmed in the dusk coming down over the island.

"He's just guessed wrong again," announced Mildred, looking up with her mouth full from her swiftly emptying plate. "He told me today it wan't goin to be a bad storm atall."

"Oh, you shut up!" Haral suddenly leaned across the table and gave her a stinging slap on one bulging cheek. The charged atmosphere of the last few hours had been a little too much for his nerves, already frayed by the week-end's sobering experience.

Mildred's mouth opened wide in a shattering roar, disclosing various objects of food lying unresolved on her tongue.

"Oh, God," said Haral, closing his eyes.

"Haral!" burst out Josie. "You go straight upstairs to bed. That was uncalled for."

"I don't think so," said Leonard. "I don't much like the way that kid talks about Pa. She's done it two-three times lately, right in front of him."

Mildred's yells, which had died down somewhat while she observed what punishment Haral was going to get, burst out again, redoubled.

"Somebody shut that blasted little sireen up," snorted Grammy. "I'm goin crazy!"

Leonard reached out and put a big hand over Mildred's mouth. "Tell her to stop, Ma, and I'll let her go."

Josie reached out and took Mildred by the arm. "Mildred," she said, "you ain't hurt. Now stop it, or upstairs you go to bed."

Leonard experimentally took his hand away, then clapped it back firmly. He picked Mildred up and carried her upstairs. "Now, look," he said. "You get un-

[153]

dressed and into bed. You show downstairs again tonight and I'll beat a pickle out of you."

She stopped obediently, her breath catching in pitiful gasps. Leonard stood uncertainly a moment, then reached in his pocket and pulled out a quarter. "Look, you can have this," he said, and fled from the room.

"I don't know's I should 'low it," he heard Grammy say as he came back into the kitchen. "She never said no more'n any of us know is so. Hardy Turner never had no mind in his life. He—"

Leonard let out a roar. "You lay off Pa!" he shouted furiously. "If he can't make up his mind, it's because you womenfolks have picked at him till he's half out of it! You say any more, Gram, and you'll go to bed, too!"

He dragged on his sou'wester and oilcoat and slammed out of the house after Hardy.

"My!" said Grammy, wagging her head. "If that didn't sound like his grandfather!"

Hardy stood for a while in the quickly thickening darkness, watching as long as he could see the malignant heads of the big combers rear up over the ledges and go crashing down through the weir. So far as he could tell in the dim light, nothing had carried away yet, but his senses, clear now as glass, told him that it was only a question of time. Growing in him was a feeling of relief, strong and warm as a long drink of whisky. The thing he had been afraid of for so long was happening at last. He stood quietly watching until it was too dark to see, then he walked home, bending his head against the rain that cracked like bullets against his stiff oiled hat and jacket.

Halfway up the hill he met Leonard coming down to

meet him. Leonard said nothing, but swung around and fell into step with him.

"Anything we can do?" Leonard asked, as they stepped up on the porch.

"Just go to bed," said Hardy quietly. "That's where I'm headed now."

AT four-thirty in the morning it was light enough to see what damage had been done. The storm had not eased off in the night, even on the ebb tide. At low water, big breakers were still curling across the channel from shore to shore, shattering on the shallows, and turning the usually still water around the weir into a weltering tumult. The wind came pouring in steadily from the southeast, carrying rain that cut the skin almost like sleet. All around the islands to the east the water was steel-gray slashed with white, and the ledges on Canvasback were buried under tons of green and white water. The spray from the crashing combers shot fifty feet into the air, falling among the flecked branches of the spruce trees a hundred yards back from the shore.

As Hardy walked along the eastern side of the beach, his boots went out of sight well over the knee in dirty yellowish foam that had blown off the combers and lay like a soiled meringue burying the beach rocks above high-water mark.

He felt at peace this morning for the first time in months. The weir, so far, was not gone, but a gap had been smashed out of one side of it, and so far as he could see from the shore, all the nets had carried away. Even as he looked now, his shoulders squared against the push of the wind and braced against his hands driven deep into his pockets, he saw a denuded pole piling shoot into the air and fall over, buried under the top of a big comber.

"Jeezus, Hardy," said a voice at his shoulder, "how come you didn't drop them nets down yistiddy, boy?"

It was old Jarvis Willow, staring blearily past him at the wreckage.

"Wouldn't a done no good if I had," said Hardy composedly. "Carried away a little slower, maybe, but it would a gone all the same."

"If you don't beat hell!" Jarv eyed him curiously. "Here I thought you'd be flat on your belly this mornin, the way you've worried about that weir. And you don't act as if you cared a hoot in hell, Hardy."

Hardy grinned. "Oh, I care," he said. "Ayeh, Jeezus, I care, Jarv."

He went along the beach past the New York House and down to the shore of the Pool where his weir dory was hauled up. The dory was half full of water, and Hardy tipped it out, puffing as he turned the heavy boat on its side.

"Hi, Hardy." Perley Higgins had spied him from the fishhouse door and had followed him down across the flats.

"Hi, Perley."

Perley's whole face drooped with unmitigated melancholy. Even his ragged mustache, wet, with the drops rolling off the ends of it, was depressed. He shifted from one rubber boot to the other, waiting for Hardy to say something, turning his eyes sidelong toward the weir. He wanted to let on to Hardy that he was sorry for him, but even a man of words like Perley couldn't seem to think of anything to say.

[156]

"Gi'me a hand haulin the dory down, will you, Perley?"

"Haul her down? Jeezus, you ain't goin off there now, are ya, Hardy?"

"The's a few nets driftin around I didn't know but I might haul aboard."

Perley looked out at the white harbor, then back to the dory. His face, twisted with unexpressed sympathy, twisted still further with relief that here was a way of showing Hardy he was sorry without talking about it. He grabbed hold of the bow of the dory and put his back into hauling her down into water deep enough to float her. Then he piled in, taking the rowing thwart and setting the tholepins into their sockets.

Hardy acknowledged his offer of assistance by saying nothing. If Perley wanted to come, he was glad to have him. He'd need someone to handle the boat while he hauled in the nets. Some of them were drifting around out there in the breakers around the weir. How many he didn't know.

Joe Comey and Leonard, walking down the road to the Pool, were electrified to see the dory heading out into the harbor.

"Hey!" said Joe. "Your old man must be goin after nets."

The boys broke into a run. The other dory was turned bottom up for safe-keeping a few hundred feet up the beach. They rolled her over and took her down the sand at a run.

Old Jarv Willow, with battle in his eye, stuck his head in at the end door of the New York House. His voice, coarsened and roughened by years of hollering two-masters from Nova Scotia to Boston, had not weakened any with his age. "Hi!" he roared. "Who's comin off with me and help Hardy pick up his nets?"

Josie, happening to look out of the window a few minutes later, was horrified to see the four or five dories heading out of the Pool. Hardy, she thought, with a cold lump of apprehension at the back of her throat. He hadn't been acting right. Had he done something foolish now? She cast a look at Grammy, trying to hide the fear in her face, but Grammy had left the west window already and was furling her heavy woolen out-door shawl over her head and around her shoulders.

Other women in the village had already seen the dories, Josie realized, hurrying down the hill. Cack Comey, in one of Eddy's old pea jackets and her head bare, was waddling down the road ahead as fast as her flesh-impeded thighs could travel. A bunch of kids was already climbing the rocks on Crab Point. Josie only half wondered, with a worry in the back of her mind, if Mildred was among them. Haral went past her on a dead run, headed for the shore, and she heard the rising volume of voices, excited and shrill, as women and girls came out of the houses and down the path behind her. Grammy, outdistanced, screamed at the top of her cracked voice for Josie to wait, but Josie was running.

She passed Cack, and Cack called out after her, "What is it, for God's sake, Josie? Who's drownded?"

"Nobody's I know of," Josie tossed back. "You know as much as I do."

She saw soon enough, when she reached the shore, what the men were doing. A dory with Jap Comey and Morris in it was tossing only a hundred feet or so off the rocks. Jap was handling the oars, his big shoulders bent with the effort of holding the boat into the wind, while

Morris, his feet astride the thwart as if it were a saddle, was fighting a big weir net in over the side. The net twisted and sucked away from him like something alive, and even as she looked, a gust of wind turned the dory half around in spite of all Jap could do. Morris let go of the net and it slithered away into the water out of reach, while he helped Jap shove on the oars and turn the dory back into the wind.

"My Lord in the landlocked heaven, look at Morris!" wheezed Cack, suddenly beside her. "What's he doin out there with a white shirt on?"

Josie located Hardy at last. He was in a dory with Perley Higgins, inside the gaping brush sections of what had been the wall of the weir. The dory was deep in the water, whether from salvaged nets or from water, Josie couldn't tell.

Leonard! she thought, her eyes hunting swiftly through the crews of the scattered dories. Yes, there he was. He and Joe Comey. She was glad he was with Joe. What Hardy had been thinking of, going off there in a dory with that fool of a Perley Higgins, she didn't know. But Hardy's dory was headed inshore now, both he and Perley pulling at the oars, and Josie saw as they came nearer that the dory was indeed loaded with nets.

"My Lord!" said Cack. "Hardy must think an awful lot of his property, lettin people risk their lives gittin drownded to save it."

May Higgins, Perley's wife, swung around on her, her eyes darkening. "It ain't property they're doin it for, as you well know, Cack Comey," she said.

Cack reddened. She started to say something, then thought better of it.

May means they're doing it for Hardy, Josie thought. Something inside her chest suddenly warmed and spread outward and she stood with tears running down her cheeks looking at the plunging dories, the harbor white and murderous, the wrecked weir against which the combers poured unceasingly.

THEY'D saved half the nets, Hardy thought, walking slowly toward the fishhouse along the beach. Half of them. He could probably pick up some more over on the Canvasback Island beaches if he was a mind to go over there after the storm.

Well, with what he had, that meant he could rebuild the weir without too much loss and with hope of a profit, before the herring season was over.

What to God I went and done that for? he asked himself, feeling the old tumult starting up again in his mind. To rebuild the weir, maybe make a little money to carry his family through the winter and pay for Haral's schooling, that was what he hadn't thought of when he'd started out to save the nets. If I'd only let them go! he thought. If I hadn't saved a one of them, maybe it would a been worth my while to quit here and go somewhere else to start over.

Yet he knew in his heart that even if he had thought of it in time, he couldn't have let the nets be lost.

THE damage to the weir was bad, Hardy saw a day later when the sea went down, but it was not so great as he had at first thought. Standing on Crab Point at the peak of the gale, watching the big combers carve through the brush and pole structure, he had expected to see very little worth rebuilding, once the storm was over. True, all the nets had been ripped off the seine poles and many had been carried away and lost, but when he came to count, he was surprised at the number that had been salvaged.

A gap fifteen feet long was gone from the wall of the inner pound, the brush and piles torn clean away, and a good many of the other piles were seriously weakened. But Hardy had reluctantly to admit that three weeks' work with the right kind of help would put the weir in fishing condition again.

He could not whip his mind to a decision. Should he rebuild the weir or put down a string of lobster traps and use Leonard's boat to tend them for the rest of the season? He knew he could have the boat for the asking, every other day. To rebuild would mean hiring labor, and breaking in on the slim reserve of cash he had laid by for winter. It would mean buying some new nets, though he had a few old ones hanging up in the loft of his fishhouse. He'd have to patch them up and put on a new coat of tar. He'd have to get the heavy pile driver down from above high-water mark in the cove where it had been hauled up until it should be needed in the spring. And above all, to have the weir fishing again would mean starting all over on the old round of worry and exasperation every time the weather looked smurry.

But fitting up a string of traps would mean a cash investment too, and the return from them, although sure, would be too small to pay for them. He didn't know which he hated worse, tending weir or going lobstering. It seemed to him, he told himself, that he hated both so bad it didn't make any difference.

The possibilities went round and round in his mind, already frayed with anxiety. He shied away from the finality of a decision. He spent hours of acute miserableness trying to force his mind one way or another, while the soft September days rolled on and Josie fumed and sputtered at his delay.

She could see and understand his misery, but she could neither see nor understand a cause for it. To her intensely practical mind, most issues were simple . . . either she did a thing or she didn't. Whatever she made up her mind to do, she abided by, unless reasons came up which convinced her she shouldn't. Why Hardy couldn't see things as simply as that, she didn't know.

There were three months left of valuable fishing—herring and mackerel were just starting in to run—before winter set in, and no reason in the world, if bad weather didn't come too early, why the weir shouldn't fish up to the end of November.

"Take a chance on its bein a mild fall," she implored Hardy. "S'pos'n it was and the herrin run good, you might make your everlastin whack."

"Yes, I s'pose I might," Hardy agreed.

"That fall Charley Warren made his three thousand, he made most of it in October," she pointed out.

"I remember."

"Hardy, you've got to do *somethin*. You can't just set and mourn because you can't make up your mind. Do one thing or the other, or we won't be able to get through the winter without goin into debt."

"Yes. Guess I'll have to," he said uncertainly. The sickness of spirit in his eyes as he looked at her might have softened her heart, but she had seen it so much lately, and she was convinced that he was making a mountain out of the molehill of his indecision. He took his cap and went out, and from the window she watched him go slowly down the path to the shore.

My heavens above, she thought, whatever's goin to happen to him! Something in the sag of Hardy's shoulders, the dejected droop of his head, snapped her patience even while she worried about him. He's just got to stiffen himself up, she told herself grimly. I ain't goin to aid and abet him no more in his foolishness till he makes up his mind. He'll feel better anyway when he knows definite what he's goin to do.

But in spite of her anger, she knew her heart was heavy for him. She turned away from the window and went back to her task of getting Haral's socks mended and in a neat pile to put with the rest of his things to be packed for school on Monday.

They were not going to have to mortgage the house. For on the day after the wrecking of the weir, Grammy had dug down in her knitting bag and had produced seven ancient ten-dollar bills, large and yellow, and belonging to a time many years before the government had made paper money smaller.

"My buryin money!" Gram grumbled bitterly. "You spend this right, Hardy, and you see that boy gets some good out a that school or I'll wring his cussed neck!"

❧

ON the Monday after Labor Day, Haral and Sayl, clad in identical dark red sweaters, new corduroy pants, and virginal white sneakers, started school.

Sayl had not gone without a final protest which had very nearly got him a thrashing from Joe. In fact, Joe would have thrashed him if Sarah hadn't interfered. Left alone, Sarah would not have insisted on Sayl's going, but she ran into an unexpected streak of stubbornness in Joe.

"He's goin," Joe said. "I never went and I've lived to be sorry. He's goin to work hard at it—or I'll take him over."

"We can't afford it," said Sarah mildly. "You've got your new boat, Joe."

"I'll handle that. You never mind it."

"All right," Sarah said. "Sayl won't make a go of it."

"He better," said Joe grimly.

The unfamiliar surroundings and routine in the classrooms made Haral embarrassed at first, and Sayl sullen. But Haral found out quite quickly that it wasn't so bad. If you played along and used your head and gave the teachers back what they wanted, you got by without much fuss. He couldn't see any sense in what they wanted him to learn, but apparently it was what you did if you expected to "make something of yourself." In one way or another he found enough to keep from being bored, and at least he was off the island. He tried to explain this to Sayl, to make him see that you could manage without so much misery, but Sayl said, "Four years of it, my God!"

The first week-end, Sayl took samples of his assignments to Joe.

"Joe, look a here, for God sake! Look a this crap I got to learn. What d' I care bout what some ole Greek done? Look a how long the guy's been dead!"

But Joe was unsympathetic. "How'd you know what they're leadin you up to?" he asked. "Them teachers, they know more'n you do about what you ought a learn."

[164]

"They're leadin me up to a guts-ache," said Sayl. "That's all I get out of it."

"You learn," said Joe, "or I'll bust an oar on you, Sayl."

LEONARD had planned to go back and see Alice in a day or so. But the weather after the storm came off fine and moderate, the fishing was excellent, and Morris was determined to make the most of it before the fall gales set in for good. Joe and Leonard agreed with him, since they wanted to earn all the money they could this fall to put into their new boat. For ten days their dragging trips almost overlapped—they would get in at five o'clock on one day, stop long enough at the Harbor fish wharf to unload their haddock, go home for a few hours' sleep, and start out on another three-day trip at two the next morning.

Generally Leonard enjoyed the long hours of hard work which always accompanied a good spell of fishing. He liked camping out on the boat—waking up in the calm early mornings twenty miles out from land, or standing his watch at night while the others slept.

But for a whole week he caught himself wishing the weather would change and give him a chance to go to the Harbor for at least an evening without balling up Joe and Morris's schedule.

At last he made up his mind to go anyway. He could plan to get back a little earlier than he ordinarily would and, after all, what was a few hours' sleep? The business of not knowing just where he stood with Alice troubled him more the longer he let it go.

He arrived at Lacy's at about seven-thirty to find

Alice gone and old Brad in possession of the hammock.

"I dunno where she is," Brad said sourly. "She went off with that Hammond sprig in his car—'f you could call it a car. He ought a be driv off the road with that thing, fer the pertection a life 'n limb."

"They didn't say where they was goin?" Leonard persisted.

"Said so, didn't I? What you want with her, any-way?" Brad hawked and spat copiously over the piazza rail. "She ain't no good to ya. She don't like men."

"Dunno's I blame her," said Leonard shortly.

The front of Brad's shirt was unbuttoned and his fat belly, covered by a grimy undergarment, rolled unpleasantly over the top of his belt.

Wonder where in hell Alice came from, Leonard thought, turning away. Her mother must've been nice.

He went back slowly down the shore road, wondering what he'd better do. He supposed the smart thing would be to go home and go to bed, seeing he was tired and he had to be up at one-thirty. But Orin had to bring Alice back sometime, and maybe when they came it wouldn't be too late for him to see her for a little while.

He stopped in at the poolroom and shot pool for an hour with some of the hangers-on whom he knew, but his aim was bad and he didn't win any games.

"Guess it ain't my night," he said, dropping his cue into the rack. "Well, I'll see ya."

It was ten o'clock when he walked up the road again toward Lacy's. As he passed the Hammond house he could see at the back the outline of the open garage doors and the empty interior in the darkness. Orin's car wasn't back yet.

Lacy's shabby frame house was dark and silent. Brad, of course, was in bed. According to Alice, his chief brag was that he always went to bed before it got dark under the table.

Leonard sat down on the steps to the piazza and leaned wearily against one of the weathered posts. He wondered what was the matter with him, why he didn't plain give up and go home. He felt like a fool, hanging around a girl's house when she was out with another fellow. Serve him right if Orin took a poke at him when he got back and found him there. Only, of course, being Orin, he wouldn't. He'd probably just grin.

Besides, Leonard thought, I ain't really chiselin in. Alice ain't let on she likes either of us better'n the other.

Maybe she had, though. After all, he hadn't seen her for ten days, and they hadn't exactly parted friends. The idea made him feel uncomfortable, and stiffened his purpose to wait until Alice got home. He got to his feet, went determinedly up the steps, and stretched out in the hammock.

The old couch mattress was lumpy, but it felt surprisingly good to his aching muscles. He took a deep breath of the sweet night air and stuck his hands behind his head. It was kind of nice to lie here in Alice's hammock and to know that not so long ago she had been sitting in this very place. He'd have to keep track of the time, though. He couldn't stay, anyway, much after twelve-thirty.

A violent rocking motion seemed to be going on underneath him, accompanied by hollow thumping sounds. For a moment he thought the boat had certainly stuck on a ledge in a heavy sea, then he opened his eyes bewilderedly and sat up. It was broad daylight. The sunlight was streaming brilliantly across Lacy's piazza, and old Brad stood over him with a red face of fury. He

[167]

had been bouncing the hammock and thumping on its canvas with a stick.

"By God, I've told that hussy to keep her drunks out a my house! I wun't hev nobody sleepin off a toot on my piazza. Go on, now, you git!"

"Hey," said Leonard, blinking, "cut it out, Brad. I ain't drunk." His face flushed slowly brick-red as he realized what he had done. "I only sat down here for a minute and went to sleep by accident. I'll clear out before . . . anybody's up."

"Well, I'm up, ain't I?" Brad eyed Leonard with suspicion. "You was, too, drunk!"

"Ssh!" said Leonard. He got up hastily and began wriggling his rumpled coat back into place. "I'll beat it. But it was like I told you, Brad. I stopped by last night to see if Alice and Orin was here yet and sat down a minute. I didn't plan on goin to sleep."

"You do look kind of unpremeditated," said Alice from the doorway. "How about it, Pop? You think he was really drunk?"

"Huh, course he was drunk!" said Brad. "Smell it on him yet!"

Leonard looked at her. She had on a bright blue cotton dress with darker blue tabs at the shoulders. Her light gold curls were brushed up into a fluff, and her skin looked rosy, as if she had just scrubbed it with cold water. The sheepish smile on his face slowly changed into a grin of appreciation. "Well," he said, "looks as if I'd got caught dead to rights. You better call up the constable, Brad, and I'll sleep it off in the cooler."

"Want some breakfast?" asked Alice, grinning back at him. "You look as if you could use some."

"Now, Alice, you ain't goin to feed him my food. I ain't runnin no flophouse for bums."

[168]

"Oh, take it easy, Pa," said Alice. "You know I bought the eggs and the oatmeal. Swallow it, now," she went on, as he took a deep breath to yell at her, "or I'll give Leonard your egg."

"That's the way she is all the time," said Brad. "I dunno who'd want to live with her." He stalked, muttering, in through the kitchen door.

"You'd better come in and wash," said Alice practically. "And if you'll take off that suit coat, I'll give it a quick press while you have your breakfast."

She led the way into the kitchen and Leonard followed, a little embarrassed, but nevertheless pleased. Apparently she was going to let bygones be bygones, and that was a load off his mind.

The inside of the Lacy house was starkly shabby, like the outside, but it was spotless and neat, especially the kitchen. The ancient cook-stove shone with polish, although the top of it was cracked and the nickel on the trimmings scabbed off in ugly patches. On the stained panel wall around it, Alice had hung scoured pots and pans, and she had put a big burnished copper kettle behind the woodbox. The worn boards of the bare floor were scrubbed until they were white and their splinters furry.

"Looks nice in here," said Leonard. "I didn't know you went in for housekeepin, Alice."

"She don't." Brad plumped down at the kitchen table and picked up his knife and fork. "All she does is stick a lot of trash around for me to fall over while I starve to death."

The breakfast didn't look much like starvation rations, Leonard thought, watching the old man stow away oatmeal and eggs and hot muffins and coffee. It wasn't a company breakfast, either, because Alice had

had it ready. Brad must be something to live with. He stayed by himself winters while Alice was away. Probably he resented being cleaned up and made to live like a human being each time she came back. Leonard could imagine the tough job she had every spring, to get the old house in such good shape as this after seven months of Brad's housekeeping.

He slipped his arms into his freshened-up suit coat, which was still warm from the heat of Alice's flatiron. "Well," he said, "I guess I better get back and face the music. Joe and Morris likely went without me when I didn't show up at one-thirty. But if they didn't, Morris'll be fit to tie. Thanks for fixing the coat, Alice, and it was a swell breakfast."

"Oh, that's all right. We don't have much company," she added, looking at him with a gleam of amusement, "that is, to stay all night."

" 'Tain't *your* fault," muttered Brad malevolently.

Alice shrugged. "Have it your own way, Pop. You'll feel better when your breakfast settles."

She walked with Leonard to the gate. "I guess we'll have some trouble living this down," she said, glancing up at the neighbors' houses across the road. "Every sash-curtain over there is shaking."

"My gosh!" said Leonard concernedly. "How about that?"

"Oh, I'm used to it. Travel's supposed to do a girl no good. People talk about me, anyway. Don't worry."

"I'm sure a prize boob," he said contritely. "I wouldn't a waited, but it was the only chance I had to see you. We was out draggin all last week or I'd been over before."

"I know," she said. "Fishing weather. It's all right, Len."

"Good," he answered. "I'll come again when I can. It might not be for a while, though, if the weather lasts."

"I'll be here," said Alice. "That is, until November."

"Oh! That's not long, now, is it?"

"No. A month and a half."

The realization of her going struck him suddenly with a new and unresolved emotion. He thought, aghast, of not seeing her for seven months. "What makes you go this year?" he asked.

"Don't be silly. I've got to."

"No, you haven't."

"Look," she said, "in five years down there I've saved five hundred dollars. It would take Pop and me through till spring, and then what? He won't work when I'm home."

"You could get married. To me."

"Oh," she said softly, "Leonard! No."

"You like me, don't you?"

"Yes, I do."

"Well, then, why not?"

Alice did not speak for a moment, then she turned and faced him. "I can't, Leonard," she said steadily. "It's nice of you."

"Somebody else?" he asked. His eyes held hers, forlornly, and as she hesitated, he added, "Orin?"

"I don't know, Len." What could she say, she thought, not to hurt him? She couldn't explain the way she had felt, seeing him sit down at her breakfast table, because the way she had felt wouldn't make sense to any man— one side of her glowing with satisfaction at having him there enjoying her good food, the other side shriveling with fury at the way, just like her father, he had pulled up to the table and took for granted that her province was to feed and wait on him. How could you explain that something you liked tremendously at the same time belittled and affronted you?

"It *is* Orin, ain't it?" said Leonard. "Well, okay, Alice. Sorry I mentioned it. He's lucky. So long."

She put out her hand toward him but he had already turned and was going down the road to the shore.

Well, she thought, her eyes on his receding back, I guess I got what I asked for.

He would not come back, she realized, now that he thought it was Orin she wanted.

I don't want Orin, she said fiercely to herself. I want Leonard—only I want him different. I want him to like what I've made of myself and to think I'm as much of a person as he is.

But as she turned back to the house it seemed to her that never in her life had she felt so lonely or had to make so empty a choice.

Leonard strode rapidly along the shore path and climbed down the wharf into his boat. He didn't feel like seeing anyone. He was blaming himself bitterly for not having had the sense to know, earlier in the summer, how he was going to feel. If he had only put forth a little more effort, been a little more serious, in time, he was pretty sure, he wouldn't have lost out.

I argued too much with her, too, he told himself. We didn't really need to have all those fights. But I never could seem to tell how I feel about things without makin her mad.

He had started up the engine and was morosely casting off the stern line when he heard rubber boots crunching on the barnacles of the wharf ladder and looked up to see his father coming aboard the boat.

Hardy was looking relieved to see him, and Leonard managed a grin. "Hi," he said. "You think I'd got lost?"

"Pretty nigh," said Hardy. "Have engine trouble? Your ma was kind a worried last night when you didn't come home, so I thought I'd cruise over with the mail boat and see if you'd got marooned somewhere."

"No," said Leonard. "I was just makin a fool of myself, I guess." He spun the wheel as the boat backed away from the wharf, and stared miserably out over the water as he headed her bow for home.

Hardy watched him for a while in silence, breaking up crumbs of tobacco from his pouch and packing them methodically into his pipe.

"Brad Lacy's girl, ain't it?"

"Ayeh. She turned me down," said Leonard briefly.

"Your own fault?"

"Ayeh. In a way."

"That's too bad, son," said Hardy. "She's a nice girl. She'll think it over, maybe."

"No," Leonard said slowly, "I don't guess she will. I better forget about it."

ON the fifteenth of September, Hardy started rebuilding the weir. He went at the job practically and with all the trained skill of which he was master.

He hired Perley Higgins and Will Comey to help him, at two dollars and a half a day apiece. Will at first was lukewarm about working for Hardy, on account of the feud between the two families, but when Hardy told him calmly that he could work out some of his mother's store bill that way, Will's attitude changed. Hardy suspected that Cack had got after him.

Leonard promised to give a hand when he could take

a day off from fishing, but Hardy wisely didn't count on him. Leonard was really busy now, or he made himself so, plunging into work as if a devil were riding him. He was having a bad time of it, Hardy knew, and was trying to let work straighten things out for him. Maybe, in time, it would. Hardy was glad that the lumber for the new boat had arrived and that soon she would begin to take shape on Harry Fenner's ways.

Hardy, with Perley and Will, hauled the heavy pile driver out of the cove on the first high-run tide and anchored it in the Pool to be ready for use. Then they spent a week cutting piles and seine poles and alders for brush foundation over on Canvasback Island, and towed them across the bay, using Leonard's boat for a tug. For two days the acrid clean smell of boiling tar blew across the village from the tar pot on the shore where Hardy was tarring nets, and for another week the clear September air rang with the bell-like *chung-plok* of the pile-driver strokes. Standing in the dory, weaving the alder brush in and out between the new piles and tamping it down to bottom with an iron-shod pole, Hardy built his pound wall sturdy and strong. He nailed up and braced seine poles and stretched between them freshly tarred nets, taut and shipshape, as he had done so many times before in the spring of the year.

When the weir was finished again it was a work of hands of which he might well have been proud. But all the time the heart within him was black with misery.

⌒⌒

FROM the beginning the new boat had meant something to Joe that Morris's boat never had. Whenever he could take time from fishing, he headed for the Harbor and Harry Fenner's boat shop, rowing the three miles and a half in his skiff, if none of the island boats happened to be going across the bay at the time. All through the critical period when the plans for the scale model were being talked over, Joe sat around the shop, not saying much and seeming to want to avoid making decisions. He referred everything to Leonard, and always seemed pleased with Leonard's choice.

"Look here, Joe," Leonard said, a little exasperated with him one day when Joe passed on to him the question of using mahogany or oak trim. "She's as much yours as she is mine. More so, really. Why don't you say what you want?"

"Oh, I dunno," said Joe. "She'll turn out okay if you do the sayin."

"Don't you give a damn?"

Joe flushed. "God, yes, sure I do. I think honest that mahogany's too high and oak'd be better for a fish boat, but us buildin her was your idea, so I thought—"

"Okay, let's have oak."

Joe was pleased. "I didn't know but you wanted her with everything like Morris's."

"Gosh, no. We'll have enough of Morris in this as it is."

They were planning to use the model and molds which Morris had made for his boat, and which he still had stowed away in the shed loft at home. But when Leonard went to ask Morris about them, rather taking his consent for granted, Morris said casually, "Sure—if you're willin to pay what I want for them."

"Pay?" said Leonard, dumfounded. "We hadn't planned to *pay* nothin."

"That so?"

"It ain't likely we did. They ain't worth nothin to you layin in that shed, rottin. I s'posed of course you'd let us use em."

"Well," said Morris, "no."

Leonard looked him up and down. "Okay," he said disgustedly. Might have known, he thought. He moved away, not missing the look, half amused, half derisive, that Morris gave him.

It hadn't occurred to Leonard and Joe that Morris would refuse the molds. They wanted a dragger as much like his as possible, for the simple reason that she was the best design for the purpose that they had ever seen. And it was something of a tradition along the coast that when one fisherman discovered something new in the way of boats or marine engines or equipment, he was glad to pass it along to the others.

In Willard Hemple's store at the Harbor, on the sunny side of the New York House on Comey's Island, where the plank laid across the pickle kegs was worn smooth by the sturdy butts of men who had time to kill talking, the design of Morris's dragger had been thoroughly discussed. She had been turned inside out verbally from engine to stern post.

In the opinion of some oldtimers, she was built too high for'ard—she'd roll too much in a heavy sea. She did roll smashingly at first, but they soon saw that Morris had allowed for that. When she had been overboard long enough for the water to soak into her timbers and weigh her down a little, she was as steady as a church.

Now she was considered far ahead of any of Harry Fenner's designs, and it had been a foregone conclusion that any new dragger built would be built like her. It came as something of a shock to know that Morris didn't intend to pass around his model and molds without being paid for them.

Not being able to use them meant that Leonard and Joe would either have to draft their own blueprint or let Harry Fenner build them a boat from one of his own designs. Harry's designs were excellent, and the boats he turned out were fine, sturdy boats.

"I could make a stab at buildin one like Morris's," Harry said, "but as for duplicatin her, I can't do it for the simple reason that I ain't got the specifications."

"Do you need all of em?" asked Joe.

"I know what her length and her beam is, but Morris done a lot a work on her himself, you know. He'd be down here fuddlin round with a plane, takin a scrape here and a scrape there some nights till twelve-one o'clock. That sheer on Morris's boat is what makes her. I ain't got that, and I couldn't build it, not without the model. I'd ruther build one to my own design than go it blind that way."

"We'll think it over," Leonard said, "and let you know, Harry." He was bitterly disappointed.

Joe said next to nothing on the way home. He didn't want to talk about what design they would use if they couldn't have Morris's, and finally Leonard gave up in disgust and let him alone. They arrived in the Pool and rowed ashore in glum silence.

Before Leonard went to sleep that night, he had made up his mind that he would ask Morris what price he would take for the model and molds.

THE next morning when he rowed out to the dragger, he found Morris aboard alone.

"Where's Joe?" he asked, when he had anchored his punt and Morris had started the engine, without Joe putting in an appearance.

"The big booby's sick," Morris said briefly. "Don't you want to go without him?"

"Ain't crazy about it," said Leonard. "What's wrong with him?" He had never known Joe to be sick.

"Disappointment, I guess. Or he et too much. He always eats like a hog."

"That so? He very sick?"

"Couldn't say," answered Morris. "I left him pukin. After he gits through he'll either be a lot better or a lot worse. You never know."

Morris himself seemed to be feeling on top of the world this morning. He spun the steering wheel with a jaunty flourish and sent the big boat roaring at full speed through the narrow channel that led out of the Pool . . . too fast for comfort, with the tide at half-ebb. The big underwater ledges off Crab Point flashed past so close that Leonard could see through the shallow water the sea urchins and wrinkles clinging to their tan, mottled sides. He realized, when the boat was out of the shallows and the channel widened to plenty of room on either side, that he had been sitting with his muscles tense. He relaxed them quickly, but Morris grinned and said, "Scared?"

Leonard stood up, feeling for a cigarette. "No. I was just hopin you'd plunk her."

From where Morris stood on the short platform built up extra high so that he could see out through the windscreen, his head was on a level with Leonard's shoulders. "Was you, now?" he said. "Be too bad to plunk this boat when she's the only one of her kind on the coast."

"And likely to be," said Leonard shortly. "I never said I wouldn't be sorry for the boat."

"Ain't feelin friendly, very, this mornin, are you?"

"No." Leonard took a long drag on his cigarette and let the smoke out slowly. "I ain't. We'll prob'ly drag just as many fish, though, if I don't kiss you every three minutes."

"Wouldn't be surprised. You're feelin pretty sore, ain't you?"

"Well, I doubt if I die of it. Look, Morris, how'd it be if you was to wait and have your pretty fun after we get back from the trip? We're likely to be two days alone on this boat."

"You wouldn't even think a tryin to see my side of it, would ya?" said Morris.

"Your side of it, if that's what you call the way you do things, don't make sense to me."

"It wouldn't. You was born on Comey's Island and you ain't never been nowheres else. Away from here, you'd starve to death."

"Think so?"

"I know so."

"All right, I'd starve to death. So what?"

"So you ain't never learnt to do nothin alone. Somethin tough comes up, some hard job, you fellers here on the Island, what do you do?"

"Okay. What do we do?"

"Squawk for help. Run to the neighbors." Morris's voice was sharp with disgust. "Then everybody turns to and does the job."

"The hell they do!" said Leonard, looking at him curiously. "You could rot here before your neighbors'd help you out."

"How about your pa's nets the other day?"

"That was different. He couldn't do that alone."

"No? I could have. But then, I wouldn't a lost em in the first place."

"Oh, go to hell! I've had enough of your chawmouth!"

"Don't sound good to you, does it? Well, if you ever go away from here, you'll see what I mean. You and Joe and kids like you is soft. Your old man's rotten soft, and so was mine. I'd see you in hell before I'd give you my model for nothin. I worked hard on that boat. Jeezus, I *invented* her. She's property. Other people besides you is goin to want them molds someday. Know what they'll pay me for em? Five hundred dollars."

"You're crazy," said Leonard slowly.

"Crazy like a rattrap," said Morris. "A guy's got a damn good right to cash in on his own work. Chrise, the way you people round here feel, if a man's got a good thing, he ought to share it with everybody. Well, it's you that's out a line with the rest a the world. It ain't me."

AS soon as Sarah Comey heard Morris's boat go out of the Pool, she went into Joe's room and shook him lightly by the shoulder. Joe raised an anguished face into which a little normal color was beginning to creep. "My God, Ma, what was that stuff, rat poison?"

"Ipecac." Sarah looked at him with a keen and professional eye. "You ought a be feelin better by now."

"I am, a little. But I thought for a while there somethin was goin to carry away." Joe swung his long legs out of bed and reached shivering for his pants. He looked woebegone and boyish, and Sarah smiled to herself at his tousled hair, his big bare feet, toeing-in and curling up sensitively as they touched the cold floor.

"What'n thunder you gi'me so much of it for? The idea was to make me puke, not to gowel my insides out," he said plaintively.

"You'll be all right in a little while," Sarah said crisply. "It takes more than half-measures to fool Morris, and it would a took more'n half a dose of ipecac. If you hadn't been turnin wrong-side-out when he left, he'd a straightened you out and made you go along with him."

"Ayeh, I guess likely," said Joe with a sigh. "I dunno's I think much a this business, Ma."

"You will, after you've had some coffee. Last night you was all for it."

He got up limply and followed her to the kitchen. "Ayeh, but it looked like it would work, last night."

"It'll work. You keep quiet and leave things to me." She handed him a cup of steaming black coffee. "Look out for that. It's hot."

Joe burned his mouth on it and set the cup on the kitchen table. He sat glumly beside it, waiting for it to cool, his hands hanging limply from his knees.

Sarah looked at him sharply. Then she came over, took the coffee and turned some of it into the saucer, cooling it expertly with her breath. "There," she said. "Drink it now."

She sat down in the kitchen rocking chair opposite him, her big body looking taut and efficient in contrast to his lax one. "Joe, you're scared of Morris."

"I know damn well I am. I don't make no bones of it."

"Well, I ain't," said Sarah. "I don't know what kind a man he is inside, or why he acts the way he does. But

I've been one jump ahead of him since the day he was born."

"I ain't never got ahead of him."

"No. You prob'ly ain't never goin to. You're too much like your pa. Your pa had to use a stick. I don't know what he'd use now. You leave this business and all the worryin to me."

"I dunno, Ma. I don't feel right about doin it."

"Well, it *is* right, when a man's bein unreasonable, Joe. You feel well enough to come help me now?"

"Ayeh, I guess so. Gi'me some more coffee."

She sat watching him while he finished his second cupful. He was feeling better now, and his courage was coming back with his strength.

Of the three sons left to her, Joe was the one she knew best and the one she counted on. Morris needed nothing from anyone on earth, and, in a quite different way, neither did Sayl. Sayl was a big, healthy eating animal and he was all right, because he was what most people thought Joe . . . dumb. Sayl, all his life, would take things as they came.

Sarah sighed. She often wondered why the Lord seemed to throw people together so piecemeal. It wouldn't have hurt Him, she figured, to have made Morris a little more human, or Joe a little tougher, or maybe to have divided the brains between Morris and Sayl. Joe's brains were all right. They worked a little slowly, but, Sarah told herself, they worked true, if you gave him time.

"Okay, Ma, let's go." Joe set down his cup and got up from the table.

They climbed the stairs to the loft over the woodshed. In the half-light which the overcast morning sent through the streaked cobwebby window, the variously shaped pieces of lumber which were the molds of Morris's boat, looked to Joe like a cumbersome jigsaw puzzle thrown down at random.

"My God, Ma," he said in a panic, "I don't see head nor tail to it. We never can do this before Morris gets back."

Sarah's voice came muffled from a corner where she was hunting and shuffling around in some stored-away packing boxes. "I know how to do it." She emerged, staggering under a double armload of folded sheets of brown paper, which she dumped on the floor, sending up a cloud of dust. "Folks don't remember very well," she said, "and they was so used to seein your pa's boat that they never thought to notice what a good one she was. Your pa and I designed and built that boat and done all the work ourselves. As for boat buildin, Morris come by it honest. These molds of his was copied off of paper, and it ain't goin to be too big a job to copy em back again."

With Joe holding the paper for her, she began tracing the outlines of the molds with a carpenter's pencil.

They worked all that day, stopping only for a meal at two o'clock. They worked all the first night and all the second day, and it was three o'clock on the morning of the third day before the last piece of tough brown paper was numbered and folded away in a crocus bag.

"There," said Sarah. Her face was streaked with sweat and dust and her eyes bright with exhaustion. "There's your boat, Joe. If Harry Fenner can't build you one from them specifications, you bring em back to me. Because I can."

Joe did an unheard of thing for him. He put his arms around her big shoulders and hugged her, not with affection, but, Sarah sensed, with a kind of desperation.

[183]

"Morris won't do nothin," she said. "If he does, I'll tend to him. But don't you tell nobody, Joe. Don't you even tell Leonard. You fix it up with Fenner to say he's figured the molds out himself."

"Okay," said Joe. He took the sack containing the papers and the clay copy of the model and went slowly down the loft stairs.

The tired lines of Sarah's face set in grimness. I've done wrong, she said to herself. Morris'll make bad trouble over this. When Joe brings that boat home I ain't goin to be able to sleep nights.

She went over to the cobwebby window and watched Joe go down the path. The line of his big shoulders, the loose-jointed swing of his hips as he walked—how many times with pride and affection she had watched a back exactly like that receding along the road to the shore.

"Clyde!" she said suddenly, under her breath. The word came hard, with a hoarse exhalation. For a moment she stood, her hands clenched on the old dry wood of the window sill, her lips stretched back over her teeth in a grimace of agony. Then the spasm passed and she turned slowly, stumbling a little as she went down the stairs.

Sometimes, when she needed him most, it came over her like this, that Clyde was gone for good, and then she couldn't stand it.

IF Joe had been along, Leonard wouldn't have minded the trip, in spite of Morris's rankling remarks and his ready-to-pounce presence. Joe was going out of his way, these days, to take Leonard's mind off his trouble. Leonard hadn't told him about Alice, but what Joe didn't know he guessed at. And he did know that Leonard wasn't going to Lacy's any more. They always kidded and laughed a lot, and they both enjoyed tremendously the job of dragging for fish.

It took a good deal of trained skill to get the big drag over the side without mishap—more than a hundred feet of twine, ready to tangle itself into a hopeless mess of toggles and sinkers and cable if it weren't handled with the proper amount of foresight.

The drag was, actually, a big bag of twine, twenty feet wide at the mouth and narrowing down to a few feet at its other end. In operation, it was towed behind the boat at the end of a long steel cable, an ingenious rig of heavy lead sinkers, glass toggles, and two flat wooden "doors" holding its mouth open in the water. Its purpose was to drag fish, but since the weighted edge of it swept along the sea bottom, it scooped up anything movable. When the big cable wound up around the open drum and the drag broke water, anything might be in it, and both Joe and Leonard always found that moment indescribably interesting.

At sundown on the second day, however, Leonard suggested to Morris that they go home. Both days had been cold and cloudy, with a southwest wind running up a strong chop, and the work of handling the drag was wet and difficult. They had been able to make only one run the first afternoon, which brought up a few haddock, but mostly a foul mess of sea-bottom trash— sea cucumbers and sea lemons, sculpins and lamprey eels. The second day they ran on to bad bottom again and netted half a ton of rocks. It took them nearly all the second afternoon to clear the drag and mend the holes that the rocks had ripped in it.

"Well," said Leonard in exasperation, when the job was finished, "one thing about Joe, he certainly ain't a Jonah. What say we call it a trip and go home?"

"Why?" Morris asked. "We got gas enough for another day."

"The grub's runnin low. I'd rather go in." Leonard let some of the nervous irritation he had been feeling creep into his voice.

"We won't starve with all these fish aboard," said Morris. He smiled his faint derisive smile. "Or is raw fish a little strong for your stomach?"

Leonard set his teeth and said nothing. It had been a shock to him to find out that he cared a damn what Morris thought about him, and he knew he wouldn't have if Morris hadn't put into words the same criticism that Alice had implied. Maybe the reason he didn't go somewhere away and land himself a good-paying job was because he was afraid to. But something staunch and self-respecting kept protesting to him that if a man had something he did well, then that was the thing he ought to do. The question had niggled at Leonard until his temper was at half cock and his emotions sensitive and frayed.

They stayed out on the fishing grounds. But at daylight the next morning the wind blew so hard that even Morris had to admit that it was hopeless to think of running out the drag, and he headed the boat inshore.

When they shot up alongside the fish wharf at the Harbor to sell the few fish they had, Leonard was delighted to see his own boat lying at the foot of Fenner's landing slip. "Joe's off here," he said to Morris, indicating it with a jerk of his head. "Must be feeling all right again."

"He got well quick," commented Morris.

Leonard said nothing. He picked up a fishfork and began to throw haddock up on the wharf. When they were unloaded, he waited for Morris to collect the small amount of money due them at the office, and turned away down the wharf. "Don't wait for me," he said over his shoulder, "I'll go back in my boat."

"All right with me," said Morris expressionlessly.

Leonard found Joe and Harry Fenner squatting with their heads together over some rough drawings tacked to the boathouse floor.

Joe jumped and whirled around, and then looked both sheepish and relieved when he saw who it was. "You couldn't a had many fish to unload," he said. "I warn't expectin you for an hour yet."

"Lousy haul," said Leonard. "How you feelin, Joe?" He was concerned at the way Joe looked—his face pale, his eyes circled with deep purple stains made brownish by his heavy tan.

"Okay, now," said Joe. "I was up'n around all day yesterday."

Harry Fenner looked at him quizzically. "Flyin ax-handles," he said, "they don't mount to much, but they sure do break up a man's sleep." Joe met his round blue eyes of an innocent baby, and then gulped and looked away.

What goes on here? thought Leonard, glancing from one to the other. He wondered if Joe were really all right now, or if he had something on his mind.

Harry Fenner indicated the drawings with his stubby pencil. "I come across these old sketches of Morris's boat," he said. "The less said, the better; but I estimate I can build you a boat like his if you still want one."

"I'll be goddammed!" Leonard stooped to look at the drawings, but Fenner waved him away.

"You come in on me when I was right in the middle a figgerin," he said testily. "If you want me to go ahead with a model and molds, so say, and I will. Yes or no, and then clear out a here."

"Yes!" said Leonard jubilantly. "Come on, Joe. When'll you have em done, Harry? When can we see em?"

"End a the week."

"You're sure you—"

"Chrise, yes! I built that boat, didn't I?"

"Okay, we'll see you." Leonard beat a hasty retreat out of the shop, following Joe down to the landing.

Joe sat down on the engine box, letting Leonard cast off and back the boat away from the wharf.

"How in hell'd he do that, Joe? Where'd he find them drawins?"

Joe jerked his head up and looked at Leonard with sleep-clouded eyes. "Come across em stowed away in his shop. Forgot he had em."

"Well, you don't seem very pleased about it," grumbled Leonard.

"I ain't pleased about nothin, right now," snapped Joe. "I'm sleepy. I been kept awake a lot."

It didn't occur to Leonard to doubt Joe. If he hadn't been so overcome with jubilation, he might have suspected something from Joe's hangdog look. As it was, Leonard thought, Gee, he's all in. Must've been quite sick.

"You think he's got her, sure, Joe?"

"Got what?" mumbled Joe.

"Morris's boat, you dope!"

"Oh. Ayeh. Hell, yes," Joe said bleakly. "He's got her, all right."

PART FOUR

THE southwest wind that had driven Leonard and Morris in from the Mary Shoal, kept on blowing. October came in with a fine burst of gusty vigor, and all through the month the wind blew, never quite strong enough to be a gale, never quite calm enough to let the whitecaps go from the surface of the bay. It went down at sunset, allowing quiet nights and early mornings, but by ten o'clock there it was again, fraying the clothes on the line, rattling the window blinds, and keeping the lobster fishermen and the draggers in a continual state of nervous fury. It was no more fun to haul lobster traps in a bucking, slatting boat than it was to run a haddock drag. No one ever remembered such a windy fall.

Southwest wind was all right with Hardy. It was southeast wind he had to worry about. Each morning he saw with deep relief that there was still no change in the weather, no telltale thin sheaves of goose-gray cloud to warn him that the "western" weather was at an end.

The weir had been repaired for three weeks, and so far it had not caught a herring. It sat—black piles, black nets, and black brushwork—in the tranquil water sheltered by the islands from the west wind, to Hardy an object of sulky and indescribable dreariness. He tended it with a kind of resigned fatalism, and each morning he scanned the sky.

Walking down the road to the shore on the first morning in November, he saw that there was no change in the weather. The air was colder, though, and some of the distant islands to the east "loomed," their ends lost to sight in the atmosphere, as if the sea had undercut them in the night.

Perley Higgins came out of his house and fell into step beside him and they went down the road together.

"Goin to blow again today," Perley announced gloomily. "Don't it beat hell! I've had so much salt water poured over me in the last month that my guts knows when the tide's out."

Hardy laughed. "Looks to me like what's one man's meat's another man's poison. I'm hatin the day when she hauls out southeast."

"She won't. God's gone and forgut he ever made any wind but this goddam monsoon. I dunno why a man ever wants to live out his life on this island. Wind sure ain't blowin you no fish, Hardy."

"No," said Hardy, "ain't, is it?"

"See you and Josie's got your potatoes dug," Perley said. "They turn out good?"

"Fifty-eight bushel."

"That so? Done good. Scabby this year?"

"No, not so bad. A few."

"Me and May'd be willin to take some pay in potatoes if you got some to spare," said Perley uncomfortably.

"You sure that'd be all right, Perley?"

"Sure."

It was decent of Perley, Hardy reflected, since he would probably have found cash far more welcome than potatoes. He still owed Perley twenty dollars for work on the weir.

"What's Jap layin in all that fence wire for? You

know?" Perley's glance flickered slyly toward him and then away.

"Fence wire? He bought some?"

"Ayeh. Thought likely you'd seen it. Three rolls. Barb wire, too."

"Understand he plans to build a fence," said Hardy. "Told me last September he was goin to, but I thought likely he'd forgot it. I had."

Perley tittered. "Guess he was waitin till Will got through workin for you," he offered.

"Guess so," Hardy agreed. He tossed the anchor into his dory, put his shoulder against her bow and shoved her down the flats until she floated. "Well, I'll see you, Perley."

So Jap was planning to keep on with the quarrel, he thought, as he rowed the dory along the wing of the weir. He'd guessed, seeing that Will had worked out most of the store bill, and Jap and Cack now owed him only a few dollars, that they would start coming around again, as if nothing had happened. Apparently he'd been mistaken.

He shipped his oars, letting the dory drift through the outer weir gate, and caught his breath in amazement and disbelief as the smooth surface of the water inside the pound broke into spattering turmoil, as if heavy raindrops had driven down on it.

Hardy stood up in the dory. Nowhere in the pound could he see bottom. The water was literally black with fish.

Not wanting to put his oars over for fear of creating further panic in the packed water, he pulled the dory alongside the brush wall and edged her up to the gate of the inner pound. Then he scooped his bailing dish overside and sent a few drops skittering across the surface. At once the still water in the inner pound blackened and boiled as the terrified fish swirled away from the disturbance.

"Jeezus!" said Hardy.

He pushed the dory silently out of the weir and then dug his oars deep as he headed for shore to get his seine and dipnet.

Josie saw the black-and-white striped flag, that signaled to the factory on the mainland that Hardy had fish, flying from the staff on the Point, and in a half-hour or so she saw the big sardine boat come hustling across the bay and inch herself in to the weir.

Josie was so excited that she couldn't stay away from the window long enough to do her work, but kept running back and peering, trying to decide whether or not Hardy had got a good haul.

"He must have at least a hundred bushel," she said to Grammy, "or he wouldn't have got the sardine boat over."

"Dyin, ain't you?" said Grammy. "Been so long since Hardy caught a herrin, I bet you don't even know how much they are. Can't figger it out, can you?"

"They was fifty cents two weeks ago," said Josie. "Oh, dear!" she fretted. "I wish Mildred would get home from school. I could at least send her down to find out how many he's got."

She was nearly overcome with excitement when she saw the second sardine boat come plowing across the bay with a bone in her teeth and range herself alongside the first one at the weir.

Hardy himself was surprised to see the second sardine boat. He was so busy when it arrived that he barely took time to glance up and note that it was a down-east boat a long way from home. Eddy MacNair, the skipper of the Harbor boat, he saw was madder than a hornet and was glowering darkly at the newcomer. With a little lurch of excitement in his chest, he realized that the presence of two sardine boats at his weir might mean some bidding for his haul of fish.

Better not count on it, though, he thought, with the fatality of the many-times-disappointed.

Mildred, seeing the herring flag flying from her father's flagstaff, ducked into the bushes at morning recess and ran as fast as she could away from the schoolhouse toward the shore. The tide was dead low, and what few punts were left in the Pool were down beyond the long line of muddy flats. Mildred forgot that she had on the good shoes she wore to school, until she climbed aboard the nearest punt, which happened to be Eddy Comey's, and saw that in the wading process her feet had got mud on them halfway up her ankles. She stopped long enough to wash the mud off, but the shoes were so wet that her feet squelched in them.

She rowed as fast as she could off into the weir, and was annoyed when she got there to find the gate between the pounds closed so that she could not get in to where Hardy was seining herring. She tied the punt up to the piling nearest the gate and, climbing up the brushwork, thrust her head through an opening between one of the tarred nets and a seine pole. The net, because it happened to be one which Hardy had just tarred, stuck to her hands and to the side of her neck where her head went through, and a goodly portion of tar came off on her tyer and stockings. But she was where she could see what was going on, and there she stayed, clinging to the side of the weir like a wrinkle, her thin, scrawny little face rapt with excitement.

Hardy had run the seine around part of the school of fish in the inner pound and had pulled it in as tight as he dared, so that it bulged and rippled with the weight. Mildred could see the struggling silver gleams through the roiled water and the shining scales floating away. Her father, dressed in his yellow oilskins, already stood ankle deep in flipping fish in the dory. He was covered from head to foot with herring scales, and all around him and Perley Higgins, who was helping him with the long-handled dipnet, tiny scales were thrown into the air so thickly that they looked like a sparkling mist. The thousands of herring all flipping at once in the dory made a light slippery slapping sound, almost like a whisper.

As she looked, Hardy and Perley hauled up the dipnet again, emptying an eight- or ten-bushel load into the boat, and instantly the volume of the whisper stepped up louder and faster, and the mist of scales flew higher. Perley got one in his eye and swore thoroughly, and Mildred had to clap her hand over her mouth to stifle her snickers.

When the dory was full—forty bushels loaded her so that her gunnel was almost on a level with the water— Hardy eased her away from the seine, opened his outer gate just wide enough, and squeezed the logy craft through between the sardine boats.

He stood for a moment, buried in fish to his knees, glancing first at MacNair, then at the skipper of the other sardine boat. "Well, boys?" he said.

"How many you think you got in there?" asked Eddy MacNair.

"I figger a good six hundred bushel. Maybe seven."

"Ninety cents," said Eddy briefly. He popped his stubby clay pipe into the middle of the bristly growth around his lips, and sent out an ennobled cloud of smoke.

"Ninety-five," said the other skipper. He was a brawny, red-faced young fellow, about twenty-seven, Hardy guessed. Hardy wondered who he was. Hadn't seen him around before. But then, he reflected, he hadn't seen any of the sardine boats as close as this since last summer.

"What's on *your* mind, herrin-choker?" said Eddy, glaring. "Ain't they got no fish down-east?"

"Used em all up," said the other mildly. "Them's factories we got down there, not preservin kittles."

Eddy spat resoundingly into the water. "You better take that sawed-off piss-pot you're in back home before it breezes up this afternoon. You git her stern-to that southwest wind we got up here, and you'll roll her under like a puffer."

The down-east boat was a little chunky, but her skipper seemed not to mind the criticism. He grinned. "What wind you talkin about?" he asked, with the air of one who really wanted to know. "I been up around here three days, and I ain't seen no wind. That is, not what we'd call *wind*, down our way."

"I've heard a the wind down your way many's the time," said Eddy. "Blows all the time and blows hot. I'll give you a dollar a bushel for them fish, Hardy."

"A dollar-five," said the stranger.

"My God," said Eddy, "why don't you go home? What's your name, anyway? A dollar-ten, Hardy."

"Dollar-fifteen. That's where I'm headed for, soon's I buy a load of fish. Marceau's my name."

"Frog, hey?" said Eddy. "Well, bust my barrel. What

[195]

you doin round here with white men? A dollar-twenty."

"I'm lookin for some google-eyes to poke out with my thumb," said Marceau. "And it looks to me like your barrel'd bust easy. A dollar-twenty-five."

Eddy started to throw down his pipe, but stopped himself in time and laid it gently down on the steering-wheel box. "Don't you call me a google-eyes, you reptile-slaughterin son-of-a-bitch!" he bellowed. "A dollar and thirty cents, Hardy, and pray to God, sell em before I murder this inchworm!"

Marceau let go with a blast of language which lasted for two minutes before he finished with an offer of a dollar-thirty-five.

Eddy looked at him with his underlip stuck out speculatively. "Well, that's my limit," he said, in his normal voice. "Beats me."

"No more bids?" asked Marceau.

Eddy shook his head. "I'll let you have em," he said grandly. "Too bad to waste good fish, because you can't get em down-east in that hooker before they rot. Start up the engine, Bob. Le's get out a here before we begin to stink, too."

The Harbor boat backed up with a churn of foam and headed out across the bay for home. No offense had been meant and none taken.

Hardy, inching his empty dory back through the weir gate, suddenly caught sight of the tar-smeared face of his daughter hanging enraptured on the side of the weir, seemingly disembodied, like the Cheshire Cat.

"Well, for the Lord sake!" he said. "Where'd you come from? You hout down out of that and get home! This ain't no place for you."

To his surprise the face instantly was withdrawn with-

[196]

out argument, and he thought no more about Mildred until later, as he was bringing the empty dory for the last time back into the weir, he saw her again, in much the same place she had been before. "I thought I told you to go home!" he bellowed at her. "You're supposed to be to school."

She did climb down for good this time, and rowed docilely after him as he took the dory ashore.

"My Lord, if you ain't a sight!" he said, gasping, as he got a look at her. The morning spent hanging to the tarred nets had left Mildred with very little of her natural skin uncovered. "You look like spots comin out on a nigger! What's your ma goin to say?" He regarded her fiercely for a moment and then, unable to help it, burst out laughing. "Well, I guess you and I both had a good time. I'll fix your ma. Hold out your tyer skirt, there."

Marceau had paid him in cash, eight hundred and twenty-five dollars, mostly small bills, with some change. Hardy loaded it all, speckled with herring scales as it was, into Mildred's tar-spotted pinafore skirt, while she watched him, round-eyed and speechless.

"There," said Hardy. "Now, le's you and me go home and show that to your ma."

Together they walked up the hill to the house, both walking very grandly, with their chests out.

❦

SAYL Comey went to school every day, but it seemed to him that things got worse instead of better. He couldn't get used to the routine, and he couldn't see any sense in what went on. In class he presented a face of bleak and absolute boredom.

Something in the sight of the big sullen fellow, sitting always on the end of his spine and the back of his neck, irritated the teachers extremely. No matter what they did to interest or amuse the class, Saylor Comey's face never changed. Miss Rayne, the English teacher, carried the battle to him the first week of school by sending him out of the room for not paying attention. Once she made him go back to the door and come in quietly because his big foot had upset a wastebasket—on purpose, Miss Rayne told herself. After that, the hatred between them was cordial and enduring.

Miss Rayne was young. Her first year out of college was rapidly proving to her that a woman's place should be in the home—as soon as she could manage it—and that no teaching job was going to take the place in her heart of being president of her sorority. She had wanted a little money of her own, and she had hoped to get through a year of teaching without being bored to death. But she had never guessed that a respectable job like this would bring her into contact with so much cheapness. And some of these kids certainly were cheap!

The freshman class was getting through the English period by reading aloud their assignment from *Macbeth*. *Macbeth* properly belonged to the juniors, but the textbooks of *Washington's Farewell Address* had not come in time for the opening of the term, and *Macbeth* was the only text on hand with enough copies to supply the whole class. Mr. Benson, the principal, had decided to start the freshmen in on it.

The class did not understand what some of the passages meant, but they felt they couldn't be blamed because, after all, *Macbeth* was junior English. Everybody found at once that there was a very good reason for turning up unprepared.

There came a day when Miss Rayne also turned up unprepared, and she did not know what some of the passages meant either. She had had a date the night before with a Coast Guard fellow, for the movies and a ride afterward in his car. When she had got home, she just had not had the energy to make out lesson plans or to read assignments and look up words. She had expected to get through the period by making the kids recite and by picking up enough information that way. She hadn't counted on nobody's knowing anything. Finally she gave up altogether and set the class to reading aloud.

"At least," she told them in an offended voice, "this will be *one* assignment you've read."

She certainly felt pretty vague today. Every once in a while her mind shied away from Shakespeare and went off on little tours of its own. George was so sweet. You had to look out for that kind of smooth, good-looking fellow, though. From far off she heard the stumbling voices hesitating over the far-off unaccustomed words.

The boy who was reading stopped suddenly. Miss Rayne's attention jerked back to the class.

"What does that passage mean, Mr. Comey?" she asked automatically.

Sayl mumbled. "Dun know."

"Please stand up, Mr. Comey, and address your comments to me, not to your stomach. That's a perfectly simple passage . . . if you know how to read."

The sarcasm and the tittering from the class which followed it made Sayl turn brick-red.

"Well, Mr. Comey?"

"Them three ole wimmen was cookin rotten guts in a kittle," Sayl said desperately.

[199]

The roar of laughter made Miss Rayne furious. *Macbeth* was great literature. She had read it in high school and someday she meant to sit down and read it right through again. She certainly wasn't going to listen to coarse talk about it, or anything else, not in her classroom.

"What do you mean by using language like that?" she demanded.

Sayl fell back upon the only weapon he had in situations like this, a kind of detached and supercilious silence.

"This is no place to show how ill-bred you are." Miss Rayne, getting red herself, was determined to prick him out of it this time. "You get up on your feet and apologize to me and to the class."

Sayl did not move.

"Do as I tell you, Mr. Comey."

In the pin-dropping silence the freshmen sat immovable and delighted that something interesting was at last happening in one of Miss Rayne's classes.

"Well, then, you can go up to Mr. Benson. Take him this note from me."

She sat down and wrote a sharp little message to the principal, informing him that Sayl had used disgusting language in class and had been disrespectful to her.

Sayl piled his books together and took the note. As he went out of the room he rolled his eyes at Haral and let one black eyebrow writhe upward into his tanned forehead.

Haral sniggered, and Miss Rayne fell upon him furiously.

"What are you laughing at, Mr. Turner?"

"Nothin."

"You think your friend Comey is very funny, don't you?"

The reminder of Sayl's interpretation of the three old women was too much for Haral. His repressed laughter burst out in a loud spitting snort, and some of the other members of the class sniggered too.

"All right, Mr. Turner. Take your books and go up to see Mr. Benson. I'm sure you'll both find him very, very amusing." Miss Rayne looked over the class. "Anybody else care to go along?"

But the class looked back at her with blank, sober eyes.

Haral caught up with Sayl at the end of the long corridor.

"Teacher's pet! Well, well!" commented Sayl.

They climbed the stairs to the principal's office on the second story of the building.

No one was there. Mr. Benson had a class and would not be back until the end of the period.

The bare, ugly little office held very little except Mr. Benson's desk, littered with papers and class books, his scabby varnished swivel chair, and a small bookcase crowded with dusty notebooks and a few texts. On the windowsill was a scrawny geranium growing in a pot.

"My God!" Sayl said. "Think a spendin your life cooped up in a place like this. No wonder they all look and act screwy!"

Now that Haral was in the same boat he was, Sayl felt better. The writhing embarrassment that had swept over him at being made a show of in front of the class was gone.

"That little mush-face dame has sure got it in for us." said Haral. "She's been lookin for a chance like this ever since school started."

"All she's got to do is wait," Sayl said grandly. "We'll fix her. Rayne, Rayne, gives me a pain." His eye fell on

[201]

the geranium and he went over and lifted the pot scornfully off the windowsill. "Gawd, a plant in a pot! I bet he waters it every mornin and sets it in the sun, the big pansy!" An idea came to Sayl and a grin spread slowly over his face. "Watch the door, Haral, and le'me know if anyone's comin."

Under Haral's awestruck eyes he made water in the pot and set it back on the windowsill.

"Gee," he said. "She don't hold much. I got some to spare. What'll I do with it?"

"Out the window," said Haral in a kind of hoarse croak.

"What, waste it? Oh, no, my son." Sayl's roving eyes fell on the principal's neat black hat hanging over his coat on a rack in the corner.

When Mr. Benson arrived at his office, Sayl was sitting in the extra chair by the desk and Haral was perched on the windowsill. Both were reading studiously in their English books and both looked very downcast indeed.

"What are you boys doing here?" the principal asked.

Sayl offered Miss Rayne's note.

"I see." Mr. Benson read the note and tossed it on his desk. "Bad language in class, eh? What about you?" he demanded, turning to Haral.

Haral looked up mournfully and Mr. Benson was gratified and surprised to see traces of tears on his cheeks.

"I . . . I couldn't help laughin," he said with a hiccup.

"You think nasty talk is funny, eh?"

Haral shook his head and looked at the floor.

"You want to apologize to Miss Rayne, or quit school and clear out?"

" 'Pologize," mumbled Haral.

"All right. Now, Comey, I've had my eye on you. You don't try, and you're ill-tempered. You boys who come in here from the islands, you think you can talk and act the way you're allowed to at home. Now, here in this school, we're civilized and we act like gentlemen. The quicker you learn that, the better." Mr. Benson had been striding up and down the little office, shaking his finger for emphasis. Now, as he turned he observed that his hat had fallen off the rack and lay upside down on the floor in the corner. He picked it up and hung it back over his coat with a sharp little *clap*.

Haral's Adam's apple clicked in his throat, and Sayl turned a little pale, but Mr. Benson merely went on with his lecture.

"Swearing in front of ladies is one thing that a real gentleman never does. The next slip out of you and you'll go back to Comey's Island, or whatever other foreign country you happen to come from."

Sayl's dead-pan face did not alter. When he had first come in, a going-over like this, especially the slur on his family, would have made him ready to fight. Now his one idea was to get out of here as quickly as possible.

"You fellows get back to Miss Rayne's room and apologize to her properly. And don't forget, the next time I'll take steps."

The boys went down the stairs, two at a time. In the cloakroom on the first floor they hid among the lockers and laughed until they were weak.

"He . . . he . . . never even noticed it," gasped Haral, rocking back and forth on the floor.

"Wait till he puts it on," said Sayl. "We hadn't better be around then, had we?"

"Gee, no. What'd we better do?"

"He can't prove nothin."

"No, but he'll guess who done it.'

"You goin to 'pologize to old Rayne-in-the-face? By God, I ain't."

This was a new idea to Haral. "We got to, ain't we?" He had had in the back of his mind that they'd better go pretty soon and get this unpleasant job over.

"What you mean, *got* to?"

"We said we would."

"Sure. But what'll we say? Like's not, she'll make us do it in front of the class. Not me. Not after what ole Stinky-lid said about my family livin in a foreign country."

The descriptive nickname sent Haral off again into helpless squeaks of laughter.

Sayl himself grinned, but his mind was busy with the problem at hand. "Shut up, now, Haral, and listen. What d'you think your old man and Joe's goin to say when we tell em what he said about Comey's Island?"

Haral sobered. The insult to his home and his family appeared before him in clarity for the first time. "Why, the old skunk!" he said. "That makes me mad."

"It does me, too. I ain't goin to no school where they call my family a foreigner."

"Me neither. Le's go home and tell em. Darn if they won't be mad."

"S'pose they'll believe us?"

"Sure they will. Look, you stick that damn English book in your pocket so's we can show em how it started. By God, I looked up a lot of them words in the dictionary to see if I could make some sense of it, and I guess the' ain't very much difference between the way that feller writes and the way I talk. Only, with him you have to look it up in the dictionary," said Sayl.

They sneaked out of the cloakroom, down the stairs to the school basement, and crawled out a cellar window. By the time they had walked the half mile to the shore and had hunted up transportation to the island, they were afire with the injustice done them, and Mr. Benson's slurs on the people of Comey's Island burned in their minds with the flame of righteous and unpunishable justice.

That the man they found to take them over to the island was Perley Higgins was better luck than they had dared to hope for. Perley made a wonderful audience, and they poured the full story out to him in all detail, except the part about the flowerpot and the hat, which seemed not to have much bearing on the matter.

Perley was indignant. "Why, the domineerin old suds-bucket!" he growled. "We're jest as good people as he is, and if your folks don't go over'n tell him so, I'll go myself, by God. The' ain't a one of us over here on Comey's but what paid taxes to help maintain that high school, too. You jest wait till I git a chance to talk to some a the Harbor fellers!"

Haral left Sayl at the cross-path that turned off toward Sayl's house, and continued on up the hill toward his own. His mind was so full of the story he had to tell his family that he did not notice Jap Comey's new fence until he walked almost into it.

The peeled spruce fence posts looked raw and yellow, and Jap and Eddy were just finishing stringing the last reel of barbed wire.

Eddy let out a yell. "Hey, look where you're gcin!"

Haral backed up and stood looking at the fence, his mouth hanging open. "Well!" he said, at a complete loss. "Well!"

[205]

"And a couple a holes," mocked Eddy. "You Turners too dumb to know a good hint when you see one?"

"What's the matter with you?" said Haral. "Huh?"

"Huh?" mimicked Eddy. "Ain't they learnt you nothin but 'huh' over to the high school?"

"Shut up, Ed." Jap advanced on Haral, his dark lean face menacing. "This fence means I don't want your folks trampin acrost my land no more. After this, you got to go round it, see?"

"Oh!" said Haral. "Is that so?" He put a hand on one of the new posts and vaulted the fence. "So I heard a monkey say."

Jap started over the fence after him, but Haral ran at top speed up the path and banged in at the kitchen door. "Ma," he said breathlessly, "you see what they're doin? You see what Jap 'n Eddy's doin?"

Josie turned sharply from the breadboard, taking her hands, white with flour, out of the dough she was kneading. "*Haral!* For heav'n sakes, what you doin home in the middle of the week?"

"Ma," said Haral, "they're buildin a *fence* down there. Jap 'n Eddy—"

"My land, yes, I know it," Josie said. Her cheeks glowed red, making a dab of flour beside her nose stand out clearly. "Your father'll tend to them. What I want to know is, what you're doin to home *in the middle of the week?*"

Haral sat down in a chair by the door. The look he bent on his mother was concerned and serious. "Ma," he said, "Sayl and I, we just can't bring ourselves to stay at no school where they say such awful things about our folks."

"Haral!" Josie was scandalized. "What kind of a story

you tryin to tell me? Have you got into a mess? If you have, don't you try to lie out of it!"

"I ain't! It's every word the truth! Mr. Benson said that we folks over on Comey's Island talked and acted nasty in our homes and that we never had no manners, and that we ain't no better'n foreigners, that's what he said! And I quit school and so's Sayl, and we ain't goin back, not to no place where they talk about our folks like that!"

Josie sat down weakly and stared at him.

"He ain't fit to be no schoolteacher, the lyin old fool!" Grammy leaped happily into the fray. "If he said that, your father'n Leonard better go right over there and beat the arse off him. Where's my money, Haral? You ain't goin to set foot inside this house till I git my money back!"

"You'll get it," said Haral. "I ain't goin back there and that's all!" He shot a quick glance at his mother and was instantly stricken to see that tears were rolling down her cheeks. "Aw . . ." he said. "Aw . . ."

Heavy footsteps sounded on the porch and Joe Comey came in. Behind him was Sayl, scared and sobered.

"I come to hear Haral's side a this yarn," Joe said grimly. "What happened over there, Haral? What started it?"

Haral told the story from beginning to end, blessing the forethought that had made them bring home the English book.

"Look," he said, turning over the pages. "Here 't is. That line right there. Sayl and I both looked up the words. That one there, it means guts. Sayl never wanted to say what it meant, but Miss Rayne made him."

"Enteruls!" said Grammy, peering over his arm. "Of course it means guts. What's the matter with that woman? She a fool? You leave that book home, Haral. I want to read it."

"She sounds like one," said Josie, the light of battle in her eye. She had dried her tears, now that Haral's story was beginning to make sense to her decent and practical mind, and she was beginning to believe that he was not entirely to blame. "I want to go see them school people, Joe, before I make up my mind about this. It don't sound to me like they've done right."

"I do, too," said Joe, setting his jaw. "I'll fix Benson."

"No," said Josie, thoughtfully. "I don't think you better, Joe. I think I and your mother had ought to go see him."

"Ma?" Joe stared at her. "She won't go. She don't like fights."

"It won't be a fight," said Josie. "My land, if it turns out to be a fight, Mr. Benson'd have a right to think we don't have any manners over here."

Joe grinned. "I guess you better see him, at that, Josie. My manners'd prob'ly be pretty lousy if it turns out he said what the kids said he did. We'll take you across in the boat tomorrow."

GRAM lay in wait for Hardy that night and pounced on him as he came through the door.

"Haral's home," she announced with relish. "Been throwed out a school for talkin nasty. Now, Hardy, I want my money back."

"Haral?" said Hardy. "Home? What you talkin about, Marm? I paid you that seventy dollars back last Tuesday."

The debt to his mother, in fact, had been the first money that Hardy had paid out of his windfall.

Gram let out a howl. "You never! You ain't goin to cheat me out a my money, Hardy Turner, lyin and sayin you paid it! Haral's come home and he don't need it now, and you gi'me it!"

"You've forgot, Marm," said Hardy patiently. "Remember, you put up a fuss about it because it was all herrin scales? You look in your bag. You'll find it."

"It ain't. It ain't in my bag!" Gram scrabbled fiercely around in the contents of her knitting bag and suddenly subsided. "Well," she said, in an abused voice, "I paid you clean bills, and them you gi'me back has made my bag stink like a blubber barrel. Herrin scales! Pu!"

His mother could certainly put on a good show of failing faculties when she wanted to, Hardy thought. He suspected she hadn't forgotten about being paid. The point was, he had a little ahead now, and she was figuring that if she made enough fuss, he might pay her again just to keep her quiet.

He looked for the milk pail, but it was gone. Josie must be in the barn milking the cow. On the way through the shed, he met Haral, staggering under a double armload of stovewood.

Hardy said nothing, waiting until Haral had dumped his load in the woodbox and returned to the shed for another.

"Warn't expectin to see you," said Hardy.

"Well, no," said Haral brightly. "I warn't expectin to be here."

"How come you are?"

Haral broke into his story, which he told quite well now.

"That all that happened?"

[209]

"That's every single thing."

"Ain't lyin anywhere, are you?" asked Hardy, eyeing him.

"No, I ain't, Pa. That's just what happened."

"You lied pretty smooth, remember, about that fish oil."

"Ayeh. I know; but I ain't now. You can ask Benson himself, but maybe he wouldn't own up to sayin what he said." Haral looked away vaguely and began to shift his feet.

"Somebody'll have to go see Mr. Benson, you know," said Hardy.

"I know they will. Ma says she's goin." Haral began to load up another armful of wood. "I'd just as soon she would."

"Where is your mother?"

"Milkin, I guess," Haral mumbled. He cast a quick look over his shoulder at his father, but Hardy had turned away and was going on into the barn.

Josie had apparently finished milking, for the tie-up was closed for the night and the pail of milk, carefully covered, was sitting on the feed barrel. In the gloomy dusk of the barn at first he did not see her, but after a moment he made out her colored dress at the far corner by the window.

"What you doin, Josie?" he asked. "It's cold out here."

"Thinkin," she said.

"What of?" He put his big hands on her shoulders and for a moment she leaned against him. "He'll go back tomorrow, Josie."

Hardy stopped uncomfortably and stood motionless. Something was going on in Josie's mind that she was trying to find words for. He sensed a struggle, feeling the tense muscles of her shoulders under his hands.

"I'm not sure I want him to," she answered finally. "That was an awful cheap way for a man to talk, Hardy."

"Most like he was mad. You can't tell what them kids had been up to. A high-school teacher's got a lot to contend with."

"I don't doubt he was tried. The trouble is, Hardy, I ain't sure but what he said was so."

"Why . . . no, it ain't, Josie."

"You know it is. I've tried to learn Haral and Mildred both their manners and to talk nice and to have sense about things. And Haral, he's wilder'n a hawk, and all he thinks about anythin is what's in it for him. And Mildred, she's a tomboy and she knows more about things she hadn't ought to than I do. I don't know what's goin to become of em, Hardy, I swear I don't."

Josie's shoulders trembled a little and Hardy dropped his hands from them in a panic. To have Josie upset by any situation shook him to his foundations. She was his refuge. He never had been, and had never thought of being, hers.

"It ain't nothin to worry about," he began. "They'll grow out of it."

"Hardy, this island ain't a good place to bring up kids. I don't know what's got into people to change em so. Look at em, backbitin and fightin with each other and gossipin, till you don't know but your best friend is your worst enemy. I've see it gettin worse and worse, and now the' ain't a one of my neighbors I'd dare to trust."

"I guess that's so," Hardy said. He moved uncertainly

away from her in the darkness and sat down on a box. "But what can you do?"

"I guess you can't do anything," Josie said. "But I'm scairt for my kids, growin up dog eat dog like this."

"Leonard's all right."

"Yes. But Leonard ain't the man he could be if we lived somewheres else but here." She drew a long breath, whether of relief or sorrow he could not tell.

He sat puzzled and shaken, trying to think of something to say that would comfort her, make her be steady again.

"It's like potaters," she said suddenly. "You grow em too many years in one place and they come up scabby."

"You want to move away from here, Josie?" he asked slowly.

To his utter desolation she put her head down on her hands and cried. "No," she said, at length. "I don't, Hardy. I like this island. I'm to home here."

JOSIE dressed herself carefully for the trip to the Harbor the next day. She put on her best black dress and the black glass beads that had been her grandmother's. The hat that she had bought two years ago and had re-trimmed twice was still in style and became her very well. When she was ready to go, she looked at herself steadily in the mirror. The neat woman who looked back at her was not Josie Turner, but the daughter of Captain Hosea Scott, of Bellport and Boston.

She had been deeply troubled at the implications inherent in Haral's story. It couldn't be, she thought, that the people over at the Harbor looked down on the islanders as they looked down on foreigners. Of course, the boys might be lying, but their story had too many logical details to be entirely made up. At any rate, Josie meant to get to the bottom of it, and she would have to do it by herself. For, as Joe had said, Sarah Comey refused to go. In fact, she obviously thought it out of the question.

"It wouldn't help matters any," she said, with a chuckle, looking at Josie with her clear blue gaze, "if I was to go in the clothes I've got."

At the school Josie waited, sensibly, until Mr. Benson came back from his lunch, and she caught him just before he left his office for his first afternoon class. He was surprised, then pleasantly flattered, to see the nice-looking, well-dressed lady in his office.

"I know you're busy," she began, "and I won't keep you long. But my boy came home from school yesterday with a queer story, and I thought I'd like to get to the bottom of it. I'm Mrs. Hardy Turner."

For a moment Mr. Benson did not make the connection. Then his jaw dropped a little. "Are you—"

Josie nodded. "Haral Turner's mother. He don't want to come back to school. His reason is that you called the people over on Comey's Island foreigners, and said that we let our youngones talk nasty in our homes. It didn't seem to me likely that you said just that."

Mr. Benson turned quite red. "Well, I—" He looked up to find her steady eyes upon his. "I don't believe I remember quite what I did say. I was . . . angry. The other boy's been hard to manage."

"I ain't got any doubt Haral has, too. But no worse'n other boys, Mr. Benson. He's had a decent bringin up."

"I'm sure he has."

[213]

"Then you didn't say what the boys said you did? I'd like to have the story straight. The people over on Comey's is pretty mad about it."

Mr. Benson was caught. He thought fast. Quite a few boys from outlying islands attended his school, and if this story got around it might make trouble for him with the schoolboard. He wanted to keep his job.

"Mrs. Turner, I think the boys repeated to you what they *thought* I meant. What I intended to say to them was that they were the representatives here of their village on the island, and if they acted badly, it reflected—er—on their people."

"I see." Josie got up quietly. "Well, thank you for explainin. They didn't understand it that way."

He opened the office door for her. "Good-by, and come in again if anything seems to go wrong."

"Good-by, Mr. Benson."

He watched her straight back go out of sight down the stairs and then breathed a sigh of relief. Most irate mothers who came to him were not so easy to deal with. He had not been aware of the desecration of his potted plant and his hat, and thus had had no telling weapon with which to meet her. He seldom looked at the plant, and the hat, by the time he had been ready to go home, had dried sufficiently to escape his notice.

Josie went out of the high-school building and down the street toward the town landing. The little weasel, she thought. Now didn't he lie out of that some slick! I ain't a one to take a part in a kids' row, but I don't think I want a man like that to educate a boy of mine.

Thanks to the weir, she and Hardy had money ahead now. There was a good high school in Bellport, and she had some cousins there. Haral could board with Deborah

Scott. She hadn't wanted to send him to her family unless she and Hardy could pay a respectable sum for his board.

～∽⌐⌐

ORIN couldn't figure out what was the matter with Alice, unless perhaps it was because she was going back to Boston tomorrow, but he couldn't see why that should make her blue, since she wanted to go. She was usually happy-go-lucky and she always kept him chuckling, but tonight she had hardly said a word. All through the movies, while he'd laughed his head off, she had sat without cracking a smile. On the way home from Bellport he pulled the car off into a side road and parked, to see if he could find out what ailed her.

"Don't you feel good?" he asked solicitously.

"M'm-h'm," she answered.

"Did I do somethin to make you mad?"

"Of course you didn't. I'm just grumpy."

"Oh," said Orin, relieved. "Like to go somewhere else? For a ride, maybe?"

"No, I guess not. After a bit we go home, h'm?"

"Okay." Orin settled down contentedly in his seat, puffing at his cigarette. Whatever she wanted was all right with him. He never had any very strong preferences, and so long as other people's did not make him actually uncomfortable, he was quite willing to fall in with any plans. He never argued and he never said positively what he himself wanted to do.

Alice found him restful, but she couldn't say he was very exciting. She figured she had paid him back for taking her around so much all summer by seeing to it that he enjoyed himself when he was with her. During

[215]

the last weeks, since she had broken off with Leonard, Orin had been a life-saver. He had, without knowing it, helped her through some pretty gloomy times.

Tonight she couldn't seem to keep on making believe she was happy. It was, she guessed, actually having made up her mind to go. Already she had stayed a week longer than she should have, letting the bunch of factory workers from the Harbor go on to Boston without her. Maybe —she hoped—after she left tomorrow and the bridges were burned, she'd feel better.

"Poor Orin," she said. "You don't know what to make of me when I ain't laughin, do you?"

Something in her voice made him turn to her with quick concern. His good-natured round face took on a sober cast which was foreign to it. Orin didn't really know how to be glum.

"Why don't you change your mind about marryin me, Alice?" he said. "A girl as good as you ain't ever goin to be happy traipsin round alone."

She thought, suddenly, how nice Orin was. He wasn't very smart, not much fun to talk to, but he was somebody to depend on. She could make him do anything she wanted, she knew that. He had already expressed his willingness to go up to the city and try for a job. And the fact remained that he did think she was wonderful.

"I'll be engaged to you, Orin," she said slowly, and then wondered, with regret, how she could have said it.

"You will? Hot dog!" Orin sat up straight with a jerk and turned toward her with an incredulous grin.

"But look, I'll have to go to Boston just the same."

He saw no reason why she shouldn't, if she wanted to. "Why, sure. We'll get married and I'll go with you."

"I don't believe so, Orin. I want some time first. Okay?"

Orin blushed bright red, partly with embarrassment, partly with acute appreciation of what he supposed was her state of mind. Of course a nice girl like Alice would want some time to get used to the idea of marriage. "Sure. We'll get hitched up when you come home, then. Or I'll come up there, if you'd rather, next June."

He leaned toward her and she closed her eyes, thinking miserably, It's fair to him because he's satisfied with so little. Just my marrying him would make it up to him.

"I'll earn enough dough trawlin this fall," said Orin happily, "for the ticket up and to buy ya a ring."

FROM the deck of the Boston boat Alice saw, for the fifth time in her life, the gray city rising out of the heavy cold water of its harbor. The boat docked at seven, and the overcast morning was hardly light enough yet for her to make out the ponderous tiers of buildings, climaxed by the shaft of the Custom House tower. Five years ago she had first stood here on the boat deck, catching her breath at the beauty of the dark tremendous pile thrusting at her out of the morning. It had seemed beautiful to her then, and did now. But five years ago she had been going to do big things in that city of Boston.

Just what those things could be, it occurred to her suddenly, she had never been quite sure. The books in high school had never given her an idea of any work she could do, nor of how she could best go about doing it if she knew what it was. What they had given her was a restless, craving energy, a determination not to let the worth she had be wasted. She didn't suppose she wanted everything in the world—only to live her life so that it made sense.

And that's a funny one, too, she thought with a wry smile.

Each year she came back to the cheap boardinghouse district, the long bench in the factory packing room, the four-cents-a-case-of-twenty-four for the cans of food she packed. She made a little more now, as a skilled worker. Two-twenty-five, two-fifty, maybe three dollars, if she felt like pushing herself—only she always paid for that by having to slow down the next day. It all averaged about the same.

The steamer's smart young first officer spoke to her courteously, and she moved aside. She had been standing beside a speed-indicator at the rail, where he needed to be to superintend docking the boat. Something about him, as he stood watchful and assured in his blue uniform, reminded her of Leonard. She watched his hand move skillfully on the lever of the indicator, the confident set of his sturdy shoulders as he edged the boat in toward the wharf. He was like a tool made especially for the work he was doing. He knew where he belonged, what he was fit for.

I wish I did, she thought, and turned away abruptly.

The factory was in Watertown, and she knew of a nice single room with a bearable landlady, on the outskirts of Cambridge. Soon she would see the few people she knew who would be her companions—not very intimate—for the winter. Soon she would drift, impersonal as a shadow and no more noticed than one, among the crowds on subway and elevated platforms and in and out of stores and cheap eating places. Straightbacked and anonymous, Alice Lacy, keeping her tryst with ambition in the city.

I'm actin like a fool with myself, she thought, pressing her lips together to keep them from trembling. I dished it out and I'd better be able to take it.

She picked up her suitcase and went down the saloon stairs, to be ready to get off the boat as soon as the gangplank was out.

⟨⁓⟩

THE weir, having not caught a herring through what had looked to be Hardy's worst summer in years, kept on fishing through the unseasonably fine November weather. All during the week when the tide served right —dead low in the early mornings—the big schools of fish poured through the shallow coves and inlets, and the wide brush wings of Hardy's weir gathered them in. Each day the herring flag snapped in the wind from its pole on the Head, and each day the sardine boats came shouldering across the rough bay and tied up to be loaded with fish.

Hardy enjoyed the sudden stir of important doings around his enterprise. For months the weir had lain in tranquil water, disturbed only by the gulls and the wash of the Island boats chugging past. Now, in addition to the sardine boats, sometimes as many as fifteen lobster and trawl boats lay off the weir in the mornings, hoping to get bait. They came from Burncoat and Tinker's and the islands up the bay, and sometimes from farther away. For the herring, the most exasperating and unpredictable of the fish schooling along any coast, seemed for secret reasons of their own to have chosen Comey's Island

[219]

waters for their rendezvous, and very few weirs outside of Hardy's were catching any.

And Hardy was the center of all, the important man, referred to and talked about, the man who was making money. The droop went out of his shoulders overnight. No one seemed to remember now that he had been made fun of during the summer.

Perley Higgins tried to keep track in his head of how many dory loads of herring went out of the weir, but somehow when he came to jot down his figures on a scrap of paper, he wasn't sure that he had remembered exactly. He guessed Hardy had made as much as five thousand dollars, and that was the sum people talked about on Perley's say-so. Actually, when the week and three days of favorable tides were over, Hardy had banked a little more than thirty-three hundred dollars.

On the morning of November 26, Hardy took a hundred bushels of herring out of the weir and sold them to Eddy MacNair for ninety cents a bushel. Then, without consulting anyone, or even stopping to wash the herring scales out of his dories, he began methodically to take the nets off the weir and boat them ashore.

Josie, glancing out of the upstairs window toward noon, was electrified to see the denuded seine poles, stripped of nets, thrusting up out of the cove. She looked anxiously at the sky, but the weather was the same—the watered blue, the high, puffy clouds, the vigorous annoying southwest wind.

"What you doin that for, Hardy?" she asked, when he came home to dinner. "I don't see no change in the weather."

Hardy said merely, "I don't like the looks of it. It's goin to blow."

But the next morning the sky was unchanged, and

the weir, even with the nets gone from one pound, caught thirty-five bushels of herring.

"Jeezus, Hardy," Perley said, " 'f you'd left them nets on, you might have got two hundred bushel. Maybe more."

"That's all right," Hardy said. "Today we'll take off the rest of em."

"You figger you got more money'n you need?" Perley asked glumly. "God Almighty, man, leave em on another week and let her fish for *me*."

By noon the nets were down and stored away in the loft of Hardy's fishhouse, spread carefully so that they would dry out and not rot. In the late afternoon, lean parings of cloud mackereled the sky, subtly changing toward night from ruffled lightness to a smooth ominous gray. The wind dropped and the air grew steadily colder. By midnight a strong northeast wind was blowing the first hard stinging snowflakes of the season over the island, and the sea was beginning to beat over the ledges with a deep-throated steady thunder.

Hardy turned over in bed with a sigh of contentment and settled himself against the comforting warmth of Josie's broad back.

Guessed right for once in my life, by God, he said to himself, and slept.

⚓

WITH the coming of winter weather, fishing at Comey's Island slacked off. Few of the lobster men cared to risk the gales and sudden snow squalls of December, or what was more dangerous, the killing cold that turned flying spray to ice. Most of them put their traps on the bank and hauled up their boats until milder weather began, usually in late March or early April.

Hardy's fishing season, of course, was over. He was free to do the fall jobs which were stacked up ahead of him and which, so far, he had had to neglect. Usually by this late in November he had the house banked. It seemed pretty slack to him to get caught by the first snowstorm without the snug banking of rockweed and spruce brush packed around the foundations. But of course the weir had taken all his time. There were other fall jobs, too, and the really big work of the winter—cutting the year's supply of wood.

Leonard and Joe had expected to quit dragging when the cold weather shut in, but they found Morris had other ideas.

"I'm goin all winter, off'n on," he told Leonard laconically, when Leonard suggested that it was time to tie up. "No use quittin if you've got a boat steady enough to stand the weather. If you and Joe don't want to come with me, I'll hire somebody."

"Kind of a diehard, ain't you?" Leonard asked. "That drag ain't goin to be funny, you get it over on a day when ice is makin."

"Suit yourself," Morris shrugged. "Only, make up your mind."

"Far's I'm concerned, I need my time to work on the boat. Harry's countin on Joe, too."

"All right with me," said Morris.

"You sure you can get somebody to go with you?"

"Yes," said Morris, with a half-grin. "It's about time I learnt Sayl how to fish."

"Sayl? Thought he was goin to school this winter."

"Nuh," said Morris. "School ain't no place for him. He'll be crazy to go with me."

Morris was right. He put the proposition up to Sayl, offering him a third share, which was handsome for an inexperienced man, and Sayl was crazy to go. It meant the two things in the world he wanted most—no more school and money in his pocket.

Joe was furious. He actually stood up to Morris for once and might have carried his point had Sarah not suddenly come out against him.

"Morris's right, Joe," she said. "Sayl'll never be no good in school."

Joe stared at her. "He could be if he was a mind to try. He's goin back, like I've said."

"Hell, Joe," said Morris, "what you want him to be— a damn pen-pusher? *Sayl?* Have some sense. He wants to go to work and I'm offerin him a job. So shut your trap."

"I won't shut my trap. You ain't interested in Sayl any more'n you ever was, except right now you got a use for him. He'll do all right in school when he gets used to it. All he's got to do is put his mind on his books."

"Sayl ain't got no mind," said Morris. "So what he ought to do is learn to use his hands. Chrise, who are you to lay down the law around here? If you want somebody to go to school, why don't you go yourself? You sure could use a little education."

"I know that," said Joe. "If Sayl was give a chance, he'd learn."

"He's had one, and look what come of it," Sarah said patiently. "He only gets into hot water. The next time he'll do somethin worse and end up in the reform school. If he does, you'll be to blame for that, Joe. I'd rather he went to work. He wants to."

"All right," said Joe bitterly. "If that's the way *you* feel about it, I give up." He took his hat and slammed

[223]

out of the room, but after a moment he stuck his head in at the door. "I won't stand for you knockin him around, Morris," he said.

Morris laughed. "Okay. We'll take along a sugar-tit for him every day in the dinner bucket."

Sayl went jubilantly off to tell Haral, and Haral was struck dumb with envy. Then he said, "I figgered it wouldn't be so bad if both of us entered Bellport High together."

"Me, I'm goin to grow up dumb," said Sayl, stretching his big lean arms over his head as high as they would go. He stood an even six feet now, and he had passed his seventeenth birthday in November. "Can't you talk some sense into your folks, Haral?"

"No," said Haral glumly. "I don't even dare to bring it up again. They got it into their heads that I'm going to school, so I go. Don't matter what I think about it. Besides, I ain't got no job."

"Maybe Morris'd take you on, too," offered Sayl eagerly, "seein Leonard owns a third of the drag. I bet he would. Want me to ask him?"

But both Josie and Hardy vetoed that idea so definitely that Haral gave it up almost before he suggested it to them.

And so, after Christmas, when Haral entered the Bellport High School for the winter term, Sayl was not with him. Sayl was learning other things and learning them fast.

*

ON the first trip dragging with Morris, Sayl found out that his new job was going to be tough. Morris's method with him was the method of a bucko mate with a greenhorn sailor, and when he spoke, he expected Sayl to jump.

Sayl didn't know that he liked that much. He had planned to work hard, but he had also planned to work with Morris as an equal. To be spoken to in a voice that sounded like a door slamming was something he wasn't used to, and it made him mad.

He stood it well enough throughout the first day's dragging. There was too much work to do and too many things to learn for him to spend much time nursing a temper. For one thing, he found that the haddock drag and the machinery that operated it fascinated him. Anything about the boat's engine fascinated him. He followed Morris's crabbed snarling directions to the letter, and whenever he was permitted to run the boat, which was seldom, he showed quite a good deal of talent in handling and steering her. The first time they warped in the cable after a run and the drag broke water, showing a heavy haul of fish, Sayl let out a yip of pent-up excited glee.

"Grow up, will ya?" snapped Morris. "You ain't on the school ground now."

Sayl clamped his jaw shut. He made up his mind that after this, whatever they yarned up in the damn drag, he wouldn't let out a peep.

When night came and they lay to at anchor, to sleep until there was daylight enough the next morning to make another run, Sayl unrolled his quilts on the locker below with a feeling that he had certainly put in one hell of a satisfactory day. He was sliding off his rubber boots, getting ready to stretch out, when Morris came down and started to fix his own bed.

"Your watch first," he said. "You can call me at twelve o'clock."

[225]

"Watch?" said Sayl, his jaw hanging. He was dead tired and it seemed to him he'd go to sleep on his feet if he didn't lie down pretty soon.

"Ayeh. Watch." Morris got into his quilts and pulled them up around his shoulders. "Well, what's the matter? You don't run of an idea that everybody goes to sleep at once on a boat, do you?"

"I'm tired," said Sayl.

"So's everybody. What the hell of it?"

Sayl squared off. "Now, look, Morris, I'll work for ya, but you ain't goin to ride me."

"That so?"

"Yes, it's so."

Morris did not lift his head. "Look, Mama's baby," he said, "you takin your watch till twelve o'clock or do I get up and sock ya?"

"Sure, I'll take it," said Sayl, "but you don't have to be so damn mean about it, do you?"

"You go with me, you take what I dish out—take it or leave it," said Morris. "I can get another man to go with me, easy."

"All right," said Sayl. Oddly enough, that word "man" from Morris took the sting out of whatever else he had said. He started up the steps of the companionway.

"Dip up a bucket a salt water and soak your head if you can't stay awake. I've done that a good many times, myself," said Morris after him.

It was a still night, not too cold. A light breeze ruffled the water and blew salt and fresh against his hot dirty face. The boat rode easily to her anchor, swaying up and down in long low arcs of thirty feet or so, as the big ocean-going swells slid lazily under her. The stars were out, quiet and winter-clear, and on the coast line, ten or twelve miles away, a lighthouse winked steadily off and on.

As Sayl's temper quieted down, he began half to like what he was doing. This was a lonesome job, but gosh, there was something responsible in it that appealed to him. Morris couldn't think he was such a greenhorn, letting him stay on watch like this, with the handling of everything in his hands. After all, he began to see, somebody had to stay awake. You couldn't just go to sleep, out on the water this far from land. Anything might happen. At twelve o'clock he'd have his turn to go to bed. Darned if he didn't think the second watch might be harder on a fellow than the first one.

Sayl dropped a bucket overboard by its rope bail and hauled it up full of icy sea water. He proceeded to stick his face into it, holding it there until the cold ached in his forehead and the sticks went out of his eyes.

This was all right. He was going to like it in spite of Morris's being such a mean devil.

This kind of work is my meat, Sayl told himself. I've only got to stand Morris until I learn as much as he knows. But then, by gosh, he better look out.

❧

AFTER a second blizzard in early January, no more snow fell for a time, but the weather began to grow steadily colder, freezing what already lay on the ground into an icy crust. Each night the thermometer registered a little lower, each day it rose a little less high. Pale green salt-water ice thrust out from the edges of the Pool, crumbled at first by the rise and fall of the tides, then as the layers froze together, overflowed and thickened by them. Only Morris's boat and Leonard's were moored in the Pool now. The others were hauled up for the winter.

Mildred had been waked up in the very early morning, before daylight, by her nose being cold. She popped it down under the covers, pinching it between her thumb and forefinger, with a little thrill of excitement. The weather must have come off very cold in the night —way below zero, because it had been zero last week and she hadn't been waked up then. She could hear the wind blowing, too; whistling in the chimney the sad, shrill little noise that Grammy didn't like, because she said it made her feel lonesome.

Mildred hoped the cold was down to ten below, twenty even. It would be exciting and something to talk about, like a blizzard, and perhaps the breathing-hole on the John Pond would freeze over hard enough to skate on.

She giggled as she suddenly remembered how last year Haral had skated right into that breathing-hole and had gone into the water up to his neck. He had come scrabbling out of it and started to run for home without even taking his skates off. Humph, everybody thought Haral was so smart! *She* didn't.

Just as soon as the frosted square of the window got the least little bit whiter she was going to get up. She wasn't a bit sleepy. This was what happened when you went to bed before you needed to. It hadn't been nine o'clock last night when her father had begun snapping his old apple seeds. He would sit in his big chair in the corner, reading or maybe pretending to sleep, eating an apple now and then from the big dishful that always stood on the table in the wintertime, and when he thought it was time for her to go to bed, he would begin to snap apple seeds at her for a reminder. She did wish she could shoot an apple seed across the room the way he could, holding it between his teeth and snapping it somehow with his tongue, so that it would fly *zing!* against the wall or the windowpane. She had tried and tried, but she never could. The seed always fell a foot or so away from her teeth with a soft little *plup!*

Now the window not only was definitely lighter, but she could already make out some of the things in the room. The commode, with its white cover and its fat little legs, looked like Cack Comey squatting in the corner. Cack, Cack, with the pimples on her back. The mean old pig, she wished her father would hurry up and chop Cack's fence down. No matter how icy the hill got, you couldn't slide down it any more because that darn old barb-wire fence ran right across the bottom.

Mildred took a long breath, made a lunge out of the bed into the cold bedroom, scooped up her clothes from a chair in passing, and ran at top speed down the stairs and into the lamp-lighted warm kitchen.

She nearly upset Hardy, who was coming from the stove to the sink with a dipperful of warm water to wash in. The water slopped thoroughly, and Hardy said, "Blast and damn it!"

Grammy, eating her breakfast at the kitchen table, uttered a loud snort. "You're gitt'n too big a girl now, Mid, to be runnin round without no clothes on. You get dressed before Leonard comes down and ketches you in your decency."

"It was cold upstairs. I don't haf to get dressed in the cold, do I?"

"You don't haf to get up till your mother's around to tend to you. The only peace I git's in the early mornin, and I s'pose I won't even have that now." Grammy chewed vigorously on a tough piece of ham and swallowed it with a gulp.

Mildred opened the oven door and stood with her small rump close to it, feeling the warm air flow gratefully around her thin legs. "Pa, how cold is it? Pa, you looked at the thermometer yet?"

Hardy spoke through the towel. "Cold? It's cold enough to freeze the spout off a brass teakittle. It's fifteen below zero, that's what it is."

"My goodness, Hardy, you don't say so!" Josie hurried into the kitchen, buttoning the last top buttons of her dress. "It *can't* be that cold."

"That's what the thermometer says," said Hardy. "Fifteen below, and blowin a livin gale nor'west. I dunno but we better all go back to bed together and wait till it warms up."

"Br-r!" said Josie. "I feel's if I'd like to." She opened the drafts of the stove and stirred the fire vigorously.

"I fixed that fire once," said Gram pointedly. "And it's *all right*."

"I guess we better have a fire in the airtight today, Hardy," said Josie, "and warm up the other part of the house so's we can spread out a little."

"No need of it at all. It's a sinful waste of wood," said Gram, "unless the' ain't room for me in the kitchen."

"My goodness, Mid, you up?" said Josie. "What was you, cold?"

"My nose was. Ma, can I open the inside window and scrape the frost off the storm window so's we can see out?"

"No, you can't!" snapped Gram. "You'll have us all froze to death."

"But I *want* to see out."

[230]

"I'll do it," said Josie. "It won't let in much of a draft for just a minute, Mother. I'd kind a like to see out myself."

"It ain't even daylight yet," said Gram. "You can't see nothin. I dunno why you want to make everybody misable."

"You go over by the stove, Mother. You're all through breakfast."

"I ain't! I ain't had my doughnut."

Since Grammy was sitting by one west window, Josie could do nothing to clear that, but she managed, by wetting a dustcloth in hot water and rubbing, to get a good deal of the thick white frost off the other window-pane.

"My goodness!" she exclaimed. "Just look at that vapor, Hardy. I don't know's I ever see it flyin any higher."

"I know I ain't," said Hardy. "I never see it fly so high you couldn't see Canvasback. Wouldn't surprise me if it was colder'n fifteen below. That thermometer of ours is pretty old and shaky. Likely it froze and stuck."

Comey's Island in the bleak morning light had seldom looked so lonely or so forbidding. The old snow lay thinly, its crust frozen hard, with forlorn brown stubble blown stiffly flat against it by the wind. Even the spruce trees looked like thin and shrunken ghosts of themselves, their branches, normally green and lustrous in winter, whipped wildly and covered with white salt rime. For the "vapor" which Josie had spoken of—the sea smoke that rises from salt water on freezing mornings—was flying over the bay like a fog, and Comey's Island was all but lost in it.

The strong northwest wind whirled it high in the air

and blew it over the ice-covered Pool, the beaches, and the houses near the shore in ragged veils, ripped apart fleetingly to show startling green and white waves, their crests streaming ahead of them in curling lines of spray. Trees, houses, boats, even the lilac bushes were covered with white rime. Overhead, the sky was early-morning whitish blue, and against it the swirling masses of vapor were dark, like smoke.

"She's boilin her pot this mornin, all right," said Gram. "My God, it gives me the boundin shivers just to look at it." She had taken one glance out the window and then had pulled a chair up in front of the stove and planted her feet firmly in the oven.

"Someone's comin," announced Mildred from the window. "Know who it is? It's Jap Comey, tee-hee!"

"Who?" asked Hardy, unbelievingly.

But steps sounded on the porch and Jap came in, fighting the storm door shut behind him.

For an instant nobody said anything. Jap was either blushing, or his face was red from the cold—that is, what could be seen of it was red, for his sheepskin collar was buttoned up to his nose.

"Hardy," Jap said, "Eddy was down to the shore, and he says he seen a boat anchored off in the bay."

"Whoever's in it's froze to death," said Grammy.

"That's right," said Jap. He did not take his eyes off Hardy. "Eddy says he see it twice when the vapor blowed apart."

"Ayeh?" said Hardy. "He know what boat 't was?"

"Nobody from round here. That is, nobody Eddy knew."

"Well," Hardy said. He was already putting on his rubber boots, buttoning himself into warm sweaters and his sheepskin coat, covering all with a suit of oilskins.

He said nothing until he had buttoned the last button of his oiljacket. By that time he had his plan in his head.

"It ain't no use to try to get a powerboat started in this cold. We'd only fid around and lose time. We better take one a my big dories. Josie, call Leonard and get some hot coffee into him. Tell him to make time. Mid, you wrap up warm and go get Joe Comey. You goin along, Jap?"

"Ayeh," said Jap.

"Four's enough, then. Three pairs a oars and a bow man to knock ice. Hustle, Mid. Tell Joe to come runnin."

Hardy and Jap started down the hill at a half-run, both pausing at the bottom to straddle Jap's new fence. Hardy waited while Jap freed his bootstrap, which had caught on the barbed wire.

"I s'pose Eddy couldn't take marks on account of the vapor?" Hardy said.

"He figgered the boat was about half a mile off the Pool beach," answered Jap. "Near's he could tell, she's in a direct line with the no'th point a Canvasback."

"Then we can quarter the wind," said Hardy. "That's one good thing." It was the only one he could think of about this business. If the unknown boat had been drifting, he would not have taken a chance on reaching her. But the fact that she was anchored meant beyond a doubt that somebody was on board of her.

They rowed the big dory to the north end of the Pool and hauled her over the beach, all of them realizing the wisdom of Hardy's plan to row southwest in a northwest wind. They launched her in the comparative shelter of the point of land that made out from the west side of Comey's, but even here the wind picked up the water and sent it streaming up the shore in lines of freezing, stinging drops. Wherever the water struck, it froze—to beach rocks, to trees, to boots and clothes.

Leonard, sitting in the bow of the dory, holding a stout gaff, and with a short hatchet where he could lay his hand to it, realized that his job was cut out for him to keep the boat clear of ice. He looked behind him once at the shore fading out of sight in the icy bitter-tasting streams of vapor, and then ducked as the dory buried her bow in the first big ragged comber.

He was glad his father was along, taking charge, and he was glad there were four men weighting and trim-ming the dory, which seemed to be wanting to stand on both ends at once. He held on to the slippery gun-nel with one hand, peering ahead, trying to see through the shifting masses of vapor that first lightened, then closed quickly in, showing strips of green wind-ripped water, spotted here and there with heavy plunging cakes of ice. The gaff was not long enough to fend them off with, and Leonard put it down after a few moments and picked up the extra heavy ash oar, which was bet-ter, but which took both hands.

They pulled ahead for what seemed to be an endless time. Finally Hardy, sitting on the thwart next to Leon-ard, shouted something over his shoulder which ended in ". . . see anything?" and Leonard, blinking his eyes to clear them of salt, made out ahead of them the ice-piled shore of Canvasback Island.

"Canvasback!" he yelled at the top of his lungs, thumping his father's shoulder and motioning him to turn the boat around.

He saw by the movements of Hardy's jaw that Hardy was swearing, and he grinned a little, wishing he were close enough to hear, but he made out only, ". . . missed the bastard, by God."

They rested a little in the lee of Canvasback Island, then turned the dory around and pulled back to the south of the course they had come. There seemed not to be much difference to Leonard, except his clothes began to freeze on the other side.

Suddenly, ahead of him, the whipped clouds parted briefly and he saw plunging head to the wind the white side and bow of a small powerboat. She was low and logy in the water, rising and falling forlornly, as if she had had about all she could take. He noticed with surprise, as they pulled closer, that she was secured with a mooring chain, not an anchor rope.

"There!" he yelled. "Look! There she is!"

They laid the dory as close alongside as they dared, and Leonard stood up to look, steadying himself against his father's shoulder.

"Nobody aboard of her," he leaned down and shouted in his father's ear. "Unless he's up under the sprayhood."

"That's where he would be, you damn fool," Hardy yelled back. "Come on, back water there. Shove her in closer."

How Hardy managed the jockeying of the dory, Leonard did not see, for he was watching the leaping cheeserind of the stranger boat come closer and closer. He stood tense, ready to jump, as soon as he could grasp it with his hands. Then, suddenly, the dory poised alongside and he felt her loft away from under him as he jumped and made the icy platform of the other boat, ankle deep in slush and water.

Everything that could come loose aboard her was rattling and clanging, and for an instant Leonard's heart turned over with a flop as he saw a longish dark object, the size of a man's leg in a rubber boot, rolling lifelessly back and forth in the dim light under the canvas spray-

hood. Then he saw that it was only a length of stove-
pipe which had shaken loose from the small cabin stove
lying bottom up by the engine box. Another look con-
vinced him that there was nobody aboard the boat.

"What's there?" Hardy yelled. The dory was close
alongside again, and Leonard motioned his father to
come closer.

"Nothin!" he bellowed, poising for the jump back
into the dory.

"What?" yelled Hardy. "Who?"

Leonard let go and landed in a tumbled heap in the
bow, as the dory rose alongside. He felt the skin scrape
on the bridge of his nose as it met a sharp piece of ice.

"Jeezus!" he said furiously into his father's ear. "You
know what we've rescued? A goddam bastardly length
a stovepipe!"

Mildred and Josie, standing at the window now
scraped clear of frost, had watched the dory go out of
sight into the vapor. The sun had risen higher and its
vague warmth was thinning the thick streams a little, so
that twice they saw the dory as she stood away from
the island. They caught sight of her again, looking
small and forsaken against the wicked green and white
water, just as she headed out from under the lee of Can-
vasback. Then there was nothing more for a long time.
After a while Josie wiped away the clear crinkles of ice
beginning to form again on the windowpane.

Mildred pressed her nose close to the glass, not too
close, for then her breath frosted and she couldn't see.
She had given up pestering Josie to let her bundle up
and go down to the shore. Josie's no this time had meant
no.

She was thinking, What if they find a dead man

aboard that boat! Her mind occupied itself deliciously with gruesome pictures of the man, dead and horrid, being taken out of the boat into the dory.

"Ma," she said, nudging Josie's motionless thigh. "Ma, would he be *froze stiff?*"

"Sh-h!" said Josie.

Suddenly they saw the dory, tail to the wind, scudding around the end of the Head and into the lee of the Pool.

Josie sighed, as if she were tired. "Well, there they are," she said. "They're all right. I hope to God they ain't found nobody."

She turned away from the window, pushed the coffeepot forward on the stove, and opened the drafts so that the fire would burn up hot, before she went to the bedrooms to bring dry clothes to warm for Hardy and Leonard.

She watched the men come hurrying up from the shore, trying to make as good time as they could in their stiffened oilskins. They looked like ghosts, white from their hats to their knees with salt rime. Jap seemed to be doing better than the rest of them. He was fifty feet ahead, his legs fairly twinkling over the snow. He was closing his house door when Hardy and Leonard got to the fence.

Leonard straddled it and started on up the hill, but Hardy, not quite so agile, fetched up sharply against one of the sharp barbs on the taut wire. For a moment he fiddled with the stiff fabric of his oilpants, then, with an angry lunge, he ripped away, leaving a largish triangle of oilcloth hanging to the fence. He came into the kitchen fairly spitting fire and brimstone, and went on through it to the tinkle of flying ice scattered from his clothing, as he fetched his ax from the shed.

"Hardy, you're freezin! Get these dry clothes on." Josie stopped as the door slammed behind him. "Your father's gone crazy!" she gasped.

Leonard, peeling his frozen clothes off and laughing helplessly through chattering teeth, shook his head. From the hill-bottom they could hear the loud hollow thwacks as Hardy drove his ax into the frost-brittle fence posts. He cut down three of them, chopped off the wire between, and carried the wreckage across the field, where he dumped it over the pasture fence.

He came back to the house spluttering, trying to hold on to the wrath that had justified his exploding, but by the time he had changed his clothes and had had a cup of coffee, he was looking shamefaced.

The northwest gale took two days to blow itself out, and until it did, nothing could be done about salvaging the powerboat out in the bay. In the afternoon, when the vapor ceased flying so high, she could be seen from Comey's Island, low in the water and covered with ice; and incredibly, on the morning of the second day she was still there, stubbornly thrusting her small bow into the wind. On the slack tide, Morris and Joe and Sayl went out in Morris's boat, managed to worry her loose from her mooring chain, and with considerable difficulty towed her into the Pool.

She turned out to be the property of a man who lived in a coast village some twenty miles up the bay. He had moored her safely enough in a small cove, but in the night, heavy ice had frozen around her, and the ice had risen with the tide, so that the pull on her mooring-rock had lifted it off bottom. The ice had gone out of the cove with the ebb tide, carrying the boat with it, mooring and all. Out in the bay when the wind had broken up the ice, the mooring-rock had dropped down to bottom.

In a few days the boat's owner came to Comey's Island after her. He said he sure was glad to have that stovepipe back as he'd just bought it new, but the boat warn't worth much.

⟨⟩

AFTER the cold snap, a week of comparatively warm weather followed, and Hardy started cutting his firewood, wanting to get as much down and piled as he could before another snowstorm made the woods impassable. He had decided to cut the spar growth, this year, in a woodlot that for the past twenty years or so he had kept free of underbrush.

The trees were big spruces, sixty to eighty feet tall, with smooth trunks free of branches except for ten or fifteen feet at their tops. As far back as he could remember, these trees had been spar growth. Old 'Lonzo Turner had taken care of the woodlot too, and Hardy had no idea which of his great-grandfathers had cleared it.

He did not know why he had decided to cut the trees this year. He justified it by telling himself that some of them had begun to die back at the top. But on years before he had simply taken out the dying trees. Cutting the spar growth was something he had decided not to do each year since the fall old 'Lonzo had died.

Seedling spruces had come up around the edges of the stand, in a bushy hedge, head-high and a few feet thick. Hardy pushed his way through and stood for a moment, lighting his pipe and surveying the job ahead of him.

The seedlings would have to be cut down for twenty feet or so and piled for burning before he could do any work on the trees. The trees themselves looked good—strong wood, mature and ready for cutting. His eye followed into the middle of the grove the gray-black vertical boles, spaced irregularly but far enough apart to allow good growth. It was dark in there, with a wintry coldness. Gray stiff moss covered the hummocky ground, and in the hollows were pools, frozen to bottom, their surfaces covered with white brittle shell-ice. The big trunks thrust downward solidly, as if they gripped the ground.

Been there a long time, Hardy thought. Too bad to cut em. Some of them big ones is goin to be tough to manufacture. Methodically he started in on the seedlings, stacking them in a big pile in a cleared space. Might as well set em afire now, he thought, seein it may snow any day. Don't want to have to wait till spring.

The tinder-dry bunch of twigs he used for a torch caught and spread among the green branches with a fine crackling. He stood leaning on his ax helve, watching the clear flame shoot up and the gray, heavy rolling of the smoke.

He had had brush fires like this in the wintertime ever since he could remember, and so had his people, a long way back, ever since the island was settled. They had cut firewood and burned it up; and the next winter, all their lives, they had come back to cut some more. Every one of them had chopped around this grove, as if a stand of spar growth were something to look at with pride, something for a man to keep.

Keep? he thought suddenly. What for?

The man who cleared it, his grandfather's father, must have worked for weeks, rooting out running juniper and laurel, taking out a sapling here and there. so that the other trees would have a chance to grow.

The old sickening sense of futility crept over Hardy, made heavier by the sudden realization of all the work that had gone into clearing this grove and keeping it clean for so many years.

They put all that into it, he thought, and handed it on to me. And I don't even want it. And my boys, they don't scarcely know how to cut down a tree.

He turned his back on the fire and looked at the trees, trying to recover the lost gusto and hopefulness that in another time had made them mean something to a man. But they were only trees, soaring upward in secrecy and silence, and their solitude seemed to him only like an imprisonment.

That he, actually, yearned after what his father and grandfather had had, the peace of mind and security which had once been here on this island and were here no longer, did not occur to him.

It was the same island, unchanged except for the snug houses and the cleared fields, which in the seventeen-fifties had meant home and harbor to men sick of sailing everywhere—the island wrapped around by water, set off from the world by a curtain of peaceful sound, which was the sound of water hanging in the air. Existence had been sweetened and protected for them here, but a man now groped after that safety, sensing its loss and feeling more and more that, if it were not here, then it must be somewhere else.

It's this island, Hardy said to himself, gone to seed so's

a man ain't got any scope here any more. I've got to go somewheres and git my hands on somethin.

Money in the bank, he realized, with almost actual pain at his chest, only made worse the senselessness and monotony. Because money in the bank meant he could go—if only he could make up his mind.

PART FIVE

LEONARD and Joe went over to the Harbor every day, weather permitting, to help Harry Fenner with the work on the new boat. Leonard had figured out that if he and Joe put in their time and economized on fancy lumber, they could afford a first-class marine engine.

"That's what a hooker this size needs," he said to Joe. "Only thing wrong with Morris's boat, that automobile engine he's got don't develop enough horsepower to drive her."

And so, wherever they could, they chose less-expensive lumber—woods just as good, Harry Fenner said, if not so handsome.

Leonard was an expert hand with tools and Harry was glad to have him help. With Joe it was a different story. Set Joe to work on a piece of lumber with a sharp tool, and one of two things was bound to happen —either you bought a new piece of lumber or a new tool, to say nothing of the wear and tear on Joe. But where heavy lifting was concerned, or odd jobs, Joe shone; and Harry had plenty of these to keep him busy.

Joe watched the boat take shape, section by section, with something very like worship. In the stout wooden cradle, in Fenner's shop, the heavy oak keel was already in place, and new timbers went on every day. In spite of his awkwardness with the work itself, Joe had a pretty good idea of how things should be done, and he nearly drove Fenner crazy making sure every nail was in exactly the right place and every piece of joining was perfect.

"My God, Joe," Harry growled good-naturedly one day, "I thought Morris was fussy, but you're a reg'lar old puss-cat. I dunno what ails you Comey boys, anyhow. Why don't you go'n get a woman instid of wastin all this love'n kisses on powerboats?"

Joe blushed and grinned. "I couldn't handle a woman good's I can a powerboat," he said.

"Chrise!" said Harry. He ran his finger inside the cutting blade of his jack plane to clear it, and took off a long curled shaving from the piece of pine he was shaping. "I wisht that was true of me. I can sail a woman on an even keel, but I wouldn't have no more idea about handlin a powerboat than Jonah had about the whale."

The boat shop was a fine place to be, on the cold winter days, Joe thought, with a wood fire going in the big-bellied stove, and the sound of hammering and the smell of raw lumber, and the boat beginning to look like a boat instead of a lot of lumber cut to different lengths. He was beginning to forget his grinding disappointment at Sayl's not going back to school, and his worry over what being so much with Morris was going to do to the boy.

Sayl seemed to be getting along all right. He was a lot brasher and sarsier than he had been, but at the same time he seemed to be soberer, too. When Joe asked him, he said everything was okay, except Morris worked him too hard.

"He takes a hell of a lot of waitin on," said Sayl. "Fixes it so I get all the nasty jobs, too."

"You want to quit and try somethin else?" asked Joe.

"Nuh," said Sayl laconically. "I'll quit when the time comes."

So far, Morris had managed to dodge the worst weather, and he had made some highly profitable trips. Haddock in the winter sold for five times their summer price. The money Morris paid him looked good to Sayl. He had a new wrist-watch and a battery set radio, and he had quite a handsome sum salted away.

Joe couldn't see any actual reason why he should worry, but he did worry when he thought about it. However, he had the boat to absorb him during the days, and evenings he and Leonard spent together, poring over marine engine catalogs and talking endlessly about the points of the various makes. So far as almost everything was concerned, Joe was as happy as he had ever been in his life. The thing that should have worried him most, he thrust down into the back of his mind, because he did not dare to think too much about the day, steadily approaching, when Morris would discover the duplication of his boat.

⌒

BY the first of February, Fenner had the timbers in place and had finished the planking. As a professional boatbuilder, he had seen one or two slight flaws in Morris's original design, and he had persuaded Joe and Leonard to let him correct them, but the changes were not apparent in the lines of the boat. She was everything, and a little more, that Joe and Leonard had wanted.

So far, Morris had taken no interest in her whatever. He never mentioned her to Joe, never asked how the building was getting on, nor what kind of engine they planned to have. Joe, for reasons of his own, never mentioned the boat to Morris.

The other Comey's Island fishermen, however, were keenly interested. Scarcely a day went by but one or more of them dropped by at Harry's shop to watch the work and to discuss the boat's lines and her progress. It was only a question of time before her resemblance to Morris's model was noticed.

"Jeezus, Harry," said Perley Higgins one day, "that boat sure looks like Morris's."

"She does?" Harry straightened up from his nailing and shouted to Joe, who was inside the hull, tapping with a hammer on the timber to show Harry where to put the next nail. "Joe!" he bellowed. "Tunk in a place, can't ya? How'n hell can I tell anythin with you goin tunk here and tunk there and tunk, tunk, tunk?"

"Ayeh, she sure does," resumed Perley, to catch Harry's attention again. "She might be the same boat."

Harry cast an appreciative eye along the boat's stripped lines and back to her curiously flaring bow. "Well, Perley, now you mention it, I dunno b't she does." He looked soberly at Perley, and in spite of himself one eyelid flicked down in an almost imperceptible wink.

Perley's jaw dropped, and for a moment he stood paralyzed with excitement at his discovery. Then he burst into a loud guffaw and slapped his leg. "You must have a good mem'ry, Harry."

"Have to, in my business," said Harry. He bent to work with no expression whatever on his face.

Perley squatted excitedly beside him. "What'd you do, Harry, keep a model of her?" he asked confidentially.

Harry turned on him such a glare of rage that Perley recoiled. "What in the hoary old hell you talkin about?"

Perley got the point and said no more to Harry, but he left the boat shop grinning. Wherever he went for the rest of the day, talk flowed from him in a stream. Harry was not surprised when larger numbers of visitors than usual dropped into the shop. Most of them merely walked around the boat once or twice, looking her over with the keen and knowing eyes of men to whom the lines of an individual boat were as distinctive as the lines of an individual face. One or two said, "Well, by God!" All were jocular and, in an indirect way, congratulatory.

"What's your idea of that, Harry?" Leonard asked, when this had been going on for a while.

"Been expectin it, ain't you?" said Harry.

Leonard nodded. "Bound to come out, sooner or later," he said. "Well, who cares?"

Jake's bar and restaurant did a humming business that afternoon, as men dropped by to make sure that everybody knew the joke on Morris Comey. A good deal of guessing went on as to how Harry had duplicated the boat, but nobody went so far as to suspect Joe.

"Harry prob'ly kept a model and a set of specifications on the sly," Jake said. "It ain't like him to do that, though."

"That's right, it ain't," said Orin Hammond. "Harry's too upright. He's pretty smart, though. Might've done it out of his head. Or Leonard's pretty good, too. Maybe he had a hand in it."

"Leonard don't know blueprints well enough," said Perley.

"Well," said Orin, "ever since that night in the poolroom when Morris trimmed up Joe, I been hopin somebody'd put one over on him. How about havin a drink on me, boys? This ought to take some celebratin."

"I never thought it'd be old Harry, though," said Jake, setting out the drinks.

"Betcha that's who it was." Orin up-ended his glass and set it down on the bar with gusto. "They say Harry was born wropped up in a blueprint. Wonder if Morris is wise yet?"

"Sh-h," said somebody.

The door had opened quietly and Morris himself had come into the room. "What about blueprints?" he asked casually. "And do I know what yet?"

There was a delicate silence. Then Orin said jocularly, "Hello, Morris. How's the king of Comey's Island?"

Morris looked at him sourly. "You drunk?" he asked. People didn't usually speak to him in that tone of voice. But he had no way of knowing how much prestige he had lost this afternoon.

"Ayeh. Drunker'n a owl," Orin said cheerfully. "Gi'me another one, Jake. Give Morris one, too. The boys are all drinkin with me, Morris."

"Thanks," said Morris. He came and stood alongside Orin at the bar, his head and shoulders barely coming above the polished wood. "Make it Scotch, Jake."

"Ow," said Orin, wincing. "Gonna get your money's worth, ain't you? Or my money's worth."

"Always do," said Morris. "Glad to pay for it myself."

"Oh, no," Orin waved his hand expansively. "It's worth Scotch."

Morris disinterestedly sipped his drink. His eyes moved blandly from one to another of the men, not seeming to see anyone in particular. A less clever man than he would have sensed something expectant in the air, but he made no sign beyond a slight drooping of his lids.

"Nice boat Joe's buildin," Orin said boldly.

"Ayeh," said Morris.

"Hear him and Leonard's buyin a Gray engine."

"Might be."

"A big Gray sure will make that model step," said Orin. "You know, Morris, I wouldn't be surprised 'n she'd wipe yours, once she's sweet enough to be opened up."

"That so? I'll have another, Jake." Morris touched his lips to his second drink and set the glass down on the bar. "Kind of tight, ain't you, Orin? What you celebratin . . . Alice Lacy's weddin?"

"Who? Alice? She ain't married," said Orin slowly.

"That's what you think."

"Well, I ought to know. I'm the one she's engaged to," said Orin.

Morris smiled faintly. "Funny what these girls'll do, once they get up to the city, ain't it? I see an account in the Boston paper yesterday. She married a Portygee, think it was. Some kind of a foreign name."

Ordinarily, a gibe like that about Alice was the only thing in the world that would have made Orin mad. But he happened to have in his pocket a letter from her, written the day before, and taken out of this morning's mail. In it she had counted the number of days left before she would be coming home from Boston. Chrise, thought Orin, and we all been thinkin this guy was smart.

He beamed down on Morris for a moment. Then suddenly he reached behind him, caught him by the back of the pants and his coat collar, and lifted him until Morris's head was on a level with his own. "Morris," he said, "I sure do ache, seein you try to drink at a man-size bar. Ain't that more comfortable?"

"Why, yes," said Morris. "It is." He picked up his glass, finished his drink and put the glass back on the bar.

Orin, after a moment, set him back on his feet, a little uncomfortably.

Morris gave himself a twist in his clothes to settle them back around him and glanced coolly up at Orin. "Thanks, Orin. I always do appreciate a favor. Well, I'll be seein ya." He walked to the door, opened it, and went out without looking back.

"Jeezus!" said Jake. "You look out for him, Orin. First time in my life before I ever see a guy's eyes turn white."

Morris walked away from the bar and down the plank path to the landing. His boat was there, tied up to a wharf-piling, and rocking gently in the flood-tide bore which was beginning to set in the Harbor. He went aboard and down the companionway step into the cabin. The bright mahogany trim and the white painted lockers shone as polished and clean as engine waste and Sayl's elbow-grease could make them; and the tools and extra cans for gas were stowed neatly away. Everything was in its place.

Morris sat down rigidly on one of the lockers and leaned his elbows on his knees. His hands shook a little, and an occasional tremor passed over his body. He was still sitting there an hour later when Sayl came trotting down the wharf and swung jauntily aboard.

"Sayl!" demanded Morris.

"Ayeh?" Sayl's voice came startled into sharpness. "I didn't know you was back aboard, Morris. I cleaned up everything before I went upstreet."

"I don't feel good. You can take the boat home."

Sayl's big dirty tennis shoes appeared on the companionway steps. "You sick—?" he began.

"God damn it, get up there and start the engine. I said *take the boat home!*"

Sayl's feet vanished with split-second alacrity. The starter ground sharply, the engine turned over with its first low smooth throb, and the rope painter slapped against the deck with little splat sounds as Sayl coiled it expertly around the bow cleat. He slipped the gear into reverse without a jar, and the big boat backed cleanly away from the wharf.

There, by golly! Sayl said to himself, gritting his teeth. Let him find something wrong with that, the little know-it-all!

He expected Morris on deck at any minute, the soft voice at his elbow emphasizing with little sarcasms all the things he had done out of line. But there was no sound from the companionway.

Gee, he thought, Morris *must* be sick.

Sayl was finding out these days that he had been born for running a boat. His big body, his oversized hands and feet aboard this boat moved with sureness and precision, and did what he told them to do. He knew what he was doing now; he was good and he knew it. Each day Morris's domineering was getting harder to take.

When he had tied the boat up to the mooring in the Pool, and Morris had still not appeared from the cabin, Sayl peered down the companionway and saw him stretched out on the locker, apparently asleep.

"Hey," said Sayl, tentatively.

Morris got up without saying anything, and Sayl rowed him silently ashore. But when they landed and the punt grated on a sharp rock that Sayl had missed

seeing, Morris said softly that he guessed they'd have to be putting new sheathing on the bottom of the punt pretty soon, and stalked away up the beach.

⁂

THE alarm clock purring softly under his pillow wakened Morris at two o'clock. He flicked the mechanism off, swung his legs out of bed, and slipped silently and deftly into his clothes. Taking his flashlight from the bureau, he went without a sound down the stairs, avoiding the third creaky step, and climbed to the loft over the woodshed.

The air in the loft was dead and icy, the window frozen tightly shut. The accumulated frost of the winter, nearly an eighth of an inch thick on the panes, glowed palely and sparkled around the edges with the outside moonlight, throwing a whitish patch on the floorboards. The patch vanished as Morris's flashlight beam slid over it and reappeared again behind him as he bent to examine the molds of his boat piled in the corner.

He could not tell whether they had been moved. There was very little dust on and under them, but that meant nothing, since Morris was aware that his mother, for some reason, had not so long ago cleaned and swept the loft. He had wondered at the time why she had done it. Sarah wasn't noted for her neatness, especially in places that didn't show.

The beam of his flashlight, flicking here and there, fell on the boat model leaned against the wall in a corner. Morris picked it up, turning it over in his hands, holding the flashlight in his armpit.

In one place the wood, neatly joined with glue, had

[252]

spread a little, and in the crack was a whitish-gray substance, which Morris pried out carefully with his penknife. Holding it close to the light, turning it over and over in his fingers, Morris suddenly knew what it was. He had seen Sarah use stuff like this to mend cracks in the stove with, and some other metal things. Wood-ashes and blue clay mixed with salt made a plaster which could be put on and left to harden. He didn't doubt that mixed to a certain consistency it would make a perfectly serviceable modeling clay.

Silently he went back down the stairs and up through the house to his bed.

His mother followed him quietly up the stairs and saw him go into his room before she went back into her own. Ten minutes ago, when she had heard him go by her door and had got up to see what he was doing, she had known that the trouble she had waited for so long was about to begin.

Well, she thought, I can watch him. He ain't ever fooled me.

HARAL walked slowly along the street in the late February evening, headed for the lighted store windows and what excitement he could find, seeing he hadn't any money. He was bored and on edge, partly from sitting still in school all day, partly from lack of interest in the things he was having to learn. The lessons in the books never had seemed to make sense. He had studied them just enough to get by and make fairly decent grades. Deborah, his mother's remote cousin, whom he now boarded with, thought he didn't study enough, and she tried to keep him in off the streets on school nights, but

Haral generally managed to elude her. He didn't like her much. She was a flub-dub, and she was always minding his business, always jawing at him because he didn't spend all his evenings grinding at his books.

He had found out early in the term that the only course he would really want to take in the whole high school was manual training. Early in January he had looked in one day at the manual training shop, and after that had hung around there whenever he could, until the instructor had chased him out because the course was open only to second-year students.

They had a band saw and a jig saw and a power lathe, and a little electric jointer that was a honey. Haral's fingers itched to get hold of the machinery.

The stores along Bellport's Main Street were lighted for the Wednesday evening trade, and the windows were gay with things. He paused in front of the sporting goods store, his longing divided between an airplane-cloth windbreaker which could be worn either side out, and a pair of racing skates. There was a rifle in the window, too, that would make life considerably more worth living.

But darn, he thought, what's the use? He didn't have a cent of money in his pocket. He couldn't even buy an ice-cream soda or go to the movies.

I s'pose, he said to himself bitterly, that when the damn summer people come they'll buy up all them things they want, with their lousy money.

Everybody in the world, it seemed, had money but him; even Sayl. Sayl had been pretty overbearing the last weekend Haral had been home, about what he was learning on the boat, and about the dough he was making.

A hand fell heartily on Haral's shoulder and a raucous voice bellowed "Hello!" He turned gratefully to see Bud Atwood, in a soft hat and a sporty winter overcoat, standing beside him grinning.

"Well, gosh, hello, Bud!" he said. "I thought you was in Florida."

"I been there, all winter," said Bud. "But I got fired off the job, so I thought I'd hitchhike home and save dough. Got here early this afternoon. What's cookin?"

"Oh, nothin much. Same old town."

"How's about comin along with me and celebratin?"

"Gee, I'd like to. Only I'm broke."

"What the hell? I ain't. How's about the movies?"

"Gee, swell, Bud!"

"I sure had luck thumbin up Route 1," said Bud, as they walked along the street toward the gaily lighted marquee. "Found one guy in a Chrysler Imperial that took me all the way from the Tamiami Trail to Charleston, South Carolina. Boy, did we travel! He had a snootful most of the way, too."

Bud had adopted Trace Jones's nasal clipped way of talking, and he rolled off the out-of-state names with a practiced familiarity, as if all those places were old stuff to him.

Haral, his glumness gone like magic, strode along beside him, listening hungrily.

The show was a good one, and they sat through it twice. When they came out of the theater, the store lights were beginning to dim here and there, and the town was heading for home and sleep.

"Hell," said Bud, "it ain't twelve o'clock yet. I don't feel like goin to bed. You know anybody's got a car?"

"Gosh, no; nobody who'd take it out at this time of night."

"Jeese, what a town! Wonder why I came back."

"Most of the kids gone home. It's a school night."

"Well, le's go have a soda."

"Drug store's closed."

"Oh, for gosh sake! Well, might as well go home, I guess. Wish Trace was here with his Chevvy."

"Where is Trace?" asked Haral. "He still in Florida?"

Bud giggled. "Trace's in jail."

"He is!"

"Ayeh. He run foul of the Florida cops. Don't do to fool none with them ottos."

"What'd he do?"

"Oh, he had a blowout one night, and figgered he needed new front tires. So while the guy at the garage was patchin the blowout, Trace he helped himself to a couple from the rack. Jeese, the cops had him in two hours. I sure never figgered Trace was that dumb. I'd a handled it different. They'd never a caught me."

They had been walking up the steep street that led past the high school building to the residential section of Bellport. The square three-story brick building at the very top of the hill, which was the Bellport High School, was dark and deserted. The arc lamp on the corner shone obliquely across the tramped gravel yard, empty except for its two thick pine trees, and the bare group of the soldiers' and sailors' monument topped by the stiff solitary figure of a man in a granite uniform. On either side of the pedestal bronze Spanish War cannon pointed vaguely toward the four corners of the sky, and a neat pyramid of cannonballs was set symmetrically in front to complete the warlike memory.

"Damned old prison," said Bud, indicating the building. "I went there two years before they kicked me out."

"What they kick you out for?" asked Haral.

"Sarse," said Bud succinctly. "Le's sneak in there and see if there ain't somethin we can do to help out teacher."

He slid noiselessly along the tree-shadows in the yard and tried one of the basement windows.

"Hey!" said Haral in a frantic whisper. "Hey, Bud!"

"Ssh!" said Bud. "Hell, they're all locked. Might bust one, but it'd make noise." He left the windows and, still in the shadow, moved across to the monument. "That feller up there looks lonesome. Le's you'n me climb up and say hi to him."

"Some of the kids tried," whispered Haral. "It's too slippery."

"Betcha ten cents I could," said Bud. But he made no effort to try. Instead, he sat down on the base of the pedestal and stretched his legs.

"Well, I been all over the South," he said. "Here I am, back where I started from. Thought it might be different, but it ain't. Think I'll join the navy next."

"Hadn't we better start along home?" queried Haral nervously.

"Ayeh. Maybe so. Hey, you ever notice them cannonballs couldn't possibly fit in them cannons?"

"Ayeh. Be way too big, wouldn't they?"

"Ain't that foolishness?" said Bud. "Just like this damn town. Never even bothered to make their cannonballs fit their cannons. Jeese, I'd like to fire one off. Bet that would wake up the town. Wonder what them cannonballs weigh?"

"Oh, tons," said Haral.

"Betcha I could lift one."

"Betcha couldn't."

Bud went over to the pyramid, bent down, and

heaved. To his obvious annoyance he could not budge the cannonball. Grunting, he heaved again and succeeded in moving it a possible inch. "Hey, Haral, come 'n help me," he panted.

"What you goin to do with it?"

"Oh, just see what she weighs."

With their combined strength, they managed to lift the bulky object out of its place and set it down on the ground.

"Le's try another one," whispered Bud. "Come on, le's roll em all over the school yard and leave em."

Haral giggled. The plan appealed to him.

The second ball slipped when it was about a foot from the ground, and fell, clanking loudly against the first one and starting it rolling. It moved slowly at first down the slight incline of the graveled yard toward the street.

"We better stop it," breathed Haral.

"It won't jump the gutter."

Bud was wrong. It bumped a few yards along the gutter, found a low place and rolled out into the tarred street. For a moment it wee-wawed lazily toward the banked center of the tar before the slope caught it. Smoothly at first, then bouncing as it gathered momentum, the cannonball shot down the middle of the steep street with hideous clankings and disappeared in the general direction of Main Street.

Bud and Haral listened, petrified, as it fetched up against something, with a prolonged, soul-rending crash and a shattering of glass.

"Run!" said Bud.

They ducked into the shadow of a building across the way, ran along on the inside of a hedge and came out in a quiet street two blocks from the high school.

"Now dust for home," panted Bud. "If anyone asks ya, you never laid eyes on me after the movies was out, and I'll say the same about you."

Haral crept up the shadowy concrete walk of Deborah's house, and let himself in at the back entry door. Nobody heard him. His cousin was snoring loudly in her bedroom.

He took off his sweaty clothes and slipped into bed, where he lay giggling silently and stuffing the pillow into his mouth to keep from making a sound.

Deborah was talking about the desecration of the soldiers' and sailors' monument when he went down to breakfast the next morning, and Haral listened to her with wide, shocked eyes. On the way to school he saw a little knot of people gathered around the front of the fish market, from which the underpinning and the big plate glass window had been thoroughly smashed. Everybody in Bellport discussed the matter indignantly for some days, and the outrage was finally laid at the door of the CCC camp. But no one ever really knew who had committed it.

IN early March Hardy drearily set about his preparations for rebuilding the weir. So far the winter storms had been fewer than usual, but what the gales had left, the drifting ice had taken, and he faced the job of putting in new piles and brush and seine poles on almost the entire structure. By the time the ice in the coves and inlets up the bay had broken up and gone down across Comey's Island channel, Hardy knew that there would be very little left of his weir. A big gap was already

[259]

gone out of the north wing, too, and ice and tide had shifted a good many of the big stones that had anchored it.

To be ready for the actual rebuilding, in April, he ought to start at once to cut weir brush and seine poles and ferry them across the bay from Canvasback Island. But to do that he would need to hire labor—the first big inroad on the money he had put away last fall.

It seemed to him he could not bear to put that money back into the weir. Three thousand dollars was all he had to show for eighteen years of hard work and worry, and he had no sanguine hopefulness that the weir would fish again this season as it had last. By a fluke last fall he had come out on top. He had been disappointed too often to think it would happen again. So he puttered around, prolonging as much as possible the time before the evil day when he actually started the work.

The weather for once helped his designs, for after the first week of mild weather, March turned into a month of cold gales and rain. Hardy did what work he could around the house, but his movements were listless, and Josie worried at his seeming inability to keep at one job for very long before he quit on it. She dosed him with the usual home remedies for spring fever, but none of them seemed to do him any good. He ate all right, she was sure of that.

Something tough and indomitable in Josie's own make-up was affronted at the way Hardy was able to put away a big hearty meal and yet did not seem to have energy enough to do a light, simple job, like cleaning out the hen house, or carting the winter's leaves and debris out of the yard. He had always been such a worker, and she couldn't understand it.

Looking from the window, she would see him standing, his shovel in his hand, or sitting on the wheelbarrow, staring at the toes of his rubber boots.

Her worry over him made her scold him, but she found that criticism only seemed to make matters worse. He merely looked disconsolate and uneasy, and at last took to going away from the house in the early morning, spending the day with Leonard and Joe. He would go with them to the Harbor and help around the boat shop, if Fenner had anything for him to do; or failing that, he would sit in Jake's or Willard Hemple's store, passing the time of day with the men who were always there. And for a little while, when he came back from these trips, the spring would be back in his walk and the lift in his shoulders, and his voice would be animated as he told Josie the news from town.

TOWARD the beginning of April, when the ice had broken away from the shore at the Harbor, Leonard and Joe launched their boat and got her ready to bring home. It was the general consensus that she was one of the best boats—if not the best—that Harry Fenner had ever built. And she looked it the morning they tried her out, feathering jauntily around the Harbor in her finery of white-painted hull and yellow decking.

Joe took her three times around the Harbor, and then with obvious reluctance turned her over to Leonard. She felt light, and she rolled a good deal when they got into the chop outside the lee of the shore, but that was all right. She needed to watersoak some, and it would take a little time to get her ballast just right.

Leonard grinned blissfully at Joe and Joe grinned back. "All right, huh?"

Joe nodded. "Like to open her up, wouldn't you?"

"What say we do—just for a minute?"

Joe looked horrified. "My God, no, Len! Big engine like this'd heat up in no time. We'll wait till she's limbered up good."

"Okay." Leonard knew Joe was perfectly right, but he was a little disgruntled. He hoped Joe wasn't going to turn out the old maid about his boat that Morris was.

He shot the boat neatly up to the Harbor landing and jumped out on the float with a bow line. "Come on, Joe. I could use some coffee. Let's go up to Jake's."

Joe did not answer at once. He was shading his eyes with his hand to peer at a rowboat loaded with men, which was just putting out from one of the boats in the harbor and was headed ashore. "Who's them?" he asked. "Look like strangers."

"Who? Oh, I dunno. Dressed up like drummers, whoever they are."

Joe followed him up the wharf. "I thought the one in the stern looked like Ben Allen," he said.

"That so?" Leonard stopped, interested at once. Ben Allen was the coroner from Bellport. "Does look like him, at that," he said. "Wonder what he's doin down here. Jake'll know if anything's happened."

Jake's bar was deserted except for Jake himself, who greeted them with round, sobered eyes. "Jeezus, ain't that an awful thing?" he said.

"What?" asked Leonard. "We just got in."

"Ain't you heard about Orin?"

"Orin Hammond? No. He hurt?"

"He's dead."

"No!"

Jake nodded his head three times impressively. "Drownded."

"We thought we see Ben Allen. What happened?"

"They got Ben down this mornin. Orin went out yesterday to set a halibut trawl, and never come in, so last night his mother she got some of the boys to go look for him. They found his boat late last night, but they never found him till this mornin. Damnedest thing I ever heard of. Honest, as good a hand as Orin was at halibutin, it don't seem possible a thing like that could happen to him." Jake stopped for want of breath, and visibly shaken.

"You ain't told us what did happen, for God's sake, Jake!" Leonard reminded him.

"Well, they picked up his trawl buoy and hauled the trawl, and Orin was on it, that's all. Got a halibut hook slap through the middle of his hand. And on the other end of the trawl the' was a thunderin great halibut."

"That ain't possible," Joe said slowly. "Any fool'd know enough to keep a knife handy. God, a million men's got hooked on a trawl. Orin has himself, a lot a times."

"Why, sure," said Leonard. "Orin kept a knife in a leather slot right on his cheeserind, where he could lay his hand to it. I've seen it. He had his initials carved on it—done it one time when we was out together on Clay Bank, waitin to underrun a trawl. He showed me how good he done the O."

"Ayeh," said Jake. "Them that found him said the knife warn't there."

"Jeezus!" said Leonard. The full impact of the tragedy hit him, and he felt the cold crawl from the back of his collar down his spine. That had been a horrible death for a man to die. More horrible now, though, for the people who cared about Orin. Leonard's chest contracted as he thought of Alice. Did she know about it yet, he wondered. He wished, suddenly, that he could have been the one to tell her—maybe he could have eased things for her a little, not let her open up a telegram and find news like that in it.

"Might have got knocked out of his hand and fell overboard," Jake said, with a sidelong glance at Joe. "I can understand Orin's bein careless with his knife. He had his trawl rigged with them knots, you know, that come ondone easy, so when he started to yarn in a big fish he could clip off the hooks fast without spoilin his snoods. A lot of the boys does that. Prob'ly you do yourself."

Leonard nodded. "But I keep a knife handy, just the same."

"It's a good idea to," agreed Jake. "Them that looked over that trawl, though, said Orin sure had a funny rig on it. They said some of the knots was them slip-knots, but some wasn't. About every sixth gangion was tied on to stay."

"Orin wouldn't of had no rig like that," said Joe slowly.

"That's what the boys figgered. No trawler would. Or if he did, *and knowed it,* he'd sure as hell have a good knife handy."

"I'll be goddammed!" said Joe. He was leaning against the bar, and he looked greenish under the eyes.

"Ben Allen's got the sheriff with him," said Jake. "The way it looks, Orin was yarnin in that fish and strippin off hooks, and he come to one hook that didn't untie the way he thought it was goin to, and while he was foolin with it, the halibut started to run. Damn big thing it was, too—weighed nigh two hundred pounds."

Jake stopped. "You boys better have a drink," he went on, after a moment. "I swear, if I didn't have to tend to business, I'd get plastered, honest to God."

"No, thanks, Jake."

"No. Thanks just the same."

Ben Allen and the party of men with him came along the wharf and up the steps into the bar.

"Hello, Ben," said Jake, in a hushed voice. "You gentlemen want drinks?"

"Coffee, Jake."

"Okay."

Jake drew the coffee from the big urn and began setting out the steaming cups on the bar. The questions he was bursting to ask seemed somehow inquisitive and irreverent, no matter what words he could think of, and Ben, big and swarthy in his worsted suit, would have been impressive even without the gruesome connotation of his office.

"You all through, Ben?" Jake finally asked.

"Ayeh."

"Awful thing, warn't it?"

"Awful is right," boomed Ben. "Awful is right, Jake. Nothin to prove it warn't an accident, though."

"That so?"

"Ayeh. It's one of them things that looks so screwy you wouldn't think it could happen all by itself, but it does."

"That your idea of it, Mr. Warren?" Leonard asked the sheriff. The sheriff was that same Charley Warren from whom Hardy had bought the weir so many years ago.

The sheriff nodded. "I dunno what that boy was doin,

riggin a trawl like that, but it looks like he must a had his reason."

"Don't look like nobody'd fooled with it?" asked Jake casually.

"Godsake, nobody'd fool with a man's trawl! Less'n it was some kid's trick to play a joke on him. Even kids has got more brains'n that."

"Seems as though," agreed Jake. "I was thinkin, though, that'd be an awful smart way to get rid of a man, if you had a grudge against him."

Warren eyed him sternly. "That's awful loose talk, Jake, unless you got somethin to go on."

"Oh, I ain't!" said Jake hastily. "I was just speculatin."

"You better speculate to yourself, then. Well, Ben, what 'd ya say? We got a long ride ahead of us. Say," he said, suddenly noticing Leonard, "ain't you Hardy Turner's boy?"

"Ayeh, I am."

"Well, Godsake, how's your father? I ain't seen him in years. Hear he's done awful well out a that headache I stuck him with."

"Done pretty well this year," said Leonard, grinning.

"Well, say, you tell him if he's got one good year out a that thing in twenty-five, to sell out of it. That damn weir only fishes one season in a man's lifetime. Well, I sure would like to see Hardy. Fifteen years I ain't laid eyes on him, and I still figger he's the best friend I ever had. They don't cut em off the same piece of cloth, nowdays. Well, so long. So long, Jake; and button that lip a yours. You'll step on it someday."

"You go to hell, Charley," said Jake succinctly.

After everyone had gone, Jake stood motionless in the deserted bar, staring at the bright nickel of the soda fountain.

[266]

Well, by God, he said softly, to nobody but himself, I sure *did* see his eyes turn white.

❧

ALICE found the notice of the telegram stuck under the door of her room when she got home from work at six-thirty. She stood turning it over and over in her fingers with a little clutch of apprehension at her throat. Nobody would be sending her a telegram except the people at home, and then only in a case of life or death.

Something must have happened to Pa, she thought, as she went down the hall to the telephone coin-box. I wonder if it could be.

The impersonal voice of the Western Union operator said, "I'm sorry I cannot give you this telegram over the telephone. We'll send it at once by messenger."

"Oh," said Alice. Her own voice sounded flat. "That means it's bad news, doesn't it?"

"We'll send it by messenger," said the operator.

"It'll be worse to wait till your messenger gets here," said Alice firmly. "I'd like you to read it, please."

The operator hesitated. "Is there somebody in the room with you?"

Alice darted a glance behind her at the empty boardinghouse hall and its double row of closed doors. "Oh," she said with a nervous laugh, "the room's full of people."

It was from home, she thought, hearing the operator read the date and address.

ORIN KILLED STOP THINK YOU OUGHT TO KNOW
JENNIE B. HAMMOND.

[267]

Jennie Hammond was Orin's mother.

"Thank you," said Alice. She hung up the receiver, went back to her room, and closed the door.

I'll have to go home, she thought. That's the least I can do.

Poor Orin. She could see him now, his head thrown back, his face crinkled, laughing at some joke of hers.

Her letter to him was still on the bureau. She was glad now that she had forgotten to mail it. She had written it a few nights before, explaining to him why she had to break their engagement. Well, now he didn't have to know.

Alice held the letter in her hand, staring at the name in her own plain writing. *Mr. Orin Hammond.* It suddenly seemed mysterious and a little frightening.

She sat down on the edge of the bed, her fingers slowly beginning to tear the thin drugstore envelope into strips. It had been a foolish letter, almost light-hearted, kidding Orin here and there while she told him she guessed she couldn't marry him. Writing it, she had convinced herself that it was the kind of letter he would understand. He was easy-going, he'd forget her soon.

Tears welled in her eyes and brimmed over on her cheeks. What right had she to think he wouldn't have minded much? How could she know? She hadn't, more than once or twice in her life, ever stopped to think how someone else might be feeling.

Her father, a mean old man, but growing feeble and needing care, left to shift for himself. Leonard, with the discouraged droop in his shoulders, striding forlornly away from her down the road. Orin, grinning, his deep voice shaking a little . . . "I'll make enough trawlin this winter for the trip up and to buy ya a ring."

In the watery mirror over her bureau she caught sight

of her face, thin and strained from the long winter of hard work indoors, the tears runneling down in two pale lines through the grime left from the packing room.

What kind of a thing am I? Does a man have to be killed to make me realize what a cheap little lightweight I am?

She hadn't loved Orin. She couldn't have helped that. But she could have helped lying to him and letting him think she did. Now, against the bleak and irrevocable fact of his death, she saw herself for the first time, quite clearly . . . the self which, all her life, had driven blind through bewilderment and insecurity toward an impossible goal.

She got up, scattering the bits of paper in her lap, and went to the window. In the brown, thick dusk, the street lamps had come on, each cold cone of light cutting a hard, intent circle on puddled slush and wet cobblestones. Taxicabs plunged by, spattering muck, headed for the roar of traffic on Massachusetts Avenue. The lighted windows of the boardinghouses opposite seemed more blank and impersonal than if they had been closed by shutters.

The city moved in the darkness with a great sound and bustle, but not even Comey's Island, shut away by water in secrecy and silence, could be more separate or more lonely.

She was very tired, she realized suddenly. She had her washing up to do, and packing, and, not so very much later on, a train to catch.

LEONARD saw Alice at Orin's funeral, sitting up in the front of the church with the mourners. Her manner seemed composed and quiet beside old Mrs. Hammond's frantic grief and the stricken bewildered crying of Orin's young brother, Jack. Alice's neat dark blue suit and her little hat with white lace on it looked strange beside Mrs. Hammond's rusty black winter coat, its fur collar coming off in tufts, and her shabby old black-felt hat.

Funny, thought Leonard. You'd think it'd be just the other way around.

Then he was disgusted at himself. What in heaven's name did he expect the girl to wear? The clothes she had on were probably the most suitable things she had. She couldn't have been expected, on such short notice, to buy a whole new outfit of mourning. He was blaming her, he realized, because she looked nicer than any of Orin's relatives; nicer, as a matter of fact, than anyone else in the church.

I guess I wanted to see her lookin as if she hadn't made a go of it, he told himself soberly. She doped out a long time ago that that's the way my mind works, and it's why she wouldn't marry me. I don't know as I blame her.

He tried not to look at Alice, but he saw her even when he turned his eyes away. It seemed unfeeling, almost indecent, to sit here at Orin's funeral and to know that in spite of trying to forget her all winter, he still felt about her the way he had before she had gone away. There it was, he couldn't help it.

She passed by him, quite close, as the doleful little procession left the church. Her glance brushed over his, then returned reluctantly, and he saw that she had been crying.

He thought that he must find a chance to speak to her,

tell her he was sorry for what had happened, but after the service at the cemetery, he found she had gone home.

⁓

THE men who lounged in and out of Jake's in their spare time were inclined to resent his big new slot-machine. They were used to the old one, a primitive cash-register-like affair, whose habits they were able to foretell, through long practice, with a certain amount of accuracy. The law, however, had caught up with Jake in the matter of the old machine, and he had had to promise faithfully to get rid of it, which he had done. He didn't know, though, as they had said anything about not getting another one.

"What's that thing?" old Jarv Willow asked, the day the new machine was set up.

"What's it look like?" Jake countered brusquely. He himself considered it more of a work of art than his juke-box, a masterpiece of colored lights and bright plastic.

"Ain't got no outboard motor on it," said Jarv, poking it with his finger.

"Feed her a couple of them nickels you're hoardin up and maybe she'll spill you one," Jake snapped.

But he was relieved to see that after the first week or so of wisecracks about the ornateness of the machine, there was generally a crowd around it, and it made money.

Sayl Comey was one of its most devoted customers, as he had been of the old one. He sometimes had pretty good luck with the old one, but this new machine certainly wasn't paying off much today. He had put in

[271]

better than five dollars in nickels and had got back about sixty cents so far.

He dropped in another, flipped the lever, and stood back as the mechanism purred into action. The dials spun and settled into place with three separate clicks, revealing two lemons and a bunch of cherries pictured on their faces. The machine gave one last click and a sigh of finality. Nothing happened.

"Hell!" said Sayl. He felt in his pants pockets for more nickels, and finding none, came up with a five-dollar bill.

"Gi'me another dollar's worth, Jake," he said, tossing it across the counter.

"You'll have me skun out a nickels," grumbled Jake, making the change for him.

"Money in your pocket, ain't it?" said Sayl. "You should worry about it."

Three or four half-grown kids moved awedly out of his way as he came back to the machine. "You goin to keep on till you make 'er puke, Sayl?" one of them piped.

Sayl did not deign to reply, but Jake, leaning over the counter, watching, said, "She ain't goin to puke for a long time yet. She don't feel like it. Don't make no difference how many nickels you put in."

Sayl grunted. "'S what you think," he said ungraciously.

Jake's eyes snapped. If that Comey kid got much bigger for his pants, he was sure goin to bust out of em, he thought. I'd sure like to take a crack at him. Used to be a pretty nice kid, too. Goin draggin with Morris ain't done him a mite a good.

He was contemplating a sarcastic retort to Sayl when Morris himself came in and lounged over to the counter.

"Hi, Jake."

"What'll you have?" asked Jake sourly.

Morris looked over the food displayed in glass crocks and cellophane wrappers. His expression was hardly calculated to please, and Jake's face went carefully blank.

"Coffee, if it's fresh," said Morris.

Behind him the slot-machine gulped and sent a tinny spattering of nickels down into the cup. Morris turned. "How many?" he wanted to know of Sayl.

"Gawd, only three." Sayl was disgusted. "This machine's fixed. I already put in six bucks eighty."

"Six-eighty?" Morris looked interested. He went over and stood by Sayl for a moment, watching as the next two nickels went in with no results.

"Shove over," he said, giving Sayl a slight push. "Le'me try now."

Sayl looked down at him. His body, except for an almost imperceptible tensing of its big muscles, did not move an inch. "I ain't through yet," he stated.

"No?" said Morris, staring back at him. He pulled a couple of nickels from his pocket and stood tossing them idly from one hand to the other.

"It ain't likely I am, when I've put in that much. She's about ready to give down." Sayl dropped in his own coin and depressed the lever.

The machine spun and sighed to a stop and they heard the nickel drop down inside with a futile clink.

Morris grinned. "You just ain't lucky," he said, "—it would seem."

Joe would have been flustered, but Sayl didn't turn a hair. "Stick around," he offered casually.

"I will," said Morris. His hand holding a nickel flicked out toward the slot, but Sayl had been watching for it. His big paw, with less distance to travel, got there first,

[273]

and Morris's coin fell and rolled away across the floor.

Jake, watching, suddenly found that he was sweating. Jeezus, he thought, that kid don't know what he's stirrin up. "Your coffee's ready, Morris," he said aloud.

"You drink it," Morris observed over his shoulder. Then, suddenly, he laughed, and shrugged his shoulders. "Kid's gettin tough since he started hangin round with me," he said. He came over to the counter and picked up the coffee.

"Seems as though," said Jake. He turned his back and began, unnecessarily, to arrange the packets of cookies on the shelf behind him. Even so, he felt Morris's eyes centered ironically somewhere about the region of his shoulder blades.

"What's the matter with you, Jake?" Morris asked. "You look like somebody'd spit on your grave. Or maybe you been drinkin some a your own coffee. Pu!" He set the cup down and headed for the door. "When you git all your dough wasted, Sayl, you might dig up that nickel I dropped. It's a lucky one." He went lightly out the door and down the steps.

All in all, Sayl got back sixteen nickels before his money was gone. When he had left the store, swearing with disgust, Jake raked the lost nickel out from under the counter with the broom, and somewhat shamefacedly dropped it into the machine.

Gawd, he said to himself, when nothing happened, somebody ought to murder that little bastid.

⌣⌣⌣

HARDY TURNER sat on an upturned empty crate in Willard Hemple's store, watching the customers come and go, and the stream of business that went over Willard's counter. It was getting on toward late afternoon and the sardine-factory workers, on the way home, were stopping in to buy supplies for supper. He liked to sit here, feeling in the swim of things, while the smooth functioning of Willard's well-run grocery went on around him.

Willard handled a variety of things, including groceries, and he kept his shelves as neat as a pin. Everything was marked with its price, everything was stacked in its place, and young Jeddy Haslam, Willard's clerk, seemed to know where each article was without having to hunt. The big electric meat refrigerator in the corner shone with porcelain and nickel kept polished bright, and its humming went on as a peaceful undertone to the bustle of people coming in and out.

Hardy envied Willard his store. He tried not to think of his own, kept locked until a customer came in, its clientele limited to eight families, most of whom traded here with Willard anyway.

He had known Willard a long time—they had, as a matter of fact, gone to business school together. The difference was, Hardy reflected, he himself had gone off to sea and wasted his time, while Willard had buckled down and made something of the store he inherited from his father.

There was another difference between them, Hardy thought, looking over at Willard, bluff, jovial, and red-faced, waiting on customers behind his counter. His hair was as bright a carrot-color as it had been when he was twenty. Willard didn't look anywhere near his fifty years.

"Well, Hardy," Hemple said, looking over at him during a lull, "you still thinkin it over?"

Hardy grinned, almost sheepishly. "Always will be, I guess."

For years they had had the joke between them that someday Hardy would buy out Willard's store. Showing Hardy the good points of the store on the pretense of urging him to buy it, had been one way for Willard to brag a little over what he had accomplished with it. But up until this year, both of them had been well aware that Hardy hadn't the capital to do it.

Since last fall, when the gossip had gone around about Hardy's making so much money out of his weir, Hemple's urging had seemed more than half serious. Hardy wondered sometimes what Willard would do if he made him an honest-to-God offer.

Willard was disposed tonight to show off his meat refrigerator. "Come on inside of it," he invited. "Jeddie, you make do without me while I show Hardy how the cooler works."

They went inside, and Hemple latched the door behind him. "Can't waste my current," he said. "Now, look, ain't this neat? Cost me twelve hundred, installed, and it's paid for itself twice awready."

Hardy looked around at the neat rows of clean pink beef and lamb, the sausages hanging from hooks, the rolls of bologna and pressed ham. This was the way he'd keep things himself if he had this outfit. Cold and clean.

"Honest, Hardy," said Willard, "you'll never have a better chance to buy me out. I got a chance this year to rebuild my garage, and if I could sell, darned if I wouldn't go into that for a livin'."

"Damned if I don't think you mean it," said Hardy, "after all these years."

"Sure, I mean it. You got the money now, ain't you? You didn't have before."

"Depends on what you want for it."

"Sixty-five hundred dollars."

"Too much."

"Now . . . wa-ait a minute. That includes house, all furnished, sixteen acres of good wood-lot, and this store, lock, stock and barrel."

"The store just as it is, goods and all?"

"Ayeh. And this meat refrigerator, cost twelve hundred dollars. The day I sign the deed and you pay me, you can walk in here and start sellin goods."

"I ain't got that much money, Willard," said Hardy.

"Don't gi'me that. We all know you done good last year."

"Not that good."

"I'll take twenty-eight hundred cash and the rest notes."

"You will?"

"Sure. Five hundred dollars a year and the interest. The business is good for it. I'll show you the books."

"I'll have to think it over, Willard."

"You do. We'll do business tomorrow if you say the word."

Josie wondered that night what had happened to make Hardy seem so much like his old self. He was almost gay at the supper table, and he even answered Grammy back with a good deal of spirit when she took it on herself to criticize the way he was letting things go to rack and ruin. But the next morning he seemed aimless again, standing by the kitchen stove for a long time, looking into space, not saying anything.

"I thought last night maybe you'd got your mind made up to build the weir again," she said at last.

"Well, no," he said, "I dunno's I had."

[277]

"What will you do, Hardy, then? We can't live forever on three thousand dollars."

"No." He began pulling on his work gloves, fumbling his fingers into their loose folds. "I dunno. I was tryin to think." He seemed about to go on, then stopped. After a moment, he went out to the shed, and she heard him pulling over the tools as he hunted out an iron bar to pry the braces off the banking boards.

THE day Joe and Leonard took the new boat home for good was bright and blue, with a snapping April wind coming in from the west. She was ballasted right, now, and she rode lightfootedly, her lean cutwater and her big flaring bow sliding sweetly through the smart cross-chop in the bay.

Joe, at the wheel, kept the engine maternally at half-speed.

Leonard was getting annoyed with Joe. They had had the boat out a lot, and it seemed to him there was no reason now why they couldn't open her up—at least for a few minutes and find out what her top speed was. Leonard was crazy to know what she'd do, but Joe stubbornly stuck to his guns.

"You'll raise hell with a new engine like this if you get her hot before she's limbered up. We got to break her in easy."

"Ayeh, but Joe, she won't get hot to amount to anything if we just open her up long enough to see how many knots we can get out a this hooker. Five minutes would do it."

"Un-hunh," said Joe, shaking his head. "I don't want to take no chances on it."

"Oh, blast and damn!" said Leonard, impatiently. He leaned against one of the coop braces and glowered at the stubborn set of Joe's shoulders. But he couldn't stay ill-tempered long, not on the day when they were bringing the boat home, finished at last, and all ready down to the last block and tackle to yarn a haddock drag in over the side.

Even at half-speed the big Gray engine drove the boat along at a good clip. Leonard, seeing Joe's blissful face, resigned himself, with a sheepish grin. Probably the engine would be all the better for being broken in slowly.

They were half way of the three miles home when he heard the hum of a heavy engine and, looking around, saw that Morris must have come out of the Harbor right behind them and was overhauling rapidly. "Morris," he said laconically to Joe, jerking his thumb over his shoulder.

Joe looked around. "That's funny," he said. "I didn't know he planned to come home for a while yet." His brows creased anxiously. From time to time he glanced back, as if he were estimating how fast Morris was coming up.

Morris was coming up fast, there was no doubt of it. The big graceful boat had a bone in her teeth and she was smacking through the cross-chop, sending clouds of spray into the air on either side of her bow.

"He must have her wide open," Leonard said nervously, as Morris drew abreast.

"Ayeh," Joe said again. He licked his lips, and Leonard saw that the knuckles of his hands tensed on the steering wheel.

By God, Leonard thought, he's goin to let Morris wipe us. He had not said much to Joe about it, but he had been secretly looking forward to the day when a contest of speeds might come up between the two boats.

Morris drew steadily ahead. Sayl waved a jaunty hand, but Morris himself did not look around. Suddenly he rolled the wheel hard over, shot across their bow, and continued on around them in a wide arc.

Joe ducked nervously as if something had been thrown at him. "What 'n hell's he doin?"

"Doin!" said Leonard furiously, "For God's sake, Joe! He's showin us that his boat'll sail circles around this one, that's all!"

Joe turned red to his hat brim, then dark purple. "Well, by God," he choked, "he is, ain't he? Well, by . . . God!" His big hand shot out and closed on the throttle.

The jerk, as the big Gray roared into full power and the boat leaped ahead, sat Leonard down with a plop on the platform. Joe had not advanced the throttle by notches. He had simply leaned his weight on it.

Morris, preparing to cross their bow in the beginning of a second circle, straightened his boat out just in time. Even so, there was a soul-sickening scrape as the gunnels kissed, and a startled yelp from Sayl.

Leonard scrambled to his feet just in time to see Morris's blank face flash past as they drew away from him.

"Wants a race, does he?" gritted Joe. "All right, by God, let him catch me!"

Leonard, clinging to the uprights of the coop, caught his breath as he saw the speed of the white-flecked water flashing by. He yelled exultantly above the full-throated roar of the engine and the clatter of the spray against the glass windscreen, and then, facing astern, he clapped his thumb to his nose and joyously waggled his fingers at Morris's boat, already a dozen yards behind.

THE rain pouring in through his half-opened window and the wet scrim curtains snapping in the wind waked up Sayl. He considered sleepily getting up and closing the window, but the spring wind was cold in the room and he pulled the bedclothes up around his neck instead.

Hell with it, he thought. Ma'll wipe it up in the mornin.

He was drifting pleasantly off to sleep when he thought he heard the far-off muffled whirr of the alarm clock in Morris's room. It had been a mere drumming breath of a sound above the swish of wind and rain, for Morris, as Sayl knew, kept the alarm clock under his pillow.

"Now, what?" Sayl mumbled. Even Morris wouldn't be starting out on a trip in a gale like this. Still, Sayl wouldn't put it past him. You never knew what that devil would try next.

He saw by the illuminated dial of the splendid new wrist-watch that it was one o'clock. Well, that was nothing out of the way—Morris would light out at one o'clock, or the night before, if the notion took him.

Sayl guessed it couldn't have been the alarm clock, for Morris did not come in to wake him. Funny thing, though. He could have sworn he heard it. He gave a sigh of relief, and then tensed as he heard soft, stock-inged feet go past his door. He listened for the familiar creak of the third stair down, but it did not come.

[281]

Morris was up, all right, and he didn't want anyone to know it, because he had kept from stepping on that creaky third stair.

The gale outside poured around the house and in through his window, and the rain drummed on the sill and dripped to the floor. Over its tumult Sayl could not hear another sound.

By golly, he thought, what's he up to? If he'd been goin out draggin, he'd a called me.

He lay for a moment quietly thinking. Just when he had stopped being afraid of Morris he did not know, but he did know that now it was only a question of time until a showdown between them. He'd about come to the end of being bossed around aboard the boat and waiting on Morris like a slave. Besides, he was experienced now, and worth more than the small share of the money he was getting. He didn't want to do anything that would make Morris mad enough to fire him, but if he could get something on Morris . . . something he didn't want anyone to know about . . . it would just about solve the problem.

Sayl got out of bed and dressed quickly and silently. He put on a sweater under his sheepskin coat, and then realized that Morris might not be going out of the house at all. If he weren't, if he were still in the kitchen, it would be useless to try to get downstairs without being heard. Then, as Sayl stood, undecided, by the open window, he heard the unmistakable click of the latch on the outside entry door, and looking out, saw Morris's figure go out of sight into the darkness along the shore path. In a moment Sayl was out of the house after him.

The night was black, but not pitch-black. Somewhere behind the mass of tumbling clouds was a piece of moon, whose partly obscured light gave solid mass to dark

[282]

objects, and to the white path, running with water, a dim luminousness.

Sayl wished, after the first plunge into the wind-riddled rain, that he had stopped to put on his oilcoat. Already the water had soaked through his shoulders, and he could feel the dankness creeping into his armpits.

He had not the slightest idea where Morris had gone. He stood shivering in the shelter of the New York House, peering up and down the shore of the Pool.

The tide was past full, already ebbing strongly. He could hear the suck and pull of the water going past the ledges. A few hundred feet off the beach the boats rode at their moorings, their white-painted sides faintly luminous against the blackness of the water. But of Morris there was no sign.

Well, he'd lost him, and he might as well go home. He didn't know why in hell he'd bothered to come out in this jimmycane anyway.

A guarded movement inside the fishhouse brought him up with a jump, and a wan ray of light streamed dimly through a knothole a few steps away, and vanished. Morris was in there.

Sayl pressed one eye feverishly to the knothole. At first he could see nothing through the mess of cobwebs and dirt that all but filled the opening. Then he made out the dark figure of Morris stooped over his toolchest. He had a flashlight in one hand and he was hunting for something in the chest. That something was a pry bar, Sayl saw, in the moment when Morris straightened up with it in his hand and snapped out the light.

He stood perfectly still, hardly breathing, as Morris came out, carefully closing the door behind him, and went on down the beach. Sayl could hear the wet beach rocks crunching under his rubber boots, and he could hear the familiar sounds of a punt being launched—the subdued rattle of the anchor as it was laid in the bow, the swish of the wet painter being coiled, the grating roll of the smooth wood sheathing over the beach as she was pushed down to the water.

Morris was going off aboard his boat, apparently. But what in hell for, and with a pry bar, at this time of night?

Figure it out any way he would, Sayl didn't see how he could find out without getting caught. There were other punts lying hauled up above high-water mark on the beach, and he could row one out there. But what would he do—climb aboard and ask Morris what he was up to?

Sayl dashed the rain out of his eyes. He certainly was wet and cold. The hell with it, he was going home.

Suddenly he saw that Morris was not going aboard his own boat. The bobbing blackness that was the punt went on past her, headed for Joe and Leonard's boat. As Sayl watched, the punt went out of sight behind Joe's boat's hull.

He came to life with a jump. He had heard the talk, of course, about Fenner's copying Morris's model for Joe, and what a good joke it had been on Morris. Morris, so far as Sayl knew, didn't really give a damn. He'd never mentioned it to anyone. But he was plenty sore about the way Joe's boat had walked away from his the other day, coming home from the Harbor, and also, Morris's boat had a dented gunnel and some scratched paint—nothing that a little white lead and some plastic wood wouldn't fix. To Sayl's personal knowledge, however, Morris would rather have lost a patch of his own skin. If he wanted to get back at Joe, this was just the kind of thing he would do—watch his chance and then do a lot of damage when nobody was looking.

I'll fix his wagon, Sayl thought fiercely, taking Leonard's skiff down the beach at a run. I ain't scared of him.

The wind whirled the skiff away from the shore almost before he had time to pick up the oars. He was going to be abreast the boat in a moment, he realized, and he'd have to decide what to do. It wouldn't be a good idea to try to climb in over that jumping cheeserind, with Morris waiting for him with that pry bar. The best way to go aboard would be to row around to the leeward side and come up under the shelter of the hull. But Morris's punt was tied up somewhere on that side. He'd be sure to bump the skiff into her in the dark. And the thing to do was to get aboard, with his feet under him, before Morris knew he was anywhere around. No, he figured rapidly, he'd have to come up as close under the lee of the stern as he could and take his chances on jumping.

He shipped one oar, using the other as a rudder, and the wind drove the skiff swiftly and silently down toward the big boat. It looked for a moment as if he had miscalculated and were going to miss her altogether. Then, leaning far over, he managed to grip her gunnel near the stern.

The jerk nearly pulled his arms out of the sockets. The skiff sucked neatly out from under him and slid away into the darkness. Sayl made a futile grab at her, bracing his feet against the wet cheeserind, but it cost him his balance, and one of his feet went overboard with a threshing splash. For a moment he lay on his face, half in the boat and half overboard, before he found his grip again and rolled sprawling down to the platform.

Gee! he thought. He must a heard me!

[285]

He scrabbled to his feet and stood peering fearfully into the shadows forward, where the cabin was.

Nothing moved in the darkness. Except for the slash of the rain against the glass windscreen and the pluck and splash of water against the boat's planks, the only sound was the irregular bumping of Morris's punt, tied alongside. Something in the quality of that stillness set the wet hair to crawling on the back of Sayl's neck. The pit of his stomach contracted.

Jeezus! he thought. I ought a got Joe.

Sayl began edging toward the side of the boat where the punt was tied, but before he reached it, he heard from up on the bow forward of the cabin a sharp splintering of wood, a rattle of the mooring chain and a heavy splash. He jerked around just in time to see Morris's huddled figure on the bow straighten up and start rapidly aft. Instantly the motion of the boat changed and she began to drive backward with the wind.

The dirty rat! Sayl thought. He's set her adrift!

He made a dive toward the comparative shelter of the cabin and brought up with a thump against the side of the coop.

Morris landed lightly on the platform ten feet away. "Who is it?" he said coolly.

Sayl braced his back against the coop and doubled both fists in front of his face. "You ain't goin to get away with it, you bastard, see?" He tried to sound fierce, but his voice was thin with fright and the "see" came out a mere hoarse squeak.

Morris stood motionless for an instant. Then he laughed, and the laugh sounded almost contented. "You damn dumb little fool," he said. "Spyin on me, eh?"

Sayl saw the quick backward and forward lash of Morris's hand and then something that seemed to be

[286]

red hot stabbed into his shoulder. He cried out, "Don't Morris!" fumbling with his hand at the smooth handle of the knife that seemed to be stuck against his sheepskin collar.

The deck came up to meet his knees and he thought desperately, putting out a hand to shield his head, he's got that pry bar!

The platform under his cheek was slimy, and smelt of fish.

Something bumped against the boat with a hollow sound, and for an instant Sayl thought that Morris must have struck and missed him. Then a bulky body reared up over the gunnel and jumped down to the platform with a crash. A heel landed on the fingers of his outstretched hand.

Sayl yelped and snatched his hand away, but the sharp pain drove the faintness out of his stomach and cleared his head. He rolled backwards out of the way, hearing the sound of heavy blows and a kind of grunting croak of horror from Morris.

Somebody had come aboard and was helping. He managed, holding to the cheeserind, to pull himself to his feet just in time to see Morris leap from the platform to the deck and overside into the punt. Big hands closed on the gunnel of the light boat and heaved upward, and Sayl caught one dim glimpse of the blank white patch of face as the far side of the punt went under and Morris, off balance, sprawled overboard into the water.

"Oh, God." Sayl said. His breath caught in a long sob of relief. "Oh, God. Ma."

Sarah Comey's hands unclenched slowly from the wet wood. When they let go, the waterlogged punt bobbed sluggishly once or twice and then slid slowly out of sight as the big boat pulled away from her.

"You hurt, Sayl?" said Sarah.

"Some, I guess, Ma. This knife . . . it's in my coat, but I don't feel it bad." He was crying, and when she came over to him, he clutched at her with his good hand and nuzzled his head down into her breast. He felt her fingers moving swiftly around the handle of the knife stuck against his collar. Then she pushed him gently away.

"You set down," she said. "You'll be all right. I got to git some kind of an anchor over quick. We're driftin, and the Lord knows where to."

Sitting weakly down on the wet platform, Sayl was suddenly aware of the difference in the boat's motion. She was beginning to lift slowly and then to slide downward in a long swooping glide, which meant that they were already out of the Pool and somewhere in the channel, where the big swells were coming in from open water.

But it's all right now, he thought. Ma, she'll do everything. From somewhere far away the idea came to him that he better tell Sarah that she'd have to anchor the boat by the stern because Morris had pried out the bow cleat, but he felt too contented and comfortable.

She'll fix it, he said to himself. It'll be . . . all right . . . now . . .

SOOT-GRAY daylight creeping through the square of his window waked up Joe. His mother hadn't called him, he thought, rolling over lazily. Well, perhaps it was just as well she hadn't. The patch of sky he could see from the window was covered with low, bulging clouds that looked as if they might pour at any minute, and if he and Leonard were going to spend the day working inside on gear, getting started early didn't much matter.

Joe got up and padded over to shut down the window, his bare feet flinching away from an icy puddle that had dripped from the sill. The wind had gone down. The bay, he saw, was a uniform dull heavy lead-color, and the fields looked brown and flat, covered with long pools, silver in the early light.

Standing by the window, suddenly Joe froze in his tracks, his big hands tensing on the sill. The mooring in the Pool, where his boat had been last night, was empty.

Could Leonard have taken her out? But what for? It wasn't like Leonard not to let him know. Unless, maybe, somebody was sick and Leonard had gone for a doctor.

Joe dressed swiftly and went clattering downstairs, two steps at a time. He brought up abruptly in the kitchen door, staring around him with astonishment. The kitchen stove was cold, and Sarah wasn't there.

Why, she was always up by this time and had a fire going. Maybe somebody *was* sick, and they had come for Sarah. Or maybe Sarah was sick. He remembered all at once that she had been looking pretty tired lately.

Joe went back upstairs to Sarah's room. Her bed was empty. He saw through an open door that Sayl wasn't in his bed, either.

What in hell! thought Joe. What *is* this?

For a moment he hesitated outside Morris's room, then shoved the door open and looked in. Morris was gone, too.

Joe headed downstairs, two steps at a time. He grabbed his coat from the hook behind the entry door and saw, in passing, that there was nobody in the shed.

As he ran down the path toward the Pool, he tried to sort out the facts into some kind of sense. The empty

house had something to do with his boat being gone
. . . but what?

Feet came thudding down the path behind him and
he turned to see Leonard panting along trying to catch
up with him.

Joe's heart sank. "Len, where's the boat? I thought
you must have her."

"God, Joe, she's layin off Scudder's Head. You can
see her from our upstairs window. Looks like she was
anchored. Gram see she was gone off the moorin and
called me, but I thought you . . ."

"We better get out there," said Joe. "Somethin's hap-
pened. Come on. We'll take Morris's boat."

"My skiff's gone," said Leonard, surveying the empty
beach. "And Morris's punt. What in hell! Joe, where's
Morris?"

"I dunno." Joe tossed the anchor into Perley Hig-
gins's punt and started her down the beach at a run.
"Hurry."

They scrambled over the side of Morris's boat. The
engine, as always, turned over and started with an even
purr. Joe cast off, and Leonard headed her out of the
Pool at full speed.

But as he swung around the ledges at the entrance to
the Pool, he suddenly cut the throttle and let the big
boat lose way. Two hundred yards off, wide open, a
bone in her teeth, their own boat was driving up the
channel to meet them.

"Joe, for God's sake! Who's aboard of her?"

But Joe stood staring silently, and small beads of sweat
stood out on his lower lip.

As the boat drew nearer, they saw Sarah standing at
the wheel.

Joe drew a long breath and let it out in a whistling sigh.

Sarah slowed down when she was abreast and reversed the engine until the two boats drew together. Then she leaned her hands on the cheeserind and shouted across the intervening space.

"Joe," she said, "I'm headed for the Harbor. Sayl's hurt and he's got to have the doctor. You boys put Morris's boat back on the moorin and come aboard with me. The's reason to hurry."

She put the gears forward, advanced the throttle, and the boat shot ahead of them into the Pool.

Leonard followed, giving Morris's engine every ounce of horsepower it would develop. Once or twice on the way in he glanced at Joe, but Joe's mouth was clamped shut and he was staring straight ahead. Little white knots showed on either side of his tense jaw muscles.

As they shot up to the mooring, Leonard saw that his father had come down and was rowing off to meet them. He let his own breath out with a sigh of relief. He was glad to see Hardy. What had happened here he could not think, except that the whole thing was more than he wanted to handle alone.

Hardy fastened his punt to the stern of Morris's boat and climbed in with them without a word. Then Sarah swung the wheel and headed out of the Pool toward the Harbor.

"I'll steer, Sarah," said Hardy, putting his hand over hers on the wheel. "You're all in. You better set down."

Sarah had a big purple bruise across her cheek and the collar of her work shirt was ripped away. Her thick iron-gray hair had come down and was strung in wet tangles over the back of the old coat of Joe's that she wore.

"All right," she said. She sat down wearily on a covered bait tub, her hands folded tightly in her lap. "Morris set your boat adrift in the night, Joe, and Sayl tried to stop him. Morris stuck a knife in him."

Joe swallowed painfully. "Where . . . ? Is he . . . ?"

"Sayl's down below on the locker. He'll come out of it, I think, all right, if he don't get infected. It was in his shoulder, but it may have ticked his lung. I couldn't tell. He's bled. I'd been in as soon as it got light enough to see where I was, but I had a time startin the engine." She stopped suddenly and her hands twisted in her lap.

"Take your time, Sarah," said Hardy gently. "Don't talk if you don't feel like it now."

"Sayl's lost a lot a blood. We was driftin, and I had to get the anchor over before I could bandage him. The bow cleat was gone, and I like to never got the anchor to hold her stern-to. He may have to go to the hospital."

"We'll get him there quick if we have to," Hardy said. "You done all you could, Sarah."

"Yes," said Sarah. "I guess I done all anyone could. It don't seem like an awful bad cut, but you can't tell, with a stab wound, and it may be dirty and . . ."

"Ma," Joe cried out, "Ma, *where is he?*"

"He's dead," said Sarah flatly. "I had to fight him, Joe, and I knocked him overboard. The' warn't nothin else to do."

⟨⟨⟩⟩

THE doctor who came aboard at the Harbor to examine Sayl was Hadley. He bustled down the slip and into the boat, his stocky little body bristling with energy and excitement.

"Hell's bells, Sarah," he said, "what happened to you?"

Sarah pointed to the cabin. "My boy's hurt, Hadley."

Sayl lay on the locker, tucked in with Sarah's coat, some tarpaulins, a set of oilskins—anything that she had been able to find aboard to cover him. He was sleeping, or unconscious. His face showed white in the dim light of the cabin, the freckles standing out in brown blotches. He muttered something and opened his eyes as the doctor's hands touched his shoulder.

"Take it easy, Saylor," said Hadley. "Got yourself in a mess again, tch! Never mind. We'll get you out of it."

Outside, on deck again, Hadley characteristically did not ask unnecessary questions. "I'll have to take him to Bellport to the hospital, Sarah. Joe, you hop up to Jake's and telephone the Bellport Hospital to send over the ambulance."

"What if they can't send it right away?" asked Joe dully.

"Send it?" howled Hadley. "They better send it, or I'll wring that red-headed hoss doctor's head off his neck. You tell em it's me, and to come runnin."

He fumbled in his bag and came up with a phial of pills. "Now, shut up, Sarah, and take one of these. No . . . better take two. Where's your water jug, Leonard? Here, Sarah. My car's up at the head of the slip. Leonard'll drive you up to my house. Leonard, you tell Susy to fix Sarah up with some clothes, so she can drive to Bellport with me."

"I'll have to see the sheriff," Sarah said quietly.

"All right, all right. All in due time. Come on, go along with Leonard. You can tell me the whole story on the way to Bellport. We'll all go see Warren together. Hell's bells, Sarah!" he snapped, as she made no move to get up from the tub where she sat, "I'll take care of your boy."

"He's bad off, ain't he, Hadley?"

[293]

"Yes, Sarah, he is."

"How bad?"

"I wish I could say. He's a good strong boy, Sarah. I'll . . . take care of him."

"You want me to go to Bellport with you, Sarah?" asked Hardy quietly.

She got up then, with a long sigh of relief. "Seems like I need somebody," she said. "Somebody . . . solid."

WHEN the ambulance had come and gone, and Joe and Sarah and Hardy had driven away with the doctor, Leonard went back aboard the boat. The first vanguard of the curious came flooding after him to get the story, but Leonard merely started up his engine and stood down the harbor for home. He'd be damned if they were going to get any details out of him to glab around the town. He dreaded to think, anyway, of what the gossip was going to be.

He felt sick and all-gone, as if somebody had hit him across the stomach with a plank. He thought suddenly, with dismay, that he would probably be the first to bring the news back to Comey's Island, and talking about it was the last thing he wanted to do. What he'd like to do was go somewhere out of sight and not see anyone for about three days.

Well, if he told the story himself, everybody would get it straight . . . first-hand, anyway.

He tied the boat up in the Pool and rowed slowly ashore in Perley's punt, which he had left on the mooring. As he came up the beach, Perley himself came out of the New York House, looking injured.

"What was the idea, takin my punt?" he demanded aggrievedly. "I been needin her all the mornin."

"I'm sorry," said Leonard. "I had to take your punt. There's been bad trouble."

"There has?" said Perley, forgetting about the punt. "What?" He edged closer to Leonard, and Eddy Comey and Jarv Willow came at once out of the fishhouse.

Leonard told the story as briefly as possible, hating them for the way their mouths hung open with amazement and their eyes seemed to grow small with speculation.

"Well, for Chrise sake!" remarked Jarv. "That Sarah, she's quite a one. Alwuz wos."

"Jeezus," said Eddy, "I knew Morris was a tough customer, but I never thought he'd be that bad."

"Well," Perley said, "course they was talk off round the Harbor about Morris's havin somethin to do with Orin Hammond's gittin drownded, but I never more'n half believed it. Jake started it—said they had some kind of a rinktum in his place."

"What was Sarah doin down round the shore at that time a night?" asked Eddy. He pursed his lips and nodded his little bullet head up and down judiciously. "That part of the story don't jibe with me."

"She's been keepin an eye on Morris ever since Joe and I brought the boat home," snapped Leonard. "Doin what we ought a had the sense to do. Look at my boat— I s'pose you think Sarah pried that bow cleat out."

"I bet Sarah knows more'n she's told," said Eddy. "I bet she ain't told a straight story."

"Why in God's name wouldn't she?" Leonard looked him in the eye.

"Well, nobody else was there," said Eddy. "Say, you know, I wonder what else the' is behind this. Sarah was

[295]

always kind of deep. I bet if Morris's body's ever found, we'll find out she done it herself and put the blame on him, now the poor guy's dead and can't speak for himself. I bet—"

The picture of Sarah's strained quiet face flashed for an instant before Leonard's eyes. His fist hit Eddy square on the nose, and Eddy sat down with a hard thump.

Eddy sat still, too amazed to move, the blood trickling from his nose. He opened his mouth and let out a roar of rage and pain before he scrambled to his feet and dove at Leonard, swinging wildly. For a moment they traded punches toe to toe, then Eddy sprawled backward and lay on his side, sniveling.

Perley and Jarv, who had taken refuge inside the fishhouse, edged back slowly toward them.

"Look," said Leonard, standing grimly over Eddy, "you button your trap. There's plenty of proof to uphold what Sarah says. What she done somebody had to do sooner or later, and you know it, and I only wish it had been me. Sarah's lost one boy and may lose another one. I can't keep you flapjaws from hashin it over, but by God, if I find out that a one of you ain't told this story straight, I'll haul your arse up over your head and cram it down your throat!"

He stepped over Eddy and strode away up the path. His rage tasted like copper in the back of his throat. God, he thought, I've only made it worse.

He slammed the kitchen door behind him, startling Gram into dropping a couple of stitches.

"Now, Leonard," she began querulously, "look what you done! You know better than to— My Lord, what's the matter?"

"I'm sick of this goddam hole of an island!" Leonard burst out. "Blasted backbiters and gossips, they'd say anything just so it was behind your back! For a dime I'd pack up my duds and blow, quicker'n I could spit!" He dropped wearily into a chair and suddenly, to his horror and Gram's, began to cry.

⟨❧⟩

CACK COMEY let out an outraged gasp when Eddy walked into the kitchen with his bloody nose and black eye. "Ed-dy! For the Lord's sake, who's been a-foul a you?"

"Leonard Turner, damn his soul!" Eddy burst out. He did not stop to wash his face, but sat down and launched at once into the story.

Cack sat listening, her hands clasped under her breasts, her jaw dropping lower and lower with excitement and horror.

"Ain't that awful, Eddy! Right in the face and eyes of the Lord and everybody!" she ejaculated. "A murder, and somebody on this island! Go on, what else?"

"The' ain't any more to tell," stormed Eddy. "Leonard's the only one knows what happened, and he hit me for askin him a civil question."

"You mean he won't *talk* about it?" demanded Cack. "Why, that ain't natural!"

"No, he won't talk about it, and he says he'll kill anybody who does," said Eddy vindictively. "If you ask me, he's in it himself, thicker'n molasses, and that's why."

"Why!" said Cack, thinking rapidly. "You don't s'pose he is, do you?" For the first time she regretted that she was mad with Josie. When something as dreadful as this happened, neighbors ought to have their minds free to talk things over. But she hadn't spoken to Josie

[297]

for weeks, and after Hardy had chopped down the fence, she had sworn she never would. She considered going over and offering to make it up with the Turners, but she suspected Josie would see through her, especially since Leonard had just beaten up Eddy, and she ought to be madder than ever.

"I'm goin right over there now and have it out with them," she said finally with decision. "They needn't think they run this place. Sarah Comey's your father's own cousin-by-marriage, and we got a right to know all the dee-tails. It's only decent to find out what we kin."

"I'll go with you," said Eddy, jumping up with alacrity.

"Well, I just guess you better. With murder around, I may need you to protect me."

They made a curious couple as they hurried up the hill—Eddy with his smeared face and swollen eye, Cack with her shawl drawn tight over her head and clutched in a fat hand under her chin.

Gram saw them from her window and uttered a shrill cackle. "Here they come, belly first," she said. "Cack, she's lettin on to be mad, but what she wants, she's nosin."

Cack came impressively through the kitchen door, Eddy agog behind her. She brought up short against the stony stillness in the Turners' kitchen.

Josie stood by the stove. Leonard sat across from Gram at the window. All three faces stared grimly at her, and nobody said anything. If they had talked loudly and angrily, she would have known how to answer.

"I want you to see Eddy's face where Leonard hit him," she began.

"I see it," said Josie. "Quite a sight."

"Ain't you goin to do nothin about it?"

"Well, I might advise him to wash it," said Josie.

A dead silence fell again on the kitchen. Eddy shifted uncomfortably and glanced toward the door. Nobody else moved.

Cack tried another tack. "I want to know what happened last night. After all, Sarah's my cousin. *You* ain't no relation."

Josie said, "Leonard told the story to Eddy."

"Well, I want to know the whole thing. What's the matter with you, keepin things back?"

"No," Josie said. "Go on home, Cack."

"What's Leonard doin, givin people a lickin just because they ask a civil question? Is he mixed up in it, or somethin? I'd say he was, the way he wants to keep things dark . . ."

Josie came purposefully across the kitchen and Cack stepped back hastily, bumping into Eddy, who bumped into the door. Josie stepped around them, turned the doorknob and flung the door wide. "Go on," she said. "You've said enough."

"Well, I ain't goin, until . . ."

"Oh yes you are. Eddy, take your mother home."

Eddy, already outside, backed away from her advance. "Come on, Ma. Come on!"

Cack turned around on the porch to deliver a parting shot, but the door closed firmly in her face. "By God, I'll fix you, Josie Turner!" she shouted at the top of her lungs. "I'll make Jap put that fence back up! By God, I'll make him put up a stone wall ten-foot high!"

But there was no answer from the house, and she whirled and started ponderously down the hill. "Eddy," she said, as soon as she could get a good breath, "you go

[299]

down to the shore and when your father comes in, you tell him he can take me to the Harbor. I'm goin to Bellport and see Sarah herself."

LATER in the day Josie and Leonard went over to Sarah's house to pack a few things for her that she might need. Sarah apparently did not possess a suitcase. At least, Josie did not see one in her closet, and she did not wish to rummage in Sarah's belongings. So she sent Leonard home to bring over her own, and while he was gone, she made the beds and set the house as much to rights as she could.

Leonard came back to find her sitting in the kitchen quietly crying, but she stopped as soon as she saw him.

"I can't find hardly a thing to pack," she told him. "She ain't got a good dress, so I've put in a couple of clean housedresses. She ain't got no hat, only that old cap of Clyde's she wears around."

"Sarah don't think much of clothes, I guess," said Leonard soberly. "She didn't ever plan to go nowhere."

"Well, I've done all I can," said Josie. "Come on home, and I'll send her my coat and hat. We're about the same size acrost, but the coat'll be too short for her."

She got up and stood for a moment looking uncertainly around Sarah's kitchen, and Leonard, suddenly, put his arms around her.

"Ma," he said, "how *would* you feel about movin away from the island?"

"Pa wants to go," she said, not answering his question.

"I know he does. I do, too."

"You do, Leonard?"

"Yes, I do."

"Where would we go?"

Leonard hesitated. He let his arms drop and stood looking at her. "I guess you wouldn't want to move any-where, would you?"

"I used to think I wouldn't," said Josie. "That's funny, too, because when we first come here, I fit like a steer with your father not to come. I couldn't see nothin in goin on to an island to live. And now . . . well, I guess I'm used to it. But I won't hold back if the rest of you want to go."

"You won't?" said Leonard incredulously.

"No."

"Has this . . . this business with Morris made you feel that way, Ma?"

"No," said Josie. "I guess it ain't that alone. That's part of it, because we ain't none of us goin to feel happy about things for a long time to come. What it is, Leon-ard, the island's been changin for a long time. Or maybe the island's the same, but the people's different. I dunno why."

JAP persuaded Cack not to start out for Bellport that night, since it was already late when he got home. Be-sides, he had just come from the Harbor himself, where the story had spread like wildfire, taking on wonderful ramifications, and he brought enough different versions and details to keep Cack interested for the evening.

One man had told Jap that his brother had seen Sayl when they carried him from the boat to the ambulance, and that he was cut open down the front so bad that his bowels were right out into the world; and another one had said that after the ambulance had driven away, somebody had picked up one of Sayl's thumbs off the ground.

As for Sarah, she was supposed to have had her clothes torn off her back, and the doctor had had to borrow some to cover her so that she'd be decent enough to drive to Bellport to jail. Nobody seemed to know why Hardy Turner had gone along, except he was mixed up in it somehow. Prob'ly something between him and Sarah Comey—must have been goin on for years. But then, anything could happen over on one of them islands.

Jap said he'd spoken pretty short to the man that had made that last remark. "Brought him up with a round turn," he told Cack. "I guess he didn't know I was listenin."

Cack left the supper dishes and went right over to May Higgins's. She did not get home until half-past ten. She felt relaxed and rested after the evening at May's, and right with the world again.

HARDY and Joe came home to the island the next morning in a hired boat, with Warren, the sheriff, and one of his deputies. There was really very little for Warren to do or see, but he felt it his duty to go over the boat and have a look through Morris's things. They came ashore after spending a long time aboard Morris's boat. Hardy looked white and tired; Joe looked exhausted.

"How's Sayl, Joe?" Leonard asked, meeting them as they came up the beach.

"He's some better, they think," Joe said soberly. "He had a blood transfusion yesterday, and he may come out of it okay, if he don't get infected."

"That's good," Leonard said, carefully keeping all emotion out of his voice. "I was comin over today, if you hadn't come home. Ma, she got some of your mother's things and packed em in a suitcase. Thought she might need a comb or somethin."

"Ayeh. Thanks. She won't need much now."

"Sarah's down sick, Leonard," said Hardy swiftly, in a low voice. "She was soakin wet in that cold wind all last night, and I guess she was wore out to begin with. She's been settin up nights, watchin, for a long time."

"Oh-h," said Leonard slowly. The heavy sense of anger and shock that had been growing in him since yesterday suddenly gave way to an almost insupportable grief. "Bad?"

Hardy nodded. "Pneumonia," he said. "Joe's got to go right back, after Warren's through. You'll take em, eh?"

"Sure."

"You want to talk to Warren? He's got somethin he'd like to ask you. I'm bound home. Kind of done, myself."

"What's he want to see *me* about?"

"Better ask him, hadn't you?"

"Sure," said Leonard looking a little foolish. He went down the beach to where a group of men had gathered around the sheriff.

Warren drew him aside. "Not much to ask," he said, in answer to Leonard's question. "Case is open-and-shut self-defense, so far's I can see. Oh, there'll have to be a hearin as soon as she and her kid gits well enough to talk, but 't won't mount to much. Sarah Comey's a mighty fine woman." Warren wagged his head with

[303]

deep respect. "Ain't many like her. You ever see this?" He fumbled in his pocket and pulled out a plain flat fish knife, worn to a slender point from many sharpenings, its handle brown and polished from use.

"Can't say I have," said Leonard.

"Take it in your hand and look close."

Leonard took the knife and turned it in his fingers. He flushed a little with concentration, then looked up at Warren. "That's Orin Hammond's knife," he said.

"How'd you know, son?"

"The one he used to have aboard his boat. He cut his initials on the handle, two summers ago, one time we was out on Claybank, waitin on a trawl. I remember he was proud a makin such a good *O*."

"You c'n say that them's the initials?"

"Well, yes. I guess I could. Orin was handy carvin letters."

"Swear to it?"

"Why . . . yes. I could."

"That's all I wanted to know," said Warren, holding out his hand for the knife. "Joe, he thought you might remember it. You know where I found that knife? Aboard Morris Comey's boat, hid down in the bottom of a box, under some fishhooks. You recall that if Orin'd had his knife handy, he'd be alive today?"

"Ayeh."

"Well," said Warren, "I dunno how much that'd prove in a court of law, but I know what people'll think. I know what I think. Wouldn't be no reason for Orin to lend Morris his knife, would they?"

"Not likely. Not that knife. A halibut trawler don't lend the knife he keeps aboard his boat."

"Well, they warn't on good terms, either, was they?"

"I heard they wasn't," said Leonard cautiously.

[304]

Warren grinned. "Funny, ain't it, how things'll turn up? I kind of guess I owe Jake an apology for shuttin him up last winter. A feller *could* sneak out at night and fid around with another man's trawl rig, couldn't he? I mean, it ain't impossible, is it?"

"No. Shouldn't think so."

"I wish I could a talked a little more to Sarah Comey before she took sick. But near's I can find out, the' was a night last March when Morris was gone for about three hours in the middle of the night. Went somewhere in his boat. It was right around the time Orin Hammond was killed. If I can establish the date, I guess we got a case. That scalawag's better out a the world than in it. Even without this, Sarah'll be all right."

Leonard nodded. He was beginning to feel sick again. His mind took an odd flash-back to the morning in the boat when Morris had said he was soft. I guess I am, all right, he thought. I guess I'd rather be.

"Well, thanks, son," said Warren. "I'll have to send for you later on."

⌒⌒

IT seemed to Sarah Comey that the heaviness which had weighed on her heart and mind for the past three years had become a physical heaviness laid now on her whole body. She could feel the load bearing down on chest and shoulders with every breath she drew.

At first it was different, and kindlier, dulling her head, so that she could lie quiescent, willing the half-consciousness that let her slip away into the place where for three years she had lived whenever she could free her mind from work and effort.

At first she had only to lie still and the pictures of

Clyde would take shape before her closed eyes, moving one into another, real, so that she could put out her hand and touch him. Going about Clyde's woodlot and land, doing his work and wearing his clothes, she had not since his death been able to picture him so clearly. Not, actually, since the early days of their marriage had he seemed like this, unobscured by the images of his sons.

"I've missed you," she said, once, and then was sorry, because Clyde never could abide anyone to speak soft to him. He himself had always spoken through his silences, and said more that way. But he lifted his head and looked at her heavily, and it was Joe.

"How you feel, Ma?" Joe whispered, and Sarah said, "Good." He looked worn out, she thought, and it was in her mind to tell him he should be in bed.

He was the only one who had ever given her back anything of his father, and he lacked the very strength which had made Clyde Comey what he was. They had passed on too many of their twists and weaknesses, she and Clyde, in the making of their four sons. Morris had been herself, soured with bitterness, she knew that, and Joe had just escaped being Clyde. The other two, reckless, thinking only of themselves, were combinations of them both, without sweetness and without restraint. Sayl was still near enough to his babyhood to be loved, but Homer, her eldest son, drowned with his father, she had put out of her heart. If Homer had not been drunk on the day of the snow squall off Grindstone Ledge, Clyde might have come home safe and sound.

The thoughts slid wearily through her mind and she forgot to tell Joe to go home to bed. The heaviness pressed down on her shoulders and chest, and for a moment she knew, clearly, that she would not see Clyde again. If she could lie quiet, she might get back the dreams, they were better than nothing, but now she had to think of work and effort—that terrible next breath which had to be taken through smothering thickness.

It was not worth taking, that breath. It was too much like climbing a series of hills, each one steeper than the last, for the sake only of finding another hill.

Joe sat by his mother until the nurses or the doctor drove him away each day, but on the fourth night they let him stay. She died in the early morning, without knowing him. Once she cried out hoarsely some words he could not make out, except, "heavy."

Hadley walked with him to the gate of the hospital and offered to drive him to the room he had rented temporarily downtown, but Joe shook his head. "I'll walk, it ain't far," he said.

"Joe, I'm sorry for ya, son."

"Ayeh. Thanks, Hadley."

"Young Saylor, he's coming along. He's going to be all right."

"What's he?" Joe burst out. "I'd rather him and the damn boat both had gone to hell!"

"No, you hadn't," said the doctor. "Don't talk like a fool, Joe. He's a game little devil, and he's been askin for you. You've got to see him in the morning and tell him. He's going to feel bad."

"Ayeh," said Joe slowly. "I guess so. I guess I don't know what I'm sayin. I'm the one that's to blame."

HE couldn't tell him, Joe thought, standing by the high hospital bed, looking down at Sayl's white face. He couldn't think how to say that Sarah was dead.

"Well, you sure look like hell," said Sayl brightly. "Godsake, I'm the one that's got the hole in me."

Maybe it would do harm if he told him now. "How . . . how you feel?" he managed to say.

"I'd set up if they'd let me. Look, I been thinkin, Joe. What's goin to become of Morris's boat?"

"I dunno. I . . . hadn't thought."

"Well, why can't I have her? I'll work and pay off what's due the bank on her. It's mostly paid off, anyway."

"Why . . ."

"Now, look, Joe, have some sense. I can run her and I bet I know more about fishin-ground marks than you do. I'll prove it."

"I guess you can have her," said Joe, choking a little. "Sure, you can." He turned and went blindly out of the room. Hadley would have to tell Sayl. He couldn't.

PART SIX

THROUGH the forenoon of the fine May day, Leonard had been helping his father shift back into place the big rocks anchoring the weir wing, which the winter's ice had moved. He felt he could ill spare the time from working on his and Joe's dragging gear, for he wanted to be ready to fish as soon as Joe came home from Bellport to stay. Sayl was getting better slowly and would soon be out of the hospital, but Joe went over every few days to see how he was coming along.

Leonard was worried about his father. Hardy seemed more nervous and down at the mouth than he had ever seen him. The warm spring weather was well advanced, and still Hardy pottered about the site of the weir in his dory, pulling away a piece of shattered pound wall here and taking out a loose piling there, but never really getting much done. He hadn't mentioned to Perley Higgins yet that he wanted to hire him, and so far he hadn't even got the pile driver out of the cove. Leonard thought if he turned to for a day or so and helped out, maybe Hardy would take some decisive steps toward actually starting the work.

Anyway, Leonard thought, maybe it'll cheer him up a little, seeing he kind of likes to have me around.

They had been working on a big three-cornered boulder which had slipped off its foundation and was half buried in the mussel beds, prying it up on edge and ending it over into place again. The job had been a tough one, because the flats mud kept giving under the pry bars, and the rock seemed possessed to slide off to one side. Three men could have done it without much trouble, but it was a little beyond the strength of two. The idea made Leonard impatient.

"Why in hell you don't come to and hire Perley, I can't see," he said. "It certainly ain't lack a money."

The rock needed to slide only an inch or so to fall into place, and Leonard slammed down his pry bar, straddled the rock and heaved on it mightily with his hands.

Hardy swore and yelled at him, but the boulder slid with a jar and dropped, catching one of Leonard's fingers between it and the stone foundation.

"Of all the simple-minded goddam fools . . ." Hardy had gone into action instantly, and his pry bar had shot into a crevice and lifted the rock an inch so that Leonard could get his hand out, but the air burned sulphurous around his head while he worked.

Leonard's jaw dropped a little with awe and admiration. His finger was numbed and didn't hurt much, and he almost forgot it, listening to the brilliant rhythms that sputtered forth from Hardy's long-forgotten repertory.

"Hoary old, roarin old, ripped-up, red-eyed Chrise! What's the matter with you?" Hardy finished. "Take off your glove and le's see that hand. Hurt much?"

Leonard fumbled with his canvas work glove. "Don't hurt at all," he said.

The end of the finger was crushed fairly flat and was bleeding mildly.

"Kind of popped open like a grape," said Leonard, staring at it foolishly. "I'll go home and get a rag on it."

"Rag?" said Hardy. "*Rag?* Hell!"

He stood for a moment looking at the finger, then with a curiously deliberate movement, turned and glanced over the site of the weir which the slowly returning tide was beginning to cover. Suddenly he took his pry bar by the end and whirled it around his head, sending it flying eight or ten yards off into the deep water.

"There, by God!" he said. "Come on. The's that little bottle a alcohol up in the fishhouse with the buoy paint. We'll douse that finger in it and then go across and see Hadley. *Come on, you half-arsed nitwit!* What you standin there for?"

Hadley took his time fixing up the mashed finger. It wasn't too badly crushed and the bone was intact.

"You'll probably always have a funny-lookin fingernail," he said, "and it'll be sorer'n hell for a couple a weeks. How's all your folks?"

"Good," said Leonard.

"Your gram'mother all right this spring? Don't need to ask, I guess."

"Oh, sure. She's chipper's they come."

"Smartest old lady I ever see," said Hadley. "Don't grow like her, these days. Women around here, two-thirds of em got somethin the matter with em before they're half her age. Hold still, I ain't hurtin ya," he said, as Leonard winced.

"Hell," he went on, deftly winding bandage around the finger, "they don't live right and they don't eat right. Spend their days workin in the factory, breathin that sardine grease, and their nights, too, if there's a run of herrin on. You couldn't get them houses down in Shantytown clean. And up on the hill they got cancers and stomach ulcers till I go crazy. Thank God for your gram'mother, I say. She gives me back my faith in the human bowels."

He dropped a piece of bloody cotton into a tin waste can and clanked the cover back on vigorously. "Well, drop by, if that finger bothers you swellin up and throbbin."

Leonard walked back along the shore road from the doctor's house. Along by the water the places did look kind of down at the heel. He'd never thought to notice much before, the Harbor was so familiar to him. But even Jap Comey's dooryard wasn't cluttered up like the fronts of these shanties. They all showed signs of wear and weather—paint scaled off, a gutter dropped here, there a rotten doorstep replaced with a rickety box. They had gone beyond the stage where a man with a hammer and a few nails could do much good—uncared-for and forlorn, as if the people who lived in them were too tired and discouraged to mind that their houses weren't anything more than a place to eat and sleep and shelter.

Below them, the tide twice a day went over the beaches, but even its scouring never quite cleaned away the refuse and grease spilled out from the vents of the sardine factory. The salt wind never quite blew away the heavy stench of frying oil hanging in the air over the town.

The houses on the hill above the shore road were strong old-timers, like the Comey's Island houses, with

solid gables, white paint, and wide comfortable barns.
The storekeepers lived there, and the bosses of the fac-
tory, and the selectmen of the town. But even their
womenfolk came down to work for thirty cents an hour
when the sardine season was on.

The life of the town was shot through and through
by the life of the factory, and it was a town like a lady
in a crisp shirtwaist and a petticoat with a dirty hem.

That was what Alice had meant, Leonard thought sud-
denly. That was what she had tried to make him see.
But good Lord, he said to himself uncomfortably, the
Turner womenfolks ain't ever had to go out to work.
His mother, though, had boarded summer people. She
probably had put in just as tough a time as the women
who worked in the factory. Only, there was nothing
draggled or worn-out about Josie. What made the dif-
ference?

Bewildered, Leonard stopped in his tracks. Then he
turned on his heel and strode back up the hill.

Someone was at home at Lacy's—the front door was
open. Brad, probably, sitting around and waiting for
Alice to feed him, the old bum. No wonder she'd been
scared out of her life about the man she married.

Leonard stopped just inside the door, for a moment
uncertain whether to call out or to turn around and go
away.

Then he saw Alice. She was standing at the door
which led to the kitchen. She had put out her hand
against the frame and was leaning there, as if she clung
to the wood for support.

"I thought I'd drop by," he started to say, but the
words caught and choked in his throat.

"Hello," she said shakily. "I watched you go down

[313]

the road. I thought you weren't coming in. You . . . hurt your hand."

"Ayeh." He looked at the bandaged finger mechanically, turning his hand over once or twice. "Not very much. I wanted to see you again."

"Yes." She did not move from the doorway. "I wanted to see you, too."

"Well . . ." He stood helplessly, all the things he had meant to say to her gone out of his head. He couldn't even find words to tell her he was sorry about Orin, that she could count on him if there was anything . . .

"I had to tell you sometime," she went on in her clear, honest voice, "that I wrote Orin to break our engagement."

"You did!" exclaimed Leonard incredulously. "Then why . . ."

"I hadn't sent the letter when I got the telegram . . . about him."

He nodded. "You mean you didn't let on on account of his folks . . . his mother? I guess you couldn't, at a time like that."

She shook her head, her lips pressed tightly together. "I've got to explain, Len, and then you can go away if you want to. I told Orin I'd marry him because it looked like a way out for me. I knew he'd go anywhere, settle down where I wanted to. So I lied to him."

"You didn't love him?" Slow comprehension dawned on Leonard's face. He took a quick step toward her.

"Len! You don't understand. Don't you see what I did? I let you go away last fall, when I knew we loved each other. I fixed it so you'd be bad hurt, and in the end, Orin would too."

Leonard looked at her soberly. "Orin wasn't ever hurt

[314]

by you. He died thinkin you loved him. Far as I'm concerned, last winter was bad, but you just said you loved me, didn't you?"

"Yes . . . I do . . . I always have."

Leonard put his arms around her and drew her close. He could feel her heart thumping thickly against his.

"Dear," he said, "if you was to marry me, you wouldn't get that slice of the world you want so bad. I've got to stay here and do what I know how."

"I know." Her voice came muffled with sobs. "It's all right, Len."

"I dunno quite how we'd work it out," he said gently. "The trouble with a place like this, most people eat their hearts out wantin things they can't have and can't pay for. They have it hard, I ain't sayin they don't, but it ain't as if by hook or crook a man couldn't get by."

"Wherever you live, things get too much sometimes, Len."

"They won't for me," he said sturdily, his lips against her hair. "Not if I have you."

Leonard climbed gingerly down the wharf ladder into the boat, holding out his sore finger to keep it from hitting against anything. Hardy, already aboard, came over to offer help, but Leonard jumped the last two rungs and landed lightly on the boat's platform.

"You been waitin long?" he asked.

"No," said Hardy. "I just got back. You was gone long enough to have six fingers tied up. Was it broke?"

"Nuh. Just jammed. It'll be okay."

"Hurt much?"

"Oh, beginnin to tune up a little." In spite of himself, Leonard's face spread in a wide foolish grin, and he sat

[315]

down on the cheeserind of the boat, beaming up at his father.

But Hardy, for once, did not seem to notice him. "That's good," he said absently. "I was afraid it was broke."

"What's the matter—somethin wrong?" asked Leonard, concerned at once.

"I been up talkin to Willard Hemple."

"Ayeh, but—" That wasn't news. Hardy generally went up to Hemple's.

"Says he'll sell his store."

"Been sayin that for years, ain't he?"

"Wants sixty-five hundred dollars for it."

"Ain't worth it," said Leonard promptly.

"House and store and sixteen acres of woodlot?" demanded Hardy sharply.

"Nuh. Not the way property is now. Listen, Pa, I—"

"I told him I'd buy it," said Hardy.

"God Almighty, Pa!" Leonard leaned back on the cheeserind and stared wildly at his father, his own news gone out of his head. "You crazy? Didn't you talk it over with anyone? Not even with Ma?"

"I never knew, myself, when I left the house this mornin. Oh, I been thinkin about it a long time—"

"Well, Chrise, Pa, you ought a said somethin to her, or somebody, before you made up your mind."

"It's a good business. Hemple gets all the trade from the factory workers. He's made money."

"Ayeh, but you know Hemple," said Leonard. "If the's so much in it, what's he gettin out of it for?"

"He's goin to rebuild his garage."

"With your dough, it looks like to me."

"All right," said Hardy bitterly. "Go on. Chaw it over. I dunno what I could say or do that you and the rest of the family'd think was right. I s'pose you think I'm goin to build that goddam weir for the rest of my life. Well, I ain't. So shut up."

"Okay," said Leonard. He said no more all the way across the bay. The suddenness of Hardy's move had knocked the pins out from under him, and he did feel that the whole thing had been decided too precipitately.

Hardy cleared his throat once or twice and started to speak, but apparently thought better of it. They moored the boat in the Pool and rowed ashore in uncomfortable silence.

"If you've made up your mind, I guess I don't care," said Leonard gruffly, as they started up the path to the house. "I guess we got to move sometime, and I just as soon live off to the Harbor. I guess I'll have to in the end, anyway, when Alice Lacy and me gets married."

Hardy looked at him soberly. "That's so?" he said. "Don't make sense right now, Leonard, does it?"

"I was goin to tell you when we went off half-cocked," said Leonard sheepishly. He explained about the letter and the broken engagement, beginning with his misunderstanding with Alice. "So that's the way it was," he finished. "We've talked it over and we figure not to get married for a while, maybe next year. We ain't tellin anyone. Except you."

Hardy nodded. They walked along a few paces in silence before he said, "I'm glad it's straightened out for you. I been wonderin all winter how it would be. People'll talk, of course, even by next year, but they always do that, whatever a man does. I wouldn't let it worry me."

Leonard looked at him with affection. Most people would have questioned Alice's sincerity, but not Hardy. He accepted the simple facts, trusting Leonard to know

[317]

what he was doing. Compunction swept over Leonard for the way he had behaved about the store. "I'm sorry I blew up," he said. "Kind of surprised me."

"Ayeh. Figgered it would."

"Worried me, too. You want to have everything in writin, Pa, and be sure Hemple ain't puttin anythin over on you."

"I dunno why he'd want to," said Hardy. "I've known Willard for years. I'd just as soon take his say-so. Hadn't you?"

"I dunno, Pa. Off around the Harbor he's got the name of bein pretty shrewd."

"He may be, in business."

"Ain't this deal with you business?"

"Ayeh, in a way," said Hardy slowly. "I figger Willard knows I wouldn't cheat *him*, and he's got a right to expect the same from me. Besides, I ain't decided this quick. I been thinkin about it ever since I put that three thousand dollars in the bank. I been over Willard's books, and I know what I'm gittin. That sixty-five hundred includes everything—house and furniture, and all the stuff in the store, just as it stands."

"Oh," said Leonard, enlightened.

"I'd a told you that before if you hadn't gone off half-cocked at me," said Hardy, grinning at him.

Leonard grinned back. He was a little bewildered. It would not have occurred to him to handle a sixty-five-hundred-dollar deal on any such basis without looking into it a little more closely. But what Hardy said had made him feel kind of good. After all, Willard Hemple and Hardy had known each other since boyhood. Maybe they *had* worked out a deal of honest give-and-take business on each other's say-so.

His grandfather, he knew, had transacted business all

his life without half the time bothering to write anything down on paper. It wouldn't be so strange if there were a few of the old boys left who worked that way.

Josie, to Leonard's surprise, seemed almost non-committal. He thought she would at least be upset because Hardy hadn't told her in the beginning. But she only nodded briefly.

"I guess for a long time I've seen somethin like this comin," she said. "And I guess you wouldn't a been happy about it, Hardy, if it wasn't all your own doin. I don't know but it'd a been a little smarter to wait till fall and harvest a garden to take with us, though."

"We can put in a garden off to the Harbor," said Hardy. "There's plenty a room on Willard's place."

"I'll have to plan about packin. We've got an awful lot a stuff to move."

"We won't have to move furniture," Hardy said, "except what you want to take. Hemple's house is furnished."

"Good," said Grammy. "Make a clean break. I certainly am sick a seein this busted-down old furniture a yourn, Josie. I ain't goin to be without my commode, though, and my little rockin chair. You might's well make up your mind right here and now to take em with us."

"All right," answered Josie. "I expect there'll be a lot a things we'll find we can't do without."

"I dunno but you'd rather a moved to Bellport," Hardy said, a little uncomfortably.

"Well, I would have, if the' was a choice. But the' might not be any store you could buy in Bellport, Hardy."

He drew a great breath of relief. "That was what I

figgered, too. I might have had to do somethin else over there. I've wanted a good store for a long time, Josie."

Josie's eyes suddenly misted and she turned quickly away. "I guess you have, at that, Hardy," she said.

SAYL lay propped up on pillows, waiting impatiently for the hospital visiting hours to begin at half-past two. Ever since they had let him begin to sit up, a week ago, the time had sure gone slow. So far he hadn't had any company but Joe, but today Haral was coming—he'd got special permission from the school to be away for the afternoon.

He'd be pretty glad to see Haral, Sayl thought, not taking his eyes off the door. He sure had plenty to talk to him about.

He hoped Haral would have sense enough not to ask questions. He didn't plan ever to talk to anyone about his mother or about what had happened that night in the boat. Thinking, sometimes, even now, he broke out in a cold sweat of terror, and the first few nights after he had come to himself in the hospital, he kept seeing figures flicking across the dark, one after another, until it seemed he couldn't stand it. Like movies, they had been, and he couldn't make them stop coming. Well, he was beginning to get over feeling so bad now; and Hadley had promised him he'd be out of here as good as new in a week or so. He sure should think so. He'd been here a month already.

Steps came up the hall, and Sayl jumped a little; but whoever it was went right by his door, and he relaxed against the pillows.

He felt all right, except his arms and legs didn't seem to have much strength in them, and, golly, he didn't know what his face must look like but the rest of him was all skin and bone. His knuckles and knees stood out in big lumps, and there were deep grooves on the backs of his hands. When he got out of here and felt like eating a square meal again, he was going to put away one big lot of food and get some meat back on him.

Everybody in the damn hospital was having their company come but him, it seemed. He made up his mind that the next time he heard steps he wouldn't look at the door, and maybe he wouldn't be fooled.

Then, sure enough, the nurse put her head in and said, "Well, here's your company. Now you can stop flopping around. 'T isn't good for you."

Sayl flushed. Couldn't turn over but old gimlet-eye knew it, huh? He sure would be glad to see the last of her.

Haral stood in the door, round-eyed, looking at him.

Hell, Sayl thought, I don't look that bad, do I? "Them's funny lookin pants," he said aloud.

Haral was all dressed up in a dark blue sweater, lemon-yellow corduroy pants and blue sneakers trimmed with strips of white rubber. He had a different haircut from the one he'd had when Sayl had seen him last, and his face was pink and white where he had lost his tan.

He started to tiptoe into the room, then changed his mind and walked the rest of the way to the bed. "These pants? Oh, all the kids wear these," he said carelessly. "You don't look very bad. You look good." He was shocked at Sayl's whiteness and thinness, and his face showed it.

"Hunh," grunted Sayl morosely. "I'll be home in a week."

[321]

A silence fell. Haral fidgeted and looked out the window. Once he cleared his throat.

Sayl said, "What's the news with you?"

"Oh, nothin. Nothin ever happens over here. Just go to school."

"You like it better'n we did at the Harbor?"

"Some. You can get used to anything. Bud Atwood's back."

"Bud is? I thought he had a hotel job, away."

"He lost it. Boss fired him."

"Hunh!" grunted Sayl. "He prob'ly got to raisin hell."

"Ayeh. Said he and a couple a the other bellboys got to wrasslin up in their room and they tore one a the doors off the hinges." Haral giggled. "Bud's a card."

Sayl did not seem to be impressed. "What's he doin now?"

"Oh, hangin around. He and I like to got put in jail last February."

"What doin?"

"Well, you ever notice that pile a cannonballs up front a the soldiers' monument?"

"Can't say I have."

"Well, we pried out three-four of em and started em rollin down the hill. God, you ought a seen em travel! One of em took the plate glass front right out a the fish market." Haral stopped, looking at Sayl out of the corner of his eye. His story, he didn't know why, had fallen flat. "I guess you don't feel good," he said tentatively.

"Oh, hell, yes; sure, I feel okay."

"Well, they had the cops out after who done it, but we never let on, so they didn't find out."

"Bud's always up to some kind of a kid's trick," said Sayl.

"Kid's trick!" said Haral angrily.

[322]

"Ayeh, that's what I said. Little kids in fancy pants playin spit-spit at the cops."

Haral turned dark red. "Look here, you—" he began shrilly, before he remembered Sayl's sickness and his trouble. "Oh, heck," he finished. "I guess you feel lousy, huh?"

"No, I don't!"

The silence fell again, this time a thick one.

"Hey," said Haral, fumbling in his pockets. "Like to forgot. I brought ya a knife."

He dropped a many-bladed jackknife, bulging with gadgets, on the thin, white bedspread within reach of Sayl's fingers.

Sayl picked it up and turned it over. It was indeed a handsome knife. The sturdy, rough, bone handle made his hands look almost transparent, and Haral swallowed loudly, making the clicking sound into a prolonged throat-clearing.

"Le'me open it for ya," he offered eagerly, as Sayl tugged ineffectually at one of the blades. "It's got an awful stiff spring."

Actually he could open it with his thumb-nail, but he made a great show now of prying at the various blades with the point of his own knife. "Gosh," he said, "I sure didn't realize that was so stiff. Maybe I could take it back and change it. Or we could oil it till it limbers up."

"Oh, she'll be okay," said Sayl, looking at the knife. "Bet she set ya back plenty."

"Two-bucks-fifty," said Haral proudly. He did not think it necessary to mention that he had borrowed the money from Bud Atwood, and did not have a notion as to how he could pay it back. "Got a screw driver on her."

"Yup. And a nail file and a can opener. That can

[323]

opener sure will come in handy on the boat this summer."

"The boat?" said Haral slowly.

"Ayeh."

"You mean a *boat?*"

"I'm goin to have Morris's boat. Goin trawlin this summer till I earn enough to pay for the boat and fit up for draggin."

Haral sat back in his chair, dumfounded. "You mean they'll let you have her? Joe, I mean?" he finished embarrassedly.

"Why not? I ain't a kid no more. When I get some meat back on me, I'll be bigger'n Joe is. Joe says if I show him I mean business, and no funny stuff, and know how to run her, he'll let me keep her for mine."

"Ayeh, but how come?"

Sayl looked away. "Never mind how come," he said gruffly. "I was sick one night, and Joe got soft, I guess."

"You figger you know enough to run her?"

"Godsake, of course I know enough! Every time Joe comes he asks me a batch of questions, and I ain't missed one yet. I could take that engine apart and swaller it and pass it, and still put it together again."

"You learnt how, huh?"

"I'll say I did. I know the marks for the Mary Shoal and the Abner Ground and Clay Bank and Bank Comfort, and any of the others you want to talk about. Joe says if I can run a boat as good's I can talk about it, I know more'n he does. I'll take him out and show him, soon's I get out a here."

"Well, gee, that's swell," said Haral weakly. Any minor triumph of his own failed to have significance beside this. He was almost crying with envy, but he kept his face carefully expressionless.

"I was goin to make ya a proposition," said Sayl, glowering at him. Two red spots glowed in his cheeks and his hands holding the knife shook a little. "But honest to God, Haral, if you're runnin with Bud Atwood, I don't know's I dare to."

"Bud's a good guy," said Haral, looking at him soberly. "He lent me the money to buy that knife for you. He said to tell you hi."

"Ayeh. He's good-hearted, when he wants to be, I guess. I never meant he wasn't. I like him okay. I dunno's I care what he does."

"Well," said Haral. "What's your proposition?"

"That boat's got six hundred dollars due the bank on her. If anything was to happen to her, it'd come right back on Joe. But if I can use her and pay that money and the interest on it, Joe says she'll belong to me. I got to have a man to go with me, Haral, but I dunno's I want one that's hell-raisin around and likely might not be fit to run a good boat."

Haral looked at him thunderstruck. "For gosh sake, I only do it for fun. It don't mean nothin."

"It would aboard a boat. If you'd promise to settle down and quit the funny business, maybe we could talk turkey. But hell, I dunno."

"You do it yourself. Look at the time we got drunk."

Sayl grinned in spite of himself. "Ayeh, that was a time. But that's what I mean, Haral, them kind a things. Gettin in trouble. The first time I do, I lose the boat. It won't be Joe'll take it away from me, it'll be the bank."

Haral hitched his chair up closer. "Okay. You win. What's your proposition? I'd join the church and swaller the hymnbook for a chance to go on that boat with ya, Sayl."

They were still deep in plans, their heads together, when the nurse announced that visiting hours were over.

⌐⌐⌐

JOSIE could not, to save her life, look at moving off the island with any feeling of reality. She had been over her house from top to bottom in the springtime for so many years that this final sorting-out and putting to rights seemed only like one more housecleaning.

She started in as usual in the attic, taking down the accumulation of old magazines, tied in neat piles and the boxes of kept things, so that she could dust and scrub the shelves. The family's winter clothes, which she had already washed and laid away in cardboard cartons for the summer, could be taken just as they were, or perhaps it would be better to leave them in the attic and have one of the menfolks come down after them next fall. But everything had to be moved so that the attic could be scrubbed and aired. Even if she were going away for good, Josie did not propose to leave any part of her house not neat and clean.

It took a full week to finish the front part of the house to her satisfaction. Hardy had wanted to pack up and move without any delay, but she would not hear of it until after housecleaning. Besides, Haral had a long week-end in mid-May—some kind of a teachers' convention that gave him a Thursday and Friday off from school. Privately, she didn't think he would be much help, but somehow she wanted him at home when they moved. No knowing, too, what a boy would think was important to take with him.

She was working up the back stairs, down on her

knees scrubbing the rough plank floor, when the thought came to her that probably this was the last time she would clean this room. She settled back on her heels and looked around her at the bright, neatly papered walls, the ceiling with the brown stain that every spring she covered with muresco, the unfinished beams which she and Hardy had always planned to have lathed and plastered someday. How many times she had lost her patience trying to get wallpaper to stick on those rough planks!

Well, if anybody'd told me, when we first moved in here, that that would be one a the things we wouldn't get done, I wouldn't a believed em, she thought. I've swore I was goin to have this back stairs finished for as far back as I can remember.

She got up stiffly, carried the bucket of dirty water downstairs to empty and fill with clean soapsuds, and just escaped throwing it all over Cack Comey, who was starting to come up the back steps.

"Well, Cack," she said, checking herself with an effort, "I guess you'd a had something to be mad about if I hadn't seen you quite so soon."

"May Higgins says you're cleanin house," said Cack, without preamble.

"That's right, I am."

"Then you ain't goin to move away at all," said Cack triumphantly. "You've just started the story goin."

"What'd you want, Cack?" asked Josie coolly.

Cack's face grew very long. "I do wish you'd tell me the rights of it, Josie," she said.

"Well, now, I'm sorry that Jap's gone to all that trouble to haul the stone for his wall," said Josie. "You tell him he won't have to build it now, because we're goin next week. How many hundred-weight's he got hauled?"

Cack looked at her and her fat underlip began to tremble. "You don't need to go if that wall is what's the matter," she said. "Jap ain't goin to build it."

"I guess that ain't the reason," said Josie. "You been pretty nasty, Cack, but I guess we could live it down in time. Hardy's bought Willard Hemple's store, and we're goin off to the Harbor to live."

"But that won't leave no store and no post office here. If you move off, everybody will, Josie."

"That's right, I guess. Unless somebody wants to take em over."

"Well," said Cack, "I was talkin with May. What *are* you cleanin house for, Josie?"

"Why, the idea! So it'll be left clean, of course."

"What's the use?"

"Oh, no use. I just like the idea, that's all." Josie looked at her quizzically.

"You reely goin, then?"

"Yes, we're goin."

"Well, then, we're goin, too, and so's May and Perley. Jap says he's sick a fishin, and he knows he can get a job in the fact'ry, and this settles it."

Josie sat down on the step. "You mean you're movin to the Harbor, too?"

"We certainly are. I'm goin right home and start packin."

Cack went down the steps and headed rapidly for home. Josie looked after her. Suddenly she began to laugh. She laughed and laughed, until Grammy came to the door and stood looking at her disgustedly.

"What you settin there for laughin like a fool?"

"I'm fated," said Josie, gasping. "If I was to move to the moon, I'd still have the Comeys."

⤸

THE families who moved away from Comey's Island went within a few days of each other. At first, it looked as if the whole community had been excited into going. The idea, talked about wistfully for years, as if the entire world beyond the island were a land of promise, suddenly seemed to have hardened into purpose.

Hardy was going, they said to each other. There won't be any store or post office. Well, I dunno's I want to be buried till I'm dead. I'm sick of eatin salt water, and by God, lobsterin that's about all you *do* eat.

The moving away was the topic of conversation for days. Then, for a while, the talk was all about *who* was going to move. In the end, Jap and Cack, Perley and May, and, oddly enough, old Jarv Willow, were the only ones who decided to follow Hardy's example.

Except for their clothes, tools which might have to be replaced, and a few keepsakes and cherished things, the families who went left their possessions standing in their houses. They said they were tired of what they had . . . where they were going they'd earn enough to buy new. Or they didn't want to take along one thing which would remind them of that damn hole of an island.

They went away with high-heartedness and hope. Things would be different in the new place. A man could have a few possessions he wanted and not have to work his fingers to the bone.

A century and a half ago, great-great-grandparents of theirs coming away from a soiled and handled world to settle the island had felt much the same. Things would be happier in this new place, and easier.

Perley and May got away first. They had found a furnished house in Bellport, and Perley had a steady job wheeling freight on the steamboat wharf. Jap and Cack went to the Harbor. The whole family except Weeza, who was under fifteen, planned to work in the sardine factory for thirty cents an hour.

Old Jarv Willow was traveling farther afield than any of his neighbors. "I've give up tryin to git a pension out a Roosevelt," he told everybody, "same as I had to out a Hoover. I'm goin to Noo York and live on the fat a the land." He was headed for Sailors' Snug Harbor. "Staten Island, Noo York," he said proudly.

Leonard and Joe, walking past his shack on the day after he had gone, saw that he had left his ax sticking in the chopping block.

&<&

IT was hard for Josie herself to decide what household furnishings to take and what to leave. She had not seen the inside of the Hemple house, but both Hardy and Leonard assured her that there was plenty of furniture. She didn't know that she cared much about using another woman's things, and there were certain possessions of her own, like her mahogany sideboard, that she certainly wouldn't leave behind. But since Hardy had bought the Hemple furniture along with their house, it seemed too bad to go to the extra expense and trouble of ferrying a lot of stuff across the bay.

[330]

Besides, Josie had a strange feeling about this moving away.

On a bright May morning she went through her house for the last time, checking to see if she had forgotten anything. The rooms were spic and span, everything in place. The row of green lamps of graduated sizes on the mantelpiece over the kitchen stove, were clean and shining, catching sparkles of light in the rubbed glass of their chimneys, and in her cupboards the dishes stood in spotless rows. Sunlight poured through the freshly washed windows. The house smelled as sweet of soap and water as it ever had after any spring housecleaning—maybe a little close now, with everything shut and locked except the front door.

Josie stepped firmly out on the porch and locked the door behind her. If we ever want to come back, she thought, it'll be all ready for us to move in again. The house, standing like that, clean and complete, seemed like an anchor to windward.

Hardy would like his store, perhaps make some money. The children could go to school. Haral would get over this crazy idea he had of going with Sayl on the boat, by the time next fall swung around. Somewhere in the town there would surely be an old lady—maybe more than one—who would be good company for Grammy.

"I guess I'll get a chance to go to them movies once in a while now," Grammy said almost amiably to Mildred, who was thinking the same thing.

They all felt in holiday mood, leaving the island behind; except the cow, tied by the neck in the weir dory towing beside the boat. Nothing in her gentle experience paralleled this horror of going to sea, and she filled the soft May air with unkempt and terrified bawlings.

On the whole, Josie was not unhappy to go. Nevertheless, she could not rid her mind of the feeling that this trip to the Harbor was like any other. They would do their shopping at the stores, perhaps visit awhile in the town, have a holiday, and then come back home to the island.

~⚘~

THE Hemple house and store stood at the foot of the hill, midway between the more prosperous dwellings higher up and the factory shantytown. Around it were all types and conditions of houses, some fairly well cared for, others shabby and sloppy.

Hemple, it seemed, had kept both house and store in good repair. Josie noticed one clapboard that needed nailing, and one pane of glass out in the peak of the barn window.

"My," she said, "you'll have to fix that before we put hay in there, Hardy."

"Ayeh," said Hardy. He was fiddling with a keyring from which he finally detached a key to hand her. "Can you make out for a while?" he asked, eagerly. "I'd kind a like to go look in the store, maybe open it up for a little business."

She watched him stride across the street before she turned to survey her own domain.

My, she thought, unlocking the door, the neighbors are close. But that was the way it was in a town. Living on the island so long, she had forgotten. From the shape their houses were in, it looked to Josie as if she was going to have some good neighbors and some bad ones.

Inside the house, she brought up for the first time with a shock. It would have been a mess anyway, with all their boxes and trunks piled in the downstairs rooms. But aside from that, there was no getting away from the fact that Mrs. Hemple had not left things very nice.

The wallpaper was streaked and old, and the paint of the woodwork was scabby and blurred with finger-marks. The linoleums were worn in places, and they were undeniably dirty. Josie went through the house with a sinking heart. She had planned on having a job of work, but nothing like this. Already she had cleaned one house this spring.

She was aware, suddenly, that Grammy had been pattering around behind her, following her from room to room, and she turned quickly to see the old lady standing forlornly in the middle of the shabby bedroom.

"Josie, I dunno's I like this place."

Josie caught hold of herself briskly. "Well, movin in's always dismal," she said. "We'll get it cleaned up."

"Well *pu!*" said Grammy. "Allowin for it stinkin, the' ain't no window where I can set and see out on the water. I like to be where I can see out."

"Ayeh," said Josie soberly. "You come downstairs, Grammy. We'll have somethin nice and hot to eat. We had breakfast too early. Then we'll fix a place for you."

She was not prepared for the tall girl in denim slacks standing beside Leonard in the kitchen, and she had to pause an instant in the doorway to manage a smile of welcome.

"This is Alice, Ma," Leonard said, abruptly, the way he always talked when he was embarrassed.

Josie went forward, holding out her hand. She had seen the girl before, she realized, once or twice when she had been to the Harbor shopping, and remembered her with approval. "I'm glad to meet you," Josie said simply.

[333]

"Alice figured you'd have a tough day," Leonard went on. "Thought she might help you get settled."

Josie laughed. "She certainly can," she said, a little grimly. "Only I guess it'll be kind of a nasty job."

"I've brought a whole basketful of fresh cleaning rags," said Alice, grinning at her. "I'd have been down here before and seen to it that things weren't so awful for you to move into, only Brother Hemple and his brood didn't clear out of here until last night. Where'll we begin?"

"I guess most anywhere," said Josie. She was touched and for a moment uncertain. She sat down wearily on a packing crate.

"It's a shame to leave the house in this shape for you to move into," said Alice. "I guess Mrs. Hemple ain't very well. Leonard, why don't you start a fire so we can heat some water?"

"What you bossin Leonard for?" demanded Grammy acidly from the doorway. "You talk like you was his girl. Be you?" She advanced on Alice, her hands on her hips.

Alice eyed her warily, but she did not give ground. "Yes," she said, "I am."

"Pants!" said Grammy, sucking in her lips over her gums.

"Take it easy, now, Gram," said Leonard warningly.

"Humph!" said Gram. "I always told you you wouldn't have the sense to git yourself a woman that looked good in them things, but I see you have. Go on, build the fire."

AS Hardy stepped up on the store stoop and unlocked the door, he had a sudden feeling of foreboding. He had expected to find the place closed, of course, but not with such an atmosphere of finality and desertion.

He shut the door carefully behind him. For a moment he stood motionless, his jaw slowly dropping, as he looked around him.

His agreement with Hemple had been to take over the store, lock, stock, and barrel. He had paid twenty-five hundred to bind the bargain, and had signed notes for the remainder at a substantial sum a year. Hemple's books, which Hardy had gone over, had shown that the payments could easily be met out of profits. That Hardy had been sure of before he had agreed to buy the store.

The shelves were bare of goods, the counters and floors littered with packing excelsior, dust, and old cartons. The big meat refrigerator was gone, torn out, the jagged ends of its electrical connections left dangling. Even the electric light bulbs and porcelain fixtures were gone. The store was, in short, cleaned out.

Hardy sat down on an empty packing case and looked around bewilderedly. Something was certainly pretty wrong with him. He began going over carefully in his mind his conversations with Hemple when they had dickered over the bargain. He thought of the day Hemple had taken him into the refrigerator and showed him how the cooling system worked. Hemple had mentioned that refrigerator quite often when he had been persuading Hardy to buy the store.

Hardy got up and went out of the dismal place, leaving the door unlocked. Hemple, he knew, had moved to a house up on the hill, a half-mile away. He was pottering around with a hammer and nails, fixing some pickets on his fence when Hardy walked into the yard.

"Hi, Hardy," he greeted him cheerfully, wagging his red head. "Movin in today?"

"Willard," said Hardy bluntly, "you agreed to sell me that store lock, stock, and barrel."

"So I did," said Hemple. "Ain't found nothin wrong with it, have ya?"

"I understood the deal included the stock and the equipment," said Hardy. "You ain't left nothin. You've stripped it."

Willard looked astounded. "Why, Hardy! Godsake, boy, you read the deed, didn't you? I s'posed you agreed to what it says on the deed."

"Sure, I read it. The deed says house, store, and wood-lot. I never questioned what no written agreement included when I had your spoken word, Willard."

"My God, Hardy, we had that joke between us for years. I thought a course you understood I'd sell you just what the deed called for."

"You mean your word ain't worth nothin?"

"Nothin in a court a law, Hardy."

"You used that refrigerator as a sellin point."

"You got witnesses to prove it?"

"Witnesses?" said Hardy. "I never figgered I'd need witnesses to prove a deal I made with a man I've known as long as I have you, Willard."

"Well, you're crazy if you didn't. You better not try to make trouble, Hardy. You ain't got a leg to stand on."

"That the way you want to leave it?"

"What other way is the'? You bought my house and store and woodlot. The papers was all drawed up honest and shipshape. Why in God's name would I make you a present of a lot a vallable stuff you ain't agreed to pay for? 'T ain't likely. I need all that equipment to stock my new store."

"You startin a new store?" asked Hardy quietly.

"Now don't make out you didn't know it. I told ya I was enlargin my garage business and buildin on space for a store, didn't I?"

"No. If you had, I wouldn't a bought yours. You figger your old customers'll trade with you, don't you?"

"Well, you can't tell people where to do their tradin." Willard started to go on with something about healthy competition, but under Hardy's steady gaze he mumbled and stopped. "You needn't stand there and look at me like I was God's louse!" he howled suddenly. "God, you'd think a man was a criminal jest because he's drove a good bargain. If you've come out the little end a the horn, Chrise, that was your lookout, warn't it? I guess you can afford it, all the money you made last fall. Don't come squawkin to me when I had the brains to take some of it away from ya!"

Hardy stared at him. Then he turned and went out of the yard and down the hill.

He didn't have enough money left to re-stock the store, he knew that, and with those notes to meet, it wasn't likely he could borrow any. He thought for a moment desperately of Leonard, and then remembered that Leonard was saving his money to get married. Besides, he'd be damned if he'd hang himself and his troubles around the necks of his youngones.

As he went with dragging steps across the yard, Josie came out of the store to meet him, and behind her, Leonard and the tall young woman whom he knew to be Leonard's girl. He saw by their faces that they knew, and he turned away from them and went slowly on toward the house.

"They didn't clean the house very good either," said Josie, catching up with him. "Gram, she's in there mournin because she can't see out. I don't look at it that way, Hardy."

"Ayeh," said Hardy. He went up the steps to the kitchen door and closed it behind him.

Josie stood looking after him, then she opened the door and followed him in.

"I warned him," said Leonard bitterly. "I thought he knew what he was doin. I didn't think he'd let that polecat gyp him like this. I wish now I'd—"

"Ssh, dear," said Alice. "We've got to think what to do."

"Do? What can anybody do? The poor old boy, he's wanted a store like Hemple's all his life, and he thought he had one. God, he looks like the life had gone right out of him." Leonard was almost crying. "Why didn't he stay over on the island where he belonged!"

"He wasn't contented there," said Alice softly.

"Maybe he wasn't, but he was looked up to. He was a man on his own ground. Look at the way people always come to him when there was a tough job on! Look at the things he can do better'n anyone else! God, he gits tore out, but that don't make him any less of a man. And now this whole town'll bust wide open laughin at him. I'd like to kill Hemple! By God, I will! I'll go up there and—"

"No," said Alice. "That wouldn't help things. What your father needs is some dough."

The rage went out of Leonard. He looked at her, and then sat down on the store doorstep, his elbows on his knees, his hands hanging. "That's so," he said. "And I can't do nothin about it, can I? If I was makin twenty-five hundred a year, now, I guess I could be some use to him."

"Oh," said Alice, almost in a whisper. "Don't. Don't remember that now."

"I can't help rememberin it." He got up suddenly, the line of his jaw set. "I can get five-six hundred dollars from the bank on my share of the boat. I'm goin to go do it."

"Wait." She caught him swiftly by the arm. "I've got most six hundred dollars. It's ours. Let's give him that."

Leonard stopped in mid-stride and turned toward her. "You was savin that to fix us up gettin a house with," he said.

"Yes. We couldn't use it that way, not at a time like this."

"Well, I'll be damned if I'll let you do it, Alice. A dog wouldn't work the way you worked for that money. You're goin to buy somethin you want with it, and that's flat. Don't let me hear no more about it." He thrust his hands belligerently into his pockets and glared at her.

"Okay, dear. You're the boss." Her voice shook a little and she put her hand on his arm. "We'll buy us a house with it. We'll buy the Comey's Island place from your father and go down there to live."

"Good God, you ain't serious! You'd go crazy down there. You said so yourself last fall."

"Look," she said. "I've learned some things since last fall. I guess I'd sound pretty corny, if I was to try to tell you what they are. We might as well look at it honest, Len. I wasn't all wrong trying to make a go of it away from here."

"No," he said uncomfortably. "I never said you was."

"I never got what I went after."

[339]

"No?" He looked at her with a little frown. "What was that?"

"Ask your father. He knows more about it right now than anybody does."

"I guess I don't know what you mean." He looked bewildered and unhappy and she slipped her hand into his.

"I found something else I wanted more," she said. "He didn't, and he's left now with plain nothing. Let's go give him the money, Len. I . . . want to." His fingers tightened around hers, but he stood stubbornly staring at the ground. "I've got you to think about," he said at length. "I can't have us start off all wrong. Comey's Island's too lonesome for you."

"Was it lonesome for you, Len?"

"Well, no. Not with you, it wouldn't be."

"The people who went there first—your great-grand-father—those people, I mean—they got along all right, didn't they?"

"Ayeh. We ain't them, and times is different." He looked at her questioningly, and she met his gaze. "I don't know, Alice," he flung out suddenly, "I can't honest, see that there's much wrong with livin over there. Grampa Turner, he had a hell of a good life—lot a irons in the fire, and dough put by. I feel the same way as he did about it. I could do the same."

"Then what's stopping us?" she asked softly.

"I've seen too much of someone tryin to make a go of it in a place he hated," said Leonard. His voice was almost savage. "I ain't got a right to ask that of you. Your say in what we do amounts to as much as mine does." He stopped, wondering what he had said that had brought that light into her eyes.

[340]

"Len, dear—if you feel that way, what on earth does it matter where we live?"

"I thought you wanted to be where there was people," he said, "and things goin on. Over on the island, it's— well, they kind of huddle away from each other, like it was every man for himself. I never could see much sense in it, where we was all neighbors," he went on reflectively. "Oh, if somethin turns up, like trouble on the water, everybody chips in and lends a hand, the way they used to. But—"

"I've lived whole winters in a boarding house where I didn't know the names of the people in the next room," said Alice. "Far as that's concerned, Comey's Island's probably better off than most places."

"I hadn't figgered it that way." He looked puzzled. "What *do* you want, Alice? I guess you've got me mixed up."

"Len, I don't believe our grandfathers had a corner on livin a good life. Trouble with us now is, there isn't a one of us who didn't have a fire built under him the day he was born—to get some place, to be somebody. Even Pop always told me I'd damn well better be a credit to him." She flashed Leonard a quick grin. "The idea's all right. Only most people go after it head-down, as if it was a Pied Piper playin a pretty tune."

She moved closer to him, slipping her arm through his, closing her fingers over the hard muscles of his wrist.

"We're just as nice people as our grandfathers were," she went on, after a pause. "We've got a lot more to mix us up, but we've got a lot more to do with. Let's give it a try, Len. I don't think Comey's Island'd be lonesome for me now."

[341]

"You beat all," he said, grinning down at her. "You sure do beat all."

"Well, how about it, then?"

"Okay, kid. If you're sure you'll be happy."

"It wouldn't surprise me," she told him with a smile, as they moved toward the house, "if that would be the least of my troubles."